please return
to S. Mary L.

Celtic Saints: PASSIONATE WANDERERS

ELIZABETH REES

Celtic Saints

PASSIONATE WANDERERS

Illustrations by Margaret Rees

Thames & Hudson

Text © 2000 Elizabeth Rees
Illustrations © 2000 Margaret Rees

First published in the United States of America in 2000 by Thames & Hudson Inc.,
500 Fifth Avenue, New York, New York 10110

Library of Congress Catalog Card Number 99-66195
ISBN 0-500-01989-4

Printed and bound in Slovenia

Contents

Preface

CELTIC MISSIONARIES often worked not in isolation, but with the support and collaboration of their extended family. Similarly, this book has come into being with the encouragement and assistance of my parents, my brother and sisters, and my brother-in-law, who have helped with illustrations, maps, proof-reading, computer skills, Welsh, and a peaceful home in which to write.

I am particularly grateful to my sister Margaret for providing illustrations, and to Roderick Geddes for contributing a chapter on the Isle of Man. I also thank Jonathan Wooding for his helpful advice. I alone am responsible for the opinions I have expressed in the text. I apologize to Irish readers for dedicating only two chapters to Celtic Ireland. If such readers persevere, however, they will find that Irish missionaries feature significantly in almost every chapter.

With a very few exceptions, the monks who wrote the *vitae*, or biographies, of the Celtic saints lived many centuries later. It is therefore impossible to reconstruct the lives of these Celtic monks, nuns and married couples. In this book I have placed the figures of medieval legend against a Celtic background, in so far as this can be reconstructed, using archaeological and literary evidence.

I invite the reader to consider this book as 'figures in a landscape'. We can no longer view the figures except through medieval eyes, but much of the landscape remains, especially in the more remote parts of Britain and Ireland. We can come closest to the Celtic saints when we visit the sites where they chose to live and work. They had an eye for natural beauty, and chose dramatic headlands, sheltered valleys, or peaceful lake shores. Here we can fill our senses with the sounds and sights they knew and loved.

Elizabeth Rees

Chapter one
The Origins of Celtic Christianity

THE CELTIC SAINTS were passionate wanderers. Over the years, as I have visited the places where Celtic Christians lived and worked, I have become increasingly awed by the immense distances these men and women travelled without the comfort of a car, or a road atlas, or even the expectation of a warm bed at night. They travelled the length of Britain and way beyond, by land and sea, often many times over. For the Celtic saints, wandering from place to place was almost second nature. Many of them felt it was their vocation to leave home in search of unknown places where they could pray in solitude or preach their faith. In the early ninth century, Wahlafrid Strabo wrote that wandering was 'the condition of the Irish'. Men and women in Celtic times easily made themselves at home in new territory. They loved the earth, and wherever they settled, they were skilled at growing sufficient food.

Who were the Celtic saints? In one sense, our nearest parallel today is the clergy: men and women whom you can expect to meet anywhere, married or single, with the pastoral care of large or small groupings, or else retired. When priests move on, their families move with them. In the same way, Celtic saints were not holy people set apart: they were men and women, married and single, sometimes travelling as a family unit, or sometimes forming communities who came together to share food, work and worship. At this time, the term 'saint' simply meant someone wise and holy, or any good Christian who had died. Bardsey Island, off the northwest coast of Wales, was nicknamed 'Isle of two thousand saints' after the many Christians buried there.

The parish system had not yet evolved in Celtic times; instead, pastoral care was tribal. For instance, St Columba (see chapter 8) belonged to the Northern Uí Néill of Ireland, and was therefore welcomed on the west coast of Scotland where they had established a new kingdom. Monks and nuns chose to be celibate: this allowed them freedom to pray and to preach. They often lived in monasteries, alongside married clerics in minor orders (or *manaig*), and a range of craftsmen and their families. Priests and bishops were married, and frequently lived in monasteries with the monks. Bishops were more like today's civil servants: they were responsible for pastoral care of the tribe; they ordained clergy and baptized converts.

Many Celtic saints were highborn members of their tribe, often a chieftain's younger son. In early life they were sent to a nearby monastery for a good education; later they commanded the respect of their people as they spoke about their faith. They were also technological innovators: Irish monasteries developed a small flour mill with a horizontal wheel, which was useful when only a small amount of water was available. Celtic missionaries travelling to the Isle of Man and to Scotland constructed similar mills. This is the origin of such settlements as Milton Eonan ('St Adomnán's Mill') at the western end of Glen Lyon. Better known is St Fillan's mill in Killin at the head of Loch Tay, ten miles south of Adomnán's settlement.

It is difficult to be certain about the lives and journeys of the Celtic missionaries. Most of their *Lives* were written by medieval monks with the aim of edifying their hearers, or of promoting the spiritual authority of their cathedral's patron saint. Their miracle stories are patterned on those found in the gospels: people are healed and raised to life, so the saint can be accredited as an apostle of Jesus. The *Lives* of the Celtic saints derived from earlier models, the *Acts of the Martyrs*, written in the second and third centuries: these describe the martyrs' lives leading up to their arrest, their final speeches to their captors and their subsequent martyrdom.

When the Emperor Constantine became Christian in AD 313 and martyrdom ceased, monks became the new models of a holy life. The *Life of St Anthony*, written by Athanasius in the fourth century, was the first of many works in this genre. Another influential biography was the *Life of St Martin of Tours*, composed by his friend, Sulpicius Severus; this was followed by large numbers of *Lives* of the Celtic saints written between the seventh and the fourteenth centuries. Many *Lives* describe their saint making a pilgrimage to Rome to pay homage to the ruling pope; often this is simply a concern for accreditation by Rome on the part of the medieval author. It also became fashionable in the *Lives* to claim that a saint worked in Ireland, when he more probably studied in Wales.[1]

Another difficulty when trying to examine the stories of the Celtic saints is their sheer number. After visiting some four hundred places where they lived (and there are hundreds more), I feel I am attempting to describe everyone listed in the local telephone directory. However, the Celtic saints are more elusive, because most churches were named not after their founding missionary but after the founder's master or teacher, so the most we can plot is a saint's sphere of influence. The Isle of Barra in the Hebrides, for example, is named after the Irish saint Finbar, who probably travelled no further than Cork.

The situation is complicated by the fact that many saints had the same name. There were at least fifteen St Brigits, seventeen St Brendans and some three hundred St Colmáns, and these were often conflated.[2] The popularity of the name Colmán, meaning 'little dove', was a standing joke: in one *Life*, a group of Irish monks were working by a stream when their leader shouted, 'Colmán, get into the water!', and twelve men jumped in.

In the 1990s an extraordinary number of books about Celtic Christianity were published, but the work of such scholars as Charles Thomas, Grosjean and Kenney remains the foundation of more recent studies. In the early twentieth century, the Cornish vicar Gilbert Doble studied and translated the *Lives* of the Cornish saints and began to chart their travels. Doble's successors are the many vicars and other local antiquarians who have delved into history and researched their particular parish saint, each contributing a piece to the jigsaw that is the story of the Celtic saints. Our knowledge of the Celtic Churches is a growing patchwork quilt, to which various disciplines contribute: the study of early inscribed stones, of medieval writings, the geography of site and seaways, the study of place-names and of Celtic politics.

The ancient civilization of the Celts flourished for over a thousand years. Greek writers describe Celts living in the upper Danube region in the fifth century BC; they were also in western Turkey, Greece, and northern Italy. St Paul wrote in Greek to the Galatians in western Turkey, but the recipients of his letter also spoke a Celtic language. The Celts were found in Gaul and Spain; they conquered Rome in 386 BC and Delphi in 279 BC. They moved westwards from France and the Low Countries into Britain, in response to the expansion first of the Germanic tribes and then of the Romans.

Celtic languages came from an Indo-European stock, but the Celts were not a homogeneous group or a single nation. A dialect developed, spoken by Celts in continental Europe, while in Britain and Ireland, an insular language was spoken: Irish, Scots and Manx peoples used the Gaelic form of insular Celtic, while Welsh, Cornish and Breton folk spoke a different Brittonic dialect. Until the Roman conquest, Celtic-speaking language groups controlled large areas of Europe, but the Romans gradually absorbed them.

Celtic peoples engaged in a vigorous trade with the Romanized world, and developed advanced forms of art. After the Roman invasions of Britain, which took place in 55 and 54 BC and again in AD 43, native peoples were encouraged to adopt the customs and beliefs of their new masters. Rome had less impact, however, on Ireland and the remoter parts of Britain. This was particularly true of Ireland, which remained outside Roman control. In Europe, the Celtic kingdom of Armorica was largely established by migrants from Britain, and became the nation of Brittany.

Celtic society incorporated many principles which we consider to be modern developments. Chieftains were elected, and answerable to their subjects. A chief could make laws, and presided over tribal assemblies, but he was dependent on the tribe for approval. He could be a judge in the public courts and became army commander in war. At the opposite end of society were non-freemen. They were mainly law-breakers who lost their civil rights until they redeemed themselves. Other non-freemen were prisoners of war and hostages, like the Briton, St Patrick. They were usually returned to their tribe on payment of tribute.

A considerable amount of tribal administration was carried out by the druids; monks later took over this role. Druids were professional teachers and priests, trained in tribal and international law, and so were able to act as arbiters between tribes. Caesar wrote that their training lasted twenty years. Bards were poets, storytellers and minstrels; their skills were valued in a society which relied on oral tradition.

Celtic Christianity was tribal; in Ireland and possibly elsewhere, lesser chieftains were subject to a 'high king'. In Irish tradition, Christ is sometimes referred to as the 'High King of heaven'. Christianity entered Britain by various routes: through the Roman occupation and Christians emigrating from Gaul, through traders and travellers. From at least the sixth century BC, Britain was linked by trade routes with Gaul and northern Spain, and with Greece, Syria and Egypt. Celtic Christianity contains various elements of Jewish, Coptic and Egyptian Christian traditions. There was no single missionary movement to Britain; instead, incoming peoples brought various strands of Christianity.

In recent years, scholars have questioned the use of the term 'Celtic Christianity', since there was no centralized government of the Celtic Churches and no acknowledged head. In this book, the term is used to describe the Christians who lived in Britain and Ireland before the mission of St Augustine in AD 597, who continued to live for a century and more in an independent state. Celtic Christianity evolved in different ways among the various tribes and language groups, but there was considerable cultural continuity.

 Celtic society easily absorbed Christianity: druids and bards taught about immortality, the sacredness of matter and a triune God, and apparently became Christian priests and monks. This was perhaps more true in Wales than in Ireland, where we hear of opposition between monks and druids. In Wales, so many druids were killed by the Romans on Anglesey that those left may have been more easily absorbed into Christianity.[3] The Celts do not seem to have harmed or opposed Christian missionaries, unlike the Romans, who martyred Alban in Verulamium and Julius and Aaron in Caerleon; their lives are described later in this chapter.

It was perhaps because the Celts absorbed Christianity so easily that the stories of a number of Celtic saints seem to have grown out of those of Celtic gods and goddesses. In Ireland, St Brigit acquired various attributes of Brígh, the goddess of fire and light. In mid-Wales,

St Melangell's story centres around her saving the life of a hare, the sacred emblem of the goddess Eostre, while St Winifred appears to have taken over the tradition of Gwinivere, the white goddess, an ever-virgin who personified spring time, and perhaps also became King Arthur's consort Gwinivere. In north Cornwall, Nectan's Kieve is a waterfall 180 metres high where St Nectan is said to have lived as a hermit, but his story may owe its origin to Nechtán, a Celtic water god.

The lives of such men and women as Nectan and Melangell pose more questions than answers. Melangell's shrine is at the head of a remote valley in the Berwyn Mountains near Llangynog. Legend accords her a royal ancestry: she was a sixth-century Irish chieftain's daughter, and her brother was Rhydderch Hael, King of Strathclyde, a patron of St Kentigern. She was descended from the fourth-century self-styled Roman Emperor, Magnus Maximus. Yet she has no evident connections with the Celtic saints who would have been her contemporaries. She fled to Wales to escape a marriage planned for her, and came to live in the valley as a hermit. A quarter of a mile south of her chapel, rock steps in the valley side lead to her 'bed', the ledge where she lived before building her chapel.

In 604 a local chieftain named Brochwel, King of Powys, who lived in Shrewsbury, was hare-coursing at Pennant Melangell. His hounds raised a hare which fled to a thicket where Melangell was praying. The hare hid in the folds of her cloak, while the hounds fled, howling. The huntsman raised his horn to his lips, but was unable to remove it. Melangell told her story to Brochwel and he was so impressed that he gave Melangell the valley where she established a community of nuns.[4] Historical evidence neither affirms nor negates the story. The churchyard had long been a holy place, for it is the burial site of a Bronze Age chieftain, encircled by ancient yew trees, the oldest dating perhaps to 400 BC. Its yew trees have caused it to be described as a druid sacred grove.

It is impossible to determine the origin of the story of Melangell and the hare. Does Melangell represent the Celtic goddess Eostre, from whom our word Easter derives? Eostre was goddess of the spring moon, and the hare was her symbol because hares 'go mad' and mate during the spring equinox. The hare was considered sacred by the Celts and was rarely eaten, while the Romans introduced hare-coursing, as we can see from their mosaics. Is Melangell's story a Celtic statement about the sacredness of the hare?

Melangell's grave is beneath a rock in the floor of the tiny twelfth-century apse of her chapel, which is built on earlier foundations. A solid Norman font survives and the remains of her shrine, built in about 1164 and sensitively restored. The prince, his huntsman and hounds chase a hare along the fifteenth-century rood-screen into Melangell's lap. She sits with her abbatial crozier in her left hand; the story was not doubted by medieval Christians.

The Romans may have hunted hares, but the Celtic Church was profoundly influenced by Roman Christianity. The first Christians in Britain were probably baptized in Gaul or further east, some of them arriving with the Roman army in the second and third centuries. Their life cannot have been easy, since the Romans did not tolerate anyone unwilling to acknowledge the gods of Rome or the deified emperors. Christianity was a 'permitted religion' from AD 260, but Christians were periodically persecuted in AD 202, in the 250s and in the late third and early fourth centuries. Britain's first martyr, Alban, probably lost his life during the rule of Septimus Severus around AD 209 or that of Decius, in about AD 254. Towards the end of the third century, we hear of two northern British bishops martyred under the Emperor Diocletian: Nelior, Bishop of Carlisle, and Nicholas, Bishop of Penryhn, near Glasgow.[5]

St Bede (673–735) recorded the story of Alban's life and death. According to the *Acts of Alban*, which Bede followed, Alban was a pagan soldier who, during one of the persecutions, sheltered a priest and was converted by him. When soldiers were sent to search Alban's house, he dressed in the priest's cloak to enable him to escape. Alban was arrested, refused to offer sacrifice, and was condemned to death. A church was built on the site; in the time of Bede it was still a place of pilgrimage where 'sick people are cured to this very day, and wonders are frequently worked'.[6]

Alban's shrine remained popular; King Offa of Mercia established a double monastery of monks and nuns there in 793. In the thirteenth century in the scriptorium at St Albans, Matthew Paris wrote an illustrated *Life of Alban*. He described the monks venerating Alban's relics in a new shrine, hung around with embroidered curtains. The present shrine, built in 1308, was restored in 1993; its scarlet hangings glow against the pale stonework.

Drawing on information from the sixth-century historian, Gildas, Bede also mentions the martyrdom of Aaron and Julius, 'citizens of Chester'. Julius and Aaron were soldiers of the Second Augustan Legion, based in Caerleon in southeast Wales. They were probably martyred between AD 250 and 260. Much of the legionary fortress has been excavated, so one can walk along the corridors of the long barrack blocks where the two men were probably billeted, and descend the steps into the immense amphitheatre where they trained.

The later church of St Cadoc is built over the *principia*, or official residence of the legionary legate. Here the legionary eagle and standards were kept, and a statue of the reigning emperor. Julius and Aaron would have been required to worship these sacred emblems, but as Christians, they refused to do so. The third-century mosaic floor of the official residence has been removed from its original site in the churchyard and can be seen in the museum opposite. It represents a labyrinth, around which curls a stylized tree of life emerging from a vase. In the ancient world, a maze symbolized the uncertainty of life, with its dead ends and hopeless meanderings, until finally we reach our destiny. Did the two Christians stand here and look down at the labyrinth in which they were trapped?

If the two men were legionaries, they were Roman citizens, and would have been sent to Caerwent, a civil settlement nine miles to the east, to be tried by the judiciary, before being returned to Caerleon and beheaded. They were buried in the large Roman cemetery on a high wooded ridge which overlooks Caerleon. It lies across the River Usk, beside the Roman road to Caerwent, in the present parish of Christchurch. By law, cemeteries had to be outside towns, and Christians built funeral chapels in their portion of cemeteries. The *martyrium*, or chapel, over the graves of Julius and Aaron was replaced by a medieval oratory. In the twelfth century, Gerald of Wales described three churches in Caerleon: one dedicated to Julius, with a choir of nuns, another dedicated to Aaron, with a community of canons, and the bishop's cathedral.

It was easier to be a Christian in civil life than in the Roman army, particularly after AD 313, when the converted Emperor Constantine gave Christians freedom to worship. Caerwent, where Aaron and Julius were tried in the civil court, was the largest civilian settlement in Roman Wales. It was called Venta Silures, 'the Market of the Silures': it became their tribal capital when they descended from their hilltop fort a mile away, after their defeat by the Romans in AD 74. One can still walk round its walls with their impressive towers.

One of Caerwent's excavated houses seems to have been adapted as a house church, with a nave, an eastern apse, a porch and sacristies. In the early Church, wealthier Christians invited poorer ones to join them for the Eucharist, which was followed by a meal in their home: writing in about AD 57, St Paul described this custom in Corinth.[7] There may have been a second house church in Caerwent, where a number of vessels were found in a sealed urn, one of which was a pewter bowl with the *chi-rho* symbol for Christ scratched on it. This Greek abbreviation of Christ's name, using its first two letters, was used from the fourth century onwards by Christians. The vessels found in the sealed urn at Caerwent were perhaps used for the feast which followed the Eucharist. The urn was buried, evidently for safety, in the late fourth century.

Communion vessels have been found elsewhere. At Water Newton in Cambridgeshire, a hoard of silver communion plate was found which included three bowls for mixing wine, a wine strainer, two flagons, a chalice and a circular dish. By the fourth century, poorer men and women across Britain scratched Christian symbols on pots and tiles, cups, pewter plates and other everyday objects (see map 1). Places named Eccles or Eccleston indicate British centres with organized worship; their name comes from the Latin *ecclesia*, meaning church. There are twenty such sites, mainly in Lancashire and the northwest, with a few in Cumbria, Norfolk and Kent. All are close to water and to Roman roads or towns. Eccles and Ecclefechan in southwest Scotland are both beside a river and near a Roman road. Ecclefechan means 'St Féchán's church' or perhaps 'little church'.[8]

British bishops are first recorded in the attendance list of a synod held at Arles in southern Gaul in AD 314. Names of British bishops are also found among those who attended Church Councils at Sofia, Bulgaria, in about AD 343 and at Rimini, Italy, in AD 359. After Constantine's conversion, Christianity spread throughout the imperial provinces. The churches of York, London, Lincoln and Cirencester were located in the four provincial capitals of Roman Britain, and there were probably bishops in some twenty smaller towns. Other churches have been identified in St Albans, Colchester and Canterbury, with smaller chapels at Uley in Gloucestershire and in a Christian cemetery at Icklingham in Suffolk.

A small church was also found near the southeast corner of the forum in the centre of Roman Silchester. It had a nave flanked by aisles, and an apse at the west end. Set into the floor of the apse was a mosaic patterned with black and white equal-armed crosses, where perhaps the altar stood. Whereas earlier churches were designed as basilicas, with a single hall in which the congregation stood, a feature of Silchester's tiny church, thirteen metres by nine, was its transepts, which gave it a cruciform shape. East of the porch, there may have been a freestanding baptistery.[9] Unfortunately, Silchester was poorly excavated, and what has been called a church might in fact be a temple. However, other Christian finds at Silchester indicate the presence of a Christian community here.

In 1998 a fifth-century church was discovered at the site of Vindolanda on Hadrian's Wall, ten miles west of Hexham. It is thought to have been built soon after the Roman legions left Britain in AD 410. This is the second church to have been found along Hadrian's Wall. It was constructed in the courtyard of what had been the villa of the fort's commander. The villa was in use from about AD 220 until the Romans withdrew 190 years later.

When the Romans abandoned the fort, trade would have collapsed, and the population probably dwindled to about fifteen families, mainly descendants of the troops once stationed at the fort. They lived beside Stanegate, the Roman road which continued to be the main route from the northeast coast to the west. These were the families who worshipped in the church – a narrow, rectangular building with an apse. This is the fifth church to have been discovered dating from such an early period. The others are scattered among the provinces of Roman Britain, with two in the south and another in Wales.[10]

Map 1. Christianity in fourth-century Roman Britain (after Thomas).

New Christians required baptism, an initiation ceremony during which candidates symbolically enter the waters of death and emerge newborn into everlasting life. The word 'baptism' means 'immersion', and circular lead tanks have been found on Roman sites, designed to contain water in which candidates could stand, while water was also poured over them. Six of the cisterns bear the *chi-rho* symbol in relief on their sides. On what remains of a baptismal tank found at Walesby, near Market Rasen, fourteen miles northeast of Lincoln, a relief depicts a naked woman about to be baptized. She is escorted by two robed female attendants, while other Christians witness the ceremony, which was probably

15

performed by the bishop of Lincoln.[11] A Roman font also survives in the church at Richborough, which was then a shore fort, north of Sandwich in Kent.

Other Christians were baptized in the pools of wealthy villas. Chedworth villa is situated at the head of the sheltered valley of the River Coln in Gloucestershire. It was occupied in the fourth century, and its owners became Christian at some point. The villa's source of water is a spring which flows through a nympheum, or shrine to the local water spirit, into an octagonal pool surrounded by paving slabs. The apsed shrine is early fourth century, and contained a pagan altar. Three of the slabs which surrounded the pool have *chi-rho* symbols carved on them, so the pool was probably used to immerse candidates for baptism. This seems to have been a passing phase, however, for later owners turned the slabs over and used them for other purposes.[12]

The villa's dining-room floor is decorated with a mosaic depicting the four seasons. Winter is wearing a cloak, tunic and hood for warmth, and carries a dead hare which he has caught. As he grasps it by the hind legs, it dangles stiffly, unlike the hare in St Melangell's story. Hares are still common in the fields around the villa. Archaeologist Graham Webster has suggested that Chedworth may have been a healing centre, since there are too many rooms for a normal family villa, and there are a number of altars. With its nympheum and a nearby temple, pilgrims may have come here to bathe, sleep and receive healing dreams and advice. There were a number of healing sanctuaries in this region: one was discovered in 1996 at Abbey Meads near Swindon, fifteen miles south of Chedworth. It lies close to the Roman road which runs between Swindon and Cirencester. Its complex of shrines, pools and terraced gardens were visited by pilgrims between AD 100 and 350.

Before future Christians were baptized, they went through a period of preparation. They could attend the readings that formed the first half of the Sunday Eucharist, but then had to withdraw for further instruction. They were often baptized on Easter night, after intensive preparation during the forty days of Lent. The mosaic floors of two house churches in Dorset show evidence of this. One from Hinton St Mary is now in the British Museum, London; the other from Frampton is now lost, but was carefully drawn in 1813. Both mosaics have Christian themes and were constructed in the first half of the fourth century; their similarities indicate that they came from the same workshop. Each mosaic outlines a square room joined by a patterned 'threshold' to a smaller room which could be screened off with a wooden folding-door or a heavy curtain. In this way the candidates could be separated from the initiated Christians, who then gathered round the altar to share the Eucharist.

The larger of the two rooms at Hinton St Mary faced east, as churches traditionally do. They face the rising sun, a symbol of Christ rising from the darkness of death. The floor is decorated with a head of Christ as a youthful hero, with a *chi-rho* behind his head. He is flanked by pomegranates, which symbolize resurrection. The heads of four young men, one at each corner, represent both the four winds and the four evangelists spreading the gospel to the four corners of the earth.

On the mosaic floor of the smaller room, the classical hero Bellerophon, mounted on his winged horse, Pegasus, slays the evil monster, the Chimaera. This was a classical parallel to the story of St George slaying the dragon; it reminded Christians how they must struggle against evil and conquer it. At Frampton there was an apse off the larger room, facing east, with a *chi-rho* symbol on its threshold. A second mosaic floor displayed the theme of the four evangelists; Bellerophon's struggle against evil is depicted in a central roundel.[13]

There were seven Roman villas in the valley of the River Darent in Kent. The clear river was fed by

A Christian praying, from a fourth-century painted frieze in the chapel of Lullingstone Roman villa, Kent. The rich, flowing yellow tunic, decorated with blue panels edged with pearls, indicates a member of a noble family (British Museum, London).

springs off the hills, and the climate was kind. One of the villas, at Lullingstone, had Christian owners who rebuilt it in about AD 360, decorating it luxuriously with wall-paintings and mosaic floors. They blocked off three or four rooms to form a self-contained house church with its own access from outside. Earlier owners had converted the cellar beneath into a shrine to the local water spirits, for a niche still contains a painting of three female water deities: blue water flows from the breasts of the central figure and green reeds sprout from her hair.

The newly converted family decorated the upper room over the cellar as a Christian chapel; fragments of its wall-plaster have been painstakingly pieced together. Along the west wall, separated by columns painted onto the plaster, were six painted figures, a third of life size, their arms outstretched in prayer. They were perhaps portraits of the family who owned the villa. Their rich, flowing tunics with pearl-edged stripes are those of fourth-century Roman nobility. A figure in an orange tunic striped with blue stands in front of a curtain, perhaps to indicate 'passing beyond the veil' into the next life (see above).

17

The praying figures faced a large painted *chi-rho* symbol of Christ on the east wall, encircled by a gold wreath which represents eternity. It floats on a blue river of paradise; doves on either side represent human souls. A similar wreathed *chi-rho* was painted on the south wall, with a third in the anteroom. This is one of the earliest house churches in Europe. Decorating the dining-room floor is a mosaic of Bellerophon slaying the Chimaera, like those in the Dorset villas. The evidence of later coins suggests that Lullingstone continued to be a house church when the villa's domestic quarters were no longer used, after they were gutted by fire.[14]

Far removed from the rural house churches, one of the ancient world's largest cathedrals was built in AD 380 on Tower Hill, close to the present Tower of London. It was excavated in 1994 and 1995. The impressive basilica was one hundred metres long and fifty metres wide, constructed from second-hand masonry re-used from earlier nearby buildings. It was decorated with white marble and a wafer-thin veneer of black marble. Inside, the walls were painted with red and white, grey, pink and yellow designs.

The great church may have been dedicated to St Paul, like the medieval cathedral which was later built on the site. A legend was current that St Paul had brought Christianity to Britain, and in the second half of the fourth century, St Paul temporarily eclipsed St Peter in popular belief. Throughout the empire, mosaics and other fourth-century works of art show Paul, not Peter, at the right hand of Christ. The basilica at St Paul's was burnt down in the fifth century, probably by Anglo-Saxons, and its masonry was used yet again to build the Tower of London and the city wall.[15]

The basilica at St Paul's was probably the brain-child of the highly ambitious head of the Roman army in Britain, Magnus Maximus, whose name means 'Great, the Greatest'. He desperately wanted to become emperor, and since he was deeply religious, he may have decided to enhance London's status by acclaiming it as a religious centre founded by St Paul. Born in Spain, Clemens Maximus came to Britain as an official in the household of the Emperor Theodosius the Great. When Roman Britain was threatened by the Picts and Scots, Maximus led a successful war against them; he was acclaimed a hero, and used his popularity to gain personal control of Britain. The legions proclaimed him emperor in AD 383, and he assumed the title 'The Great'.

At Segontium, a Roman fort near Caernarvon on the north Welsh coast, Magnus Maximus met a Celtic princess named Helen, perhaps the daughter of Endaf, a Cornish chieftain. Helen is thought to be responsible for a network of ancient trackways, called Sarn Helen, which can still be seen. In *The Dream of Maxen Wledig*, a story chanted by medieval Welsh bards, Helen orders the roads to be constructed to improve travel between fortresses for the royal entourage: 'One day the emperor (Magnus Maximus) went to hunt at Carmarthen ... and he built a castle there, with very many soldiers. Then Helen decided to have roads built between the castles throughout Britain. That is why they are called Helen Luyddoc's roads, because she was British-born, and Britons made these great roads only for her.'[16] One can hear the patriotic pride in the Welsh bard's voice!

During the next five years, using Britain as a power base, Magnus Maximus became ruler of most of western Europe. He assembled a large British force and ferried it across the Channel to challenge the forces of the Emperor Gratian, who was then in Paris. In his book, *The Ruin of Britain*, the sixth-century historian Gildas lamented: 'Britain is robbed of all her armed soldiery, her military supplies, her rulers, cruel though they were, and of her vigorous youth, who followed the footsteps of the aforementioned tyrant, and never returned'. The Emperor Gratian and his forces retreated southwards to Lyon, where the governor assassinated him.

Magnus Maximus was now in command of Gaul, and he successfully negotiated with Theodosius the Great, Emperor of the East, to become Emperor of the West. He established his imperial court at Trier on the River Moselle, where his wife Helen and their family joined him. But Magnus Maximus was not content to remain in Trier; he decided to conquer Rome. He invaded Italy, where the Emperor Theodosius defeated him. He retreated to Aquileia, where he was arrested and executed in AD 388. His severed head was sent around the empire to proclaim his downfall.

While they lived in Trier, Magnus Maximus and Helen came to know St Martin of Tours (*c.* 316–397), a man who would greatly influence the Celtic west, and Helen saw the new monastic life that Martin was creating. She returned to Britain after her husband's defeat and death, with her sons, including Publicus and Constantine (or Peblig and Custennin in Welsh). Peblig is honoured with a church at Llanbeblig, on the southward slope of the hill below Segontium, in the area of the fort's cemetery. A Roman altar survives in Llanbeblig churchyard. Helen and Custennin have other dedications in north and south Wales.[17]

Martin of Tours was born in Hungary, the son of a Roman army officer. He too became a soldier, but converted to Christianity, and was therefore expelled from the army. He became a disciple of Bishop Hilary of Poitiers, who not only baptized Martin, but also told him about the monasteries he had seen in Asia Minor. Hilary had been exiled to Phrygia from about 356 to 360 for opposing the Arian heretics, who denied that Christ was fully divine. While in exile, Hilary had learnt about the Eastern Church, and was able to see for himself how monks now lived alone as hermits in caves, or in organized groups following a pattern of prayer, simple work and service of others. When Hilary returned to Gaul, Martin rejoined him and built a hermitage for himself near Amiens, where he lived for almost twenty years.

When Martin was asked to become Bishop of Tours in about AD 370, he took his new responsibilities seriously. He travelled through the countryside with his followers, on foot, by donkey and boat, preaching and destroying temples and holy trees. Yet he continued to live as a monk, alone at first in a hut, and later with a large group of followers in a monastic settlement which became known as Marmoutier, meaning 'place of the big family'. His friend Sulpicius Severus described how they lived: 'The bishop lived in a wooden hut. Many of the brothers lived in similar huts, but most dug out caves in the overhanging rock and lived in them. About eighty disciples followed the example of their holy master. No one owned property; everything was shared.'[18]

Monastic life spread rapidly throughout Gaul, and Martin became very well known: in France alone, four thousand churches are dedicated to him. Martin continued to influence the Celtic Churches, as pilgrims from Gaul followed the trade routes westwards to Ireland and Britain. The Irish monastic tradition owes much to the monasteries of Gaul, while St Ninian's settlement at Whithorn in southwest Scotland is dedicated to Martin, as are other foundations made by Ninian's followers. Magnus Maximus had stripped Celtic Britain of its military strength, leaving it defenceless against invading forces, but at the same time a new force crossed the Channel to Britain. From AD 400 the monasteries of north and south Gaul, with their system of leadership and their strong intellectual tradition, began to influence the monasteries of Ireland, which in turn led to the establishment of those in Wales.

Chapter two

Patrick and the Early Irish Church

WHILE BRITAIN was largely Christianized simply by being part of the Roman Empire, Ireland developed rather differently. Britain's Roman towns had bishops, who exercised pastoral care over the church in their area, and continued to do so after the departure of the Romans. Since Ireland was never under imperial administration, it had no urban bishops. However, Ireland was considerably influenced by Roman culture, and Christians from the Roman Empire travelled to Ireland from early times.

In the mid-second century, Ptolemy named locations in Ireland, implying that traders visited its shores and were familiar with its place-names. A hoard of fourth-century imperial gold coins and Roman pendants, also of gold, have been found in the passage grave of New Grange in County Meath. Such finds suggest that Romanized Britons settled in Ireland and were buried there. Most of these Roman artefacts have been found in Leinster, the kingdom closest to southeast Britain, and in northeastern Ireland, which was only a day's sail from southern Scotland.[1]

The Romanized families who settled in Ireland in the fourth century were probably traders who came from Britain and perhaps from Gaul. They would have controlled shipping and markets, and staffed establishments at the mouths of Ireland's navigable rivers, in order to obtain goods from further inland. They spoke Latin, and employed native Irish who probably needed to write a little and count in Latin. There may also have been Irish soldiers serving in auxiliary cohorts of the Roman army in Britain and elsewhere. These men returned home when they had finished their service.

Latin words entered the Irish language at this time, including such military terms as arms and soldier, tribune and legion, wall and longship. The royal seat of Cashel in southeast Ireland derives its Irish name, Caisel, from the Latin word *castellum*, meaning a fort. Other fourth-century Irish words were borrowed from Latin by traders: purple-dyed cloth, dish and brooch, quill pen and oven, and even days of the week, Wednesday and Saturday.[2]

At this time, Christians used Latin in worship, and it is likely that a number of Irish people were competent Latin speakers, particularly in the southern kingdoms of Munster and Leinster. This is where the greatest number of ogham-inscribed memorial stones are found. The concept of incised commemorative slabs came from the pagan Roman Empire, and ogham probably pre-dates the arrival of

Christianity in Ireland. The inventors of this cryptic alphabet were familiar with the sound-values of spoken Latin; the language may have been devised by Latin-speaking Irish intellectuals, perhaps even as early as AD 300.[3]

When Christians from Britain and Gaul came to Ireland, they brought books with them, some of which contained vivid accounts of Egyptian monasteries, written by Europeans who had visited the Egyptian desert. To undertake such a pilgrimage was a profound and life-changing experience. At the end of the fourth century, an Italian monk, Rufinus of Aquileia, recalled his stay in Egypt: 'When we came near, they realised that foreign monks were approaching, and at once they swarmed out of their cells like bees. They joyfully hurried to meet us.' Rufinus was deeply impressed by the solitude he found: 'This is the utter desert, where each monk lives alone in his cell.... There is a huge silence and a great peace there.'[4]

The most popular accounts of the Egyptian monasteries were those of John Cassian, whose books spread through Italy and southern Gaul, and also reached Ireland. With a companion, Cassian set out for Egypt in about 385, and spent fifteen years learning from men and women whom he met. After a further twenty years of reflection on his experience, Cassian wrote his *Institutes* and *Conferences* for a monastery in Marseilles in about 425. In these books, Cassian explained the aims and methods of monastic life; he helped western Christians to understand the life of eastern, Greek-speaking monks, and to adapt it to their own very different conditions. Cassian's Latin writings were circulated widely and were eagerly read.[5]

Other books reached Ireland: an early Irish version of the *Life of Martin of Tours* survives, written perhaps within sixty years of his death in AD 397. Later monks such as Enda (d. *c.* 530) and Finnian of Moville (d. 579) trained in Britain and later returned to Ireland as scholars and teachers; Columba was one of Finnian's pupils. Fragments of Egyptian glass and of Mediterranean pottery with Christian symbols dating from the mid-fifth century have been found at Garryduff in the hinterland of Cork harbour. Early genealogists claimed that an Irish group living in this region were the first to receive Christianity.[6]

The small Celtic monasteries around the Irish, Welsh and Cornish shores lay at the western end of the Mediterranean sea-routes. A scattering of pottery fragments found at Celtic forts and monasteries indicates that wine and other goods reached them in large amphorae from Rhodes, Cyprus and the Aegean. Map 2 shows how traders with eastern goods sailed through the Straits of Gibraltar and reached Celtic settlements in Cornwall, Wales and southern Ireland in the fifth and sixth centuries.

By the early fifth century, British Christians had introduced Latin words into Irish: *cresen* (Christian) and *domhnach* (church, from the

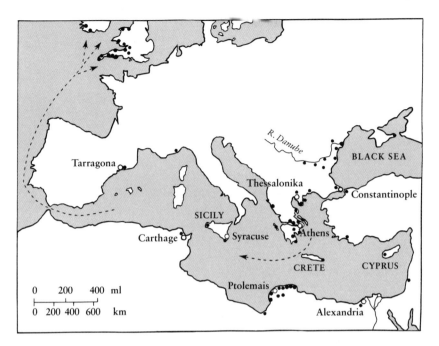

Map 2. Eastern influence on Britain's Celtic monasteries.
This map plots the distribution of pottery storage jars (amphorae type B1) in the
eastern Mediterranean, and fragments of similar jars found at Celtic sites in Britain
(after Bowen).

Latin *dominicum*). Throughout Ireland, particularly in the south, are places named *teampall* (from the Latin *templum* or church) and *díseart* (from the Latin *desertum*, or desert). This name indicates where a Celtic hermit sought out a lonely place, as did the desert monks of Egypt, Syria and Palestine. Other solitaries lived at sites named *uaimh* (cave) or *inis* (island). Scottish place-names reflect a similar story, with Dysart (desert), Weem (cave), and Inch (island).

In names such as Kildare and Killarney, the name-element *cill* comes from the Latin *cella*, a word which described the huts or cells in which monks lived. The Columban monastery of Kells simply means 'cells'. Two thirds of the parishes with the prefix *cill* are found in Leinster and Munster in the southeast, where early Christian settlements grew around small groups of hermit monks.[7] In Scotland, the name-element *kil* is also common. Kilwinning means 'cell of Finnian' (probably the Irish monk, Finnian of Moville), and Kilmarnock means 'cell of Marnoc' or, more accurately, 'cell of my little Ernán', a pet or affectionate name for the saint.[8]

23

We know of five missionaries who worked in southeast Ireland in the early fifth century before the arrival of Patrick: Ciarán of Saigir, Ibar and his nephew Abbán, Ailbe of Munster and his friend Déclán of Ardmore. Their monasteries can be found on map 3: those of Ibar on Beggary Island and of Déclán at Ardmore are coastal settlements, with easy access to south Wales and Europe. A twelfth-century *Life of Déclán* survives: it was probably written to support Ardmore's claim to authority over the Déisi tribe, before the churches of Lismore and Waterford wrested leadership from Ardmore.

Déclán's *Life* relates that he came from the royal house of the Déisi; the tribe had been expelled from Tara in Meath, and their wanderings became one of the great stories of the bards. They told how one group was reinstated, while another migrated to Wales, where St David became bishop of their descendants, and the remainder were given land in southwest Ireland after an intertribal marriage. Here, Déclán was born in Lismore and established a monastery twenty miles further south, on the coast at Ardmore in about 416. Anachronisms in the *Life of Déclán* include his visit to David in Wales (who was not born until a hundred years after Déclán's death), to remind hearers of their Welsh relatives, and an account of a Viking raid on Ardmore (which took place in 824). There are the standard miracles and a visit to Rome, but a few elements in the *Life* convey a picture of a fifth-century tribal missionary.

We are told that the area was mainly pagan at Déclán's birth, but a priest named Colmán came to his home, preached to his parents and baptized Déclán. At the age of seven he was sent to study under a monk who had been trained abroad. Déclán also went abroad to study (probably to south Wales or Gaul), and returned with his monk's bell and staff. On one journey home, his boat landed on an island whose sheep belonged to the chieftain's wife, a reminder that women owned property in their own right in Celtic Ireland.[9] Déclán made friends with Ailbe of Munster: according to Déclán's *Life* the two missionaries, who worked in neighbouring territories, 'loved one another like brothers'. Ailbe established a base at Emly, thirty miles west of Cashel, beside a lake which has now been drained.

Meanwhile, Déclán preached, baptized and built churches among the Déisi. When he went further afield and preached to King Aongus of Cashel, the king refused baptism, although he continued to let Déclán work among his people. The clan of Aongus were not on good terms with the Déisi, so the king could not bring himself to be beholden to Déclán. In his own territory, however, Prince Déclán was sufficiently powerful to depose the chieftain for refusing baptism, and appoint a kinsman as the new head of the clan.

The twelfth-century author of Déclán's *Life* wrote with an eye to Church politics. He stressed Déclán's role as patron as the Déisi, while being careful to acknowledge the superiority of Ailbe, patron of the newly created archbishopric of Munster, which was based at Cashel. The writer was even more concerned to emphasize the importance of Patrick, whose see of Armagh was now the most powerful in Ireland. The author describes Ailbe paying homage to Patrick on behalf of the other bishops, and Déclán giving Patrick land near Clonmel. As might be expected, King Aongus of Cashel agreed to be baptized by Patrick![10]

Déclán built his principal church at Ardmore; the name means 'great headland'. The site was then possibly an island in the mouth of the River Blackwater before it burst its banks in 803, and made a new channel to the sea through Youghal Bay. A gravestone inscribed in Irish ogham survives from Déclán's time in the ruined ninth-century cathedral chancel. Around the cathedral, Celtic gravemarkers mingle with medieval and modern tombstones. To the south is a small chapel on eighth-century foundations, built over Déclán's tomb. Generations of Christians have scooped earth from Déclán's grave, believing it to protect them from disease.

In the twelfth century, a graceful round tower was built beside the cathedral, tapering to a height of twenty-nine metres, perhaps the most beautiful of Ireland's sixty-five round towers. It could be entered only by ladder, and was both a belfry and a place of refuge for monks from attack by rival clans or Vikings. Books, chalices and shrines could be safely stored in the tower when necessary, and towers also served as lookout posts and landmarks, guides for sailors and travellers by land.

A mile away round the headland was Déclán's hermitage, where he went to pray, and where he retired before his death. There are ruins of a medieval chapel here, and a well to which pilgrims have always come, particularly on Déclán's feast day. His *Life* describes how Déclán sensed his death and returned from the hermitage to his monastery. He 'asked to be brought back to his own town, for at that time he lived in a narrow place beside the sea, where a shining stream flows down from the hillside above. It is surrounded by bushes and trees, and is called Déclán's Desert. The city is a mile away, and Déclán came here to avoid being disturbed, in order to fast and pray. He was carried back to his town.'[11]

We know less about the other early bishops of the south. Ciarán of Saigir was born on or near Clear Island, off the southwestern tip of County Cork, where he became a hermit after being baptized and ordained abroad. His ruined chapel and well survive on the island. He later built a monastery at Saigir (Seirkieran in County Offaly), where the kings of Ossory, his family tribe, were buried. Bishop Ibar's chief monastery was on Beggary Island in Wexford harbour; his nephew Abbán is remembered at Kilabbán in Leinster and his followers established one of the earliest chapels on the Isle of Man, Keeill Abban, high above the Baldwin Valley, where St Luke's chapel now stands. A simple seventh-century cross-slab of red sandstone has been preserved in its east wall, beneath the belfry. Like much of the higher ground on

Man, the site is often windy and wet, but on a clear day, Anglesey is visible from Abbán's hermitage.

Palladius was the first bishop to be sent from Rome to Ireland. Pope Celestine had sent Germanus, Bishop of Auxerre (d. 446), to Britain on two missions to combat the heretical teaching of the Briton, Pelagius. The bishops held a conference at Verulamium, where Germanus visited the tomb of St Alban, gathering some earth from his grave to take back

Map 3. Irish monasteries in the sixth century.
Most founders chose sites on the coast or along rivers.

to his new church in Auxerre, Germanus visited Britain twice, in 429 and 431, and recommended that Palladius, who was then a deacon in his church at Auxerre, should go and work among the Irish 'who already believed in Christ'.

Palladius came to Ireland, accompanied by three bishops from Gaul, Secundinus, Auxilius and Iserninus. According to tradition, Palladius landed near Arklow in Wicklow; his three fellow bishops have dedications in the surrounding area, each near a tribal stronghold. Map 3 shows their monasteries at Dunshaughlin (meaning '*domhnach* of Seachnal', or church of Secundinus), Killossy ('cell of Auxilius') and Aghado, which means 'field of the two yews' and was evidently selected for a church because it was already a holy place.

Many Celtic missionaries settled beside yew trees, which often marked a pre-Christian sacred site. Yews were sometimes planted on top of Bronze Age barrows, which were the equivalent of funeral chapels, where people gathered for prayer. Yew trees become hollow with age, and they sometimes served as a monk's shelter, home and chapel: Kevin of Glendalough is said to have lived in a hollow tree for some years in the sixth century. Only a hundred years ago, gypsies were living in a hollow churchyard yew at Leeds in Kent.[12]

Other types of tree were also considered holy: Irish sacred trees included the oak and ash, hazel and hawthorn. More than half of the sacred trees mentioned in Irish folk tradition are hawthorns. The word *bile*, which means 'holy tree', survives in over twenty place-names; for example, Moville, where Finnian founded a monastery, comes from *maigh bhile*, meaning 'plain of the ancient holy tree'. Sacred trees grew in forts, and some were tribal inauguration trees, under which the king was ritually married to the goddess, even into Christian times. It was an insult for an enemy to desecrate the inauguration tree of a neighbouring tribe. A rod or branch was part of the insignia of Irish kings, who were handed a 'rod of kingship' by a bard, or later by an abbot. In the *Life of Maedoc of Ferns*, when a king of Breifne was inaugurated, his wand was cut from the hazel bush beside Maedoc's hermitage. The wand was sometimes used by kings and abbots as a branch of peace, to stop a battle.[13]

While Palladius was preaching in the south, Patrick (*c.* 390–*c.* 461) was working in northern Ireland. There are few references to Patrick before the eighth century, when he was 'discovered' as a national hero and glorified as the founder of their cathedral by the monks who compiled the *Book of Armagh*. Late in life, Patrick wrote his autobiographical *Confession*; it is a journal of his inner feelings rather than a historical account. While this brings him closer to us as a person, it leaves us uncertain about the story of his life.

We do not know where Patrick was brought up: Carlisle has been suggested, or perhaps east of Dumbarton in the Romanized area south of the Antonine Wall. He may have been born at Old Kilpatrick, where a Roman garrison controlled the River Clyde. Now the site of a bus station, the garrison commanded a view of shipping for miles, both upriver and out towards the sea. Three hundred metres to the south, a modern church stands on the site of a Celtic one. On the hilly ridge above both church and garrison, the Antonine Wall marked the boundary of Roman Britain, although it had been abandoned as a fortification two hundred years earlier.

Patrick writes that his father was a Roman *decurion* or local official. The family were Christian: his father was a deacon and his grandfather was a priest. When he was fifteen, Patrick was captured by Irish raiders and shipped to Ireland as a slave. Patrick tells us how he now learnt to seek God: 'When I reached Ireland, I tended the animals each day, and I used to pray often during the day. My love of God and my fear of him grew; my faith was strengthened and my spirit was stirred. I said about a hundred prayers each day, and almost as many each night.

'I stayed in the forest and on the mountainside, and awoke to pray before dawn, whatever the weather, snow, frost or rain. I felt no harm, and was not lazy for, as I now see, the Spirit was fervent in me.'[14] Patrick's writing is simple and sincere as he recalls his late teenage years, when he poured his energy into a new-found relationship with God, oblivious of the discomfort of soaking rain and winter snow. He shows a typically Celtic perception of God in the natural world, finding it easy to pray out of doors, surrounded by creation.

After six years Patrick escaped or was freed, and returned to his family. He wrote: 'A few years later, I was back in Britain with my parents, who welcomed me home as a son, and begged me never to leave them again, after all the hardships I had endured.'[15] Patrick received training for the priesthood and became familiar with the Latin bible. He regretted that he received no 'higher education' and criticized himself for his rustic and inelegant style: 'I blush today for my lack of eloquence, for although my spirit is moved and I understand with my mind, I cannot express myself clearly and briefly.'[16] Patrick may have studied in Gaul. It is not known whether he became a monk: monasteries were still a new idea, and roving bishops were more common.

The time that Patrick spent in solitude had prepared him for ministry. He describes how Ireland continued to haunt his thoughts and dreams, and so he eventually returned as a missionary. He felt that the passing years had brought him wisdom and a depth of compassion that now fitted him for the task: 'I did not decide to return to Ireland until I was almost worn out. However, this was quite good for me, for by now the Lord had schooled me, and made me more suitable for the task than I could ever have been when I was younger. I was quite thoughtless then, but now I was a caring person, concerned for the salvation of others.'[17]

On his return to Ireland, Patrick suffered hardships and was criticized and ridiculed, but he persevered and baptized many people. He tells us that he was a bishop; he was evidently based in the northeast, and appears to have founded a settlement at Armagh, near the headquarters of the most powerful king of Ireland. Perhaps he had a school here and a small community. We cannot ascertain the truth of traditions that he landed at Saul in the northeast, or spent Lent on the mountain of Croagh Patrick, or died at Downpatrick. There are dramatic stories of him lighting the Easter fire on Slane Hill, to pre-empt the pagan new fire at the Spring equinox, which was to be lit at sunrise, and of Patrick baptizing the king of Cashel, and accidentally piercing the king's foot with his pointed staff during the ceremony.

As an old man, Patrick wrote two letters to the soldiers of Coroticus, the second of which survives. Coroticus may have been a Dumbarton chieftain; his forces had raided Ireland, captured some of Patrick's converts and sold them to the Picts. Patrick wrote demanding their release. His writings are the first to survive from the British Church, and give us a unique glimpse of the experience of a Celtic missionary. It is possible that Patrick's own handbell is preserved in a beautiful jewel-studded shrine, dating from about 1100, in the National Museum of Ireland, Dublin.

It is difficult to ascertain where the most popular saints, Brigit and Brendan, Columba and Patrick actually worked, because churches were dedicated to them throughout the Celtic world. Nevertheless, scattered across northern Ireland are thirty churches named *Domhnach Patraic*, and these are likely to indicate where Patrick and his first companions worked. *Domhnach* is a word that pre-dates monastic life; it probably indicates a non-monastic parish church, of the kind established by Patrick.[18]

The next generation of Patrick's followers travelled further afield. In Scotland, for instance, at Cardross beside the River Clyde, Kilmahew chapel is dedicated to another British Celt, St Mahew or Mochta. Writing in about 690, Adomnán, Abbot of Iona, described him as 'a Briton and a holy man, disciple of the holy bishop Patrick'. Mochta's church at Cardross is ten miles northwest of Dumbarton, where Patrick might have worked. *The Annals of Ulster* record Mochta's death as taking place in 535.

Mochta's charming fifteenth-century chapel at Cardross still contains its original 'Sacrament house' in a cavity on the inner wall of the sanctuary; the church is built on a raised, oval Celtic site, beside a swift stream. In the porch is the top of a pre-Christian standing stone on which a plain cross was carved in the sixth century. It was perhaps

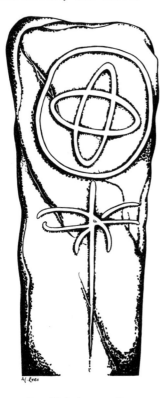

Pre-Christian standing stone at Llanbadrig, Anglesey, decorated in the seventh or eighth century with carvings of crossed fish and a palm tree; they resemble carvings found in the Roman catacombs and churches of the Near East.

chiselled by the monk who established a church there, to bless what was already a holy site. In Ireland, Mochta apparently worked first in Meath but, after opposition, moved northward to Louth, where he established a large monastery.

On the Lancashire coast opposite northeastern Ireland, a group of Celtic monks were honoured after their death with a cliff-top shrine. Heysham, overlooking Morecambe Bay, was a significant Neolithic settlement, where about twelve hundred artefacts have so far been found in the turf not far above sea level. On the headland above, built into a rocky outcrop, is a chapel dedicated to Patrick. According to tradition, he landed here after escaping from Ireland, before making his way home to Scotland, but it is more likely that a group of Patrick's followers came here, for at either end of the oratory are sixth-century reliquaries for bones, carved out of the rock, six in a row on one side, with others, less well preserved, lower down the slope. Each has a rim to take a lid, and a socket at its head into which a wooden or stone cross was inserted.

The site became a cemetery: the bodies of ninety Vikings and other Christians were buried in and around the chapel, close to the relics of the monks. The tiny oratory on the headland was built in the early eighth century by Anglian Christians, who settled in this area in the sixth and seventh centuries. Its inner walls were decorated with red and yellow, white and green-brown paintings and inscriptions. The stone arm of an elaborate seat was found, carved in the shape of a bird's head.

The chapel was enlarged by Saxons in the tenth century; an ancient stone passageway connects it with the parish church which was built in the sheltered hollow below. The base of an elegant carved Anglian cross stands near the entrance to the churchyard, and a tenth-century Viking chieftain's hogback tombstone indicates the continuing importance of the site. It is shaped like a feasting hall, with a curved roof and patterned ridge tiles, and a procession of people and creatures along each side.

Patrick did not become a popular figure in Wales, where only three churches are dedicated to him. One is at Llanbadrig on the north coast of Anglesey, a mile east of Cemaes Bay, in a particularly remote spot – perhaps a follower of Patrick drifted ashore here. Its location would have been helpful to Celtic sea-travellers, for on a clear day one can see the Isle of Man and the mountains of Cumbria, and occasionally the Irish mountains of Mourne. Half a mile out to sea is a rocky islet named Ynys Badrig (Patrick's Isle); on the mainland, a cave with a freshwater well, halfway up the cliff, is also named after him. The medieval church contains a pre-Christian standing stone which was decorated in the seventh or eighth century with carvings of crossed fish and a palm tree (see opposite). The two fish symbolize Christians, for the Greek letters which spell 'fish' also represent a title for Christ. The palm represents a tree of life; these symbols are also found in the Roman catacombs and in churches of the Near East.

Most of the Irish monasteries were built around the coast, on islands or beside major rivers, as map 3 indicates. The Celts were accomplished sea-travellers; their *Lives* depict them sailing in curraghs with a crew of three or six people. A number of churches are named after their three founding monks, whom we can imagine setting out in a three-seater curragh: churches named Llantrisant ('church of three saints') in Wales or the Scottish church of Lochgoilhead named after 'the three holy brothers'. Sometimes monks set out to make a new foundation in two six-seater curraghs, to imitate the twelve apostles following Jesus. For river travel they used the smaller, more manoeuvrable coracle. This is a shallow basket made from locally available materials, normally light enough to be carried on a person's back, and propelled by a single paddle. Coracles are one of the earliest forms of transport; they are found across Europe and Asia.

An early description of a coracle occurs in the Old Testament story of Moses (*c.* 1250 BC) when, as a baby, he was put in a floating papyrus basket coated with bitumen and pitch, and set afloat on the Nile.[19] Larger circular boats made of woven reeds or rushes, coated with pitch, are still to be found on the Rivers Tigris and Euphrates in Iraq. Most coracles and their heavier relatives, curraghs, were covered with animal hides, from Eskimo kayaks and Indian parisals to the coracles of Scotland and Wales. Our word 'boat' seems to have originally described such a leather-covered vessel; one Breton word for 'boat' is *balg* or *bak*, resembling our word 'bag'.[20]

When Julius Caesar visited Britain in 55 and 54 BC he saw coracles in use, for when he was fighting in Spain five years later, he 'ordered his men to build boats of the type that his experience in Britain a few years before had taught him to make. The keels and ribs were made of woven withies covered with hides.'[21] The main rivers under Caesar's control were the Thames, the Medway and the Stour, so he probably stood on the bank of one of these rivers to watch coracles in use.[22]

Curraghs like those used by Celtic pilgrims are still found in the Dingle peninsula and in Donegal. Some Dingle curraghs are three-man boats, used for coastal salmon-fishing. The Donegal curragh is a flat-bottomed coracle in which one or two men can skim across the sea at speed. It can travel three miles out to sea, and handle a force eight gale. It is paddled or 'pulled' with a single paddle over the bow in a sculling movement. Light as it is, it can carry a full-grown cow on its back, with its legs tethered. The Donegal curragh is used for transport, fishing and cutting seaweed, which was also gathered in Celtic times and used to fertilize crops. A circular curragh of hide and hazel withies was used on Irish lakes and rivers; it was last used on the River Boyne, with one person kneeling in the bow, paddling, and the second casting a net behind, which was secured to the shore at one end. We can picture Celtic monks fishing in this way.[23]

In 1977 a curragh was built to sail from County Antrim in northeast Ireland up through the Western Isles of Scotland, following the route taken by St Columba and many others. It was made of hazel, willow, green ash and eight salt-cured cowhides, and took four weeks to build. It was propelled by six oars and a square sail, carrying boulders for ballast. With eight men and their provisions on board, it proved quite seaworthy.[24] In the same year, Tim Severin constructed a much larger curragh of timber covered with forty-nine tanned oxhides, in which he sailed to America with a crew of four to explore the possibility of St Brendan's epic voyage.[25] We shall return to Brendan's travels in chapter 3.

Once Celtic missionaries had settled in a new location, the smaller coracle was more suitable for fishing and transport. Coracles were widely used in Britain until this century, varying in style according to the speed of the river, the purpose of the boat and the availability of materials. There were various types of coracle on the River Severn which borders England and Wales. In north Wales there were coracles on the Rivers Dee and Conwy. On the Taf in southwest Wales they were made of apple and hazel wood; on the nearby Teifi they were made of hazel and willow, with an oak sapling as a handle to carry the craft. In the 1860s there were said to be four hundred coracle men on the Teifi, with a coracle hanging by the door of every cottage. Coracles were ideal for a range of activities from dipping sheep to poaching.[26] If we were to step back in time only a hundred years, we would meet men and women in rural Wales and Ireland whose lives were not too dissimilar from those of their Celtic forebears.

Chapter three
Irish Nuns, Monks and Missionaries

S OME OF THE EARLIEST Irish monasteries were founded by women. In the fourth century, both men and women had followed St Anthony into the Egyptian desert, where some established communities. In Celtic Ireland a similar pattern emerged: Patrick's biographer, Tírechán, describes small Christian centres which Patrick founded and left in the care of 'three brothers and a sister' or 'two young women' or even one woman. There were many small groups of nuns scattered around Ireland, which have left no trace, since early Irish laws rarely allowed women to own land or pass it on. An abbess might be given land for a monastery only for her lifetime; when she died, her nuns dispersed and the land reverted to the men in her family who had given it to her.[1]

The most famous Irish nun was Brigit (c. 455–c. 525); she lived a couple of generations after Patrick, but we know very little about her. She is believed to have been born near Kildare and may have founded a small community under the bishop of Ardagh, a follower of Patrick. In about 480 or 490, the king of Leinster gave her land at Kildare (meaning 'church of the oak'), where she built a monastery beneath an ancient holy tree which survived until the tenth century. Brigit had a reputation for generosity, and Kildare came to be known as 'the city of the poor'. The earliest *Life of Brigit* describes her on the move, preaching the gospel and caring for those whom she met. She travelled in a chariot; her driver was a priest who could also baptize converts.

Brigit owes her name to Brígh, a Celtic goddess of fire and light, and inherited some of her attributes. When Gerald of Wales visited her monastery in the twelfth century, he saw a fire which her nuns carefully tended. He wrote: 'The fire is surrounded by a circular withy hedge, which men are not allowed to enter.' The communal hearth was a central feature of ancient rural communities, and was held to be holy. In monasteries, the fire lit on Easter night might be kept alive for the following year.

A *Life* of the early bishop, Ciarán of Saigir, tells how he decreed that the fire in his monastery must not go out. When it was allowed to do so, and the monks could no longer cook or warm themselves, Ciarán prayed and the fire lit itself again.[2] A similar story is told of Serf's Scottish monastery at Culross, where the young Kentigern was left in charge of the fire in midwinter, and fell asleep. The fire went out, but Kentigern broke off some frozen hazel twigs, prayed, and rekindled the flames.

33

Brigit's fire was extinguished during the Norman invasion of 1220, but was rekindled and kept alight until the monastery was destroyed at the Reformation in the sixteenth century, when Church property was appropriated by the English crown.

Of the many legends about Brigit, one describes how she was called to the bedside of a dying pagan chieftain. As she sat beside him, she picked up some rushes from the floor, weaving them into a cross, and explained the story of the crucifixion to him. Brigit's crosses are still made in Ireland, although their most ancient form has three arms, not four. In about 650, Cogitosus wrote a *Life of Brigit* which describes Kildare a century after her death. He tells us of a large double monastery, in which monks and nuns lived and worked as equals. He describes a wooden church containing the shrines of Brigit and Conleth, a hermit and metalworker whom Brigit invited to Kildare to make church vessels and to be pastor of the people surrounding the monastery. Cogitosus admired their ornate tombs on either side of the altar, each decorated with gems and precious metals. Crowns of gold and silver hung above them, and carved statues and paintings adorned the church.[3]

In the National Museum, Dublin, there is a shrine made of silver and brass, set with jewels, containing a relic of Brigit's shoe. 'St Brigit's mantle' is found in Belgium, in Bruges cathedral; it is said to have been brought there by King Harold of England's sister after the Norman invasion in 1066. It is a small square of red woollen cloth with curly tufts. Such shag-rug mantles were woven from Bronze Age times until the sixteenth century.[4]

Since Brigit was a popular saint, she has many dedications across the Celtic world, including various Scottish Kilbrides and numerous Welsh Llansanffraids ('church of St Bride'). There are a few foundations connected with her early followers: one is St Bride's church at Abernethy in Perthshire, north of the Firth of Forth. Abernethy was a Pictish royal capital, the seat of King Nechtán Morbet; the *Pictish Chronicle* relates how Nechtán was driven from his kingdom by his brother Drust, and fled to Ireland. He arrived at Kildare and asked for Brigit's prayers. He reconquered his kingdom, which he ruled from 457 to 481, and after his return one of Brigit's nuns from Kildare, named Darlugdach, came to his monastery at Abernethy. The king dedicated the wooden church to God and St Brigit, and during the Mass of consecration, Darlugdach 'sang Alleluia over the offering'.[5]

In about 590, some of Columba's monks rebuilt Abernethy's church in stone, with the blessing of Gartnaith, King of the northern and southern Picts. The scene changed, however, when another Nechtán became King of the Picts in 706. He declared his allegiance to Rome and expelled the Columban monks from Abernethy, since they followed the Celtic tradition. After his death, Abernethy once more became the Pictish capital. In the early eighth century we hear of St Donald's nine daughters entering St Bride's monastery. In 875 Abernethy's bishop Adrian, an Irish missionary, together with many companions, was killed by Vikings on the Isle of May in the Firth of Forth.

In the tenth century, perhaps as a defence against the Vikings, an Irish-style round tower, twenty-two metres high, was built beside the church, one of only two in Scotland. A Pictish symbol stone beside the round tower depicts a hammer, anvil and tongs; it is the earliest feature of the site. In the eleventh century, William the Conqueror met King Malcolm III of Scotland here. He had been attacking northern England, and so in 1072 King William mounted a daring and risky expedition by land and sea, and met Malcolm at Abernethy. Here, Malcolm paid him homage, and handed over one of his sons as a hostage. There was a Celtic bishop's cathedral at Abernethy until about 1273.

At the opposite end of Britain is Breage in west Cornwall, said to have been established by one of Brigit's followers, a nun also named Breage (Gaelic for 'Brigit'). The Tudor antiquarian, John Leland, made extracts from her *Life* which was then in Breage church and has since been lost. According to her *Life*, Breage was born in Lagonia (possibly County Laois in Leinster) and became a nun in St Brigit's foundation at 'Campus Breacae' before coming to Cornwall. Breage was one of a number of fifth-century Irish monks and nuns who, according to tradition, sailed to Cornwall and landed in the estuary of the River Hayle: legends describing them will be discussed in chapter 10. Many of the group were said to have been martyred by a Cornish chieftain named Tewdrig, but Breage escaped their fate. Several chapels are dedicated to her, as well as the village of Breage, three miles west of Helston.

The settlement was on an ancient routeway: a Roman milestone stood a few hundred metres from the church and can now be seen within it. It bears the name of Emperor Marcus Cassianus Postumus, who ruled from AD 260 to 268; if Breage lived here, she would often have passed it on her travels. The foundation grew in importance and became the mother church of the Lizard peninsula. Outside the church porch is a four-holed sandstone cross. The soft sandstone is not local; it was perhaps brought here by ninth-century stonemasons whose tools were not sufficiently powerful to work the hard local granite.

Returning to Ireland, another woman contemporaneous with Brigit was St Monenna (d. *c.* 518), who lived as a nun at Killeevy in Armagh, where she was said to have been joined by eight young women and a widow, whose child Monenna fostered; he later became a bishop. The nuns grew their own food, but not very successfully, since they were often starving. Another fifth-century Irish nun was St Gobnait who, according to tradition, was born in County Clare and went to the Aran Islands to escape a family feud. She built a church there before continuing to southern Ireland, where she eventually settled at Ballyvourney. Here, she was guided by St Abbán, whom we met in chapter 2; he was later buried in her monastery. A monk gave Gobnait some of his stock of bees which, according to legend, she not only bred for honey but also used to repel robbers. A thirteenth-century wooden image of Gobnait at Ballyvourney is one of the few surviving medieval statues in Ireland.

Among the Irish nuns who came after Brigit, the most well known was St Ita (*c*. 480–*c*. 570), a princess who was baptized Deirdre (or 'Dorothea' in Latin), but nicknamed 'Itha' ('Thirst') because of her thirst for God. According to her *Life* she was born in Waterford in the southeast, and moved westwards to Limerick, founding a small community at Killeedy ('cell of Ita'), where she lived into old age. She spent much time praying in solitude, and lived an austere life. She ran a school for young boys which became so well known that Ita was called 'foster mother of the saints of Ireland'. She was sought out for advice, and her nuns cared for the sick. Surviving in a ninth-century manuscript is a 'Lullaby for the Infant Jesus' attributed to her.

Ita has dedications in Waterford where she was brought up, and around Killeedy, and a few churches in north Cornwall, where her nephew Dagán was said to have landed, possibly with some of Ita's nuns. The Cornish church of St Issey, on an ancient burial mound two miles south of Padstow, may be dedicated to Ita. Her nephew Dagán became bishop of Wexford. He later upheld his family's Celtic traditions in the face of pressure from the Roman clergy of Canterbury, by refusing to sit down and eat with Augustine of Canterbury's successor, Archbishop Laurentius. His aunt Ita would perhaps have been proud of him! Dagán died in 640.

Most of Ireland's monasteries were established by the mid-sixth century. Some were small communities, often on islands: the illustration opposite represents a typical small monastery of this kind. Larger communities were founded in populated areas on important routeways, or on fertile land which could support a bigger population, for there was intensive settlement around the larger monasteries, which became important centres for craftsmen and for trade. Since there were no large cities in Celtic Ireland, monasteries were modelled on the pattern of the chieftain's fort or the schools of bards and druids, which were self-contained and self-supporting, surrounded by their own farmland.

In Ireland's central plain, the sixth-century monasteries developed a balanced lifestyle combining the austerity of the eastern desert tradition with a commitment to classical learning which was more commonly found in Europe. In the churches of Britain and Europe, Latin was a familiar language: Patrick wrote in Latin, although he tells us that his grammar was weak. Austerity combined with learning was also a feature

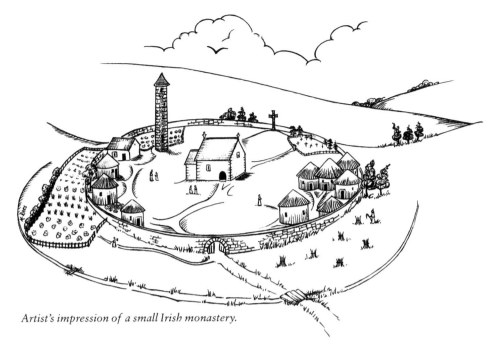

Artist's impression of a small Irish monastery.

of the great monasteries of southeast Wales founded by Illtud, Cadoc and their contemporaries (see chapter 4), and many Irish monks trained under these Welshmen.

St Finnian of Clonard (d. *c.* 549) was influential in establishing this type of community in Ireland. He was a Leinster man who went to Wales to study under Cadoc. Finnian later set up a community at Clonard in one of the most fertile areas of the central plain, which could support a large number of monks. Its access to Ireland's east coast meant that travellers could reach it via the seaways from other parts of Ireland and beyond. Finnian's *Life* describes how monks flocked to Clonard, and, after their training, each left with a gospel book, a bishop's staff or a reliquary to enshrine in a new church. Finnian was remembered as being holy and wise, and was called 'Teacher of the twelve apostles of Ireland'. Several of these 'apostles' had died before Finnian's time, or had not yet been born, but the list, which includes Brendan and Columba, indicates Clonard's considerable influence.

One of the 'twelve apostles' who studied with Finnian was Ciarán of Clonmacnoise (*c.* 512–*c.* 545). We know little about him. The author of his *Life* indicates that he was a holy man by writing that, like Jesus, Ciarán was the son of a carpenter, and died at the age of thirty-three. He is said to have taken a cow with him to Clonard to provide himself with milk. Ciarán later settled with his companions at Clonmacnoise on the River Shannon. He chose a site on the east bank of the river, on an esker or natural gravel ridge, overlooking a large marshy area through which the Shannon flows. The monastery was in a central position, and came to rival Armagh in importance, becoming the burial place of the kings of Tara and Connaght.

Ciarán worked at erecting the first monastery buildings, but died within a year, in the same year that the Yellow Plague killed his master, Finnian of Clonard. Some of the finest scholars of Ireland and Europe studied at Clonmacnoise, including Alcuin, Bishop of Tours. From the sixth century onwards, the monastery had several small churches, with a large number of wooden huts for the monks to live in, scattered among the churches. The whole complex was surrounded by a rampart of earth or stone.

Excavation has revealed intensive settlement outside the monastery, with traces of circular houses, and evidence of trades and crafts: metalworking in iron and bronze, gold and silver, and either antler-working or comb-making.[6] Stonemasons worked here too, for there are remains of seven hundred carved stone slabs, mostly grave-markers dating from the eighth to the twelfth century. Today, the large monastic site contains six ruined churches, including Temple Kierán, in which Ciarán may be buried. The Clonmacnoise crozier in the National Museum, Dublin, is said to have come from Ciarán's shrine. The largest church (the 'cathedral') was built by the High King Flann and Abbot Colmán in 909. There is a round tower and, outside the monks' enclosure, a nuns' church. The community survived many Viking raids and was plundered in various Irish and Anglo-Norman wars, but continued as a monastery until 1552, when an English garrison destroyed it.

The most famous of Finnian's 'twelve apostles of Ireland', Columba, will be discussed in chapter 8, since he worked not only in Ireland but also extensively in Scotland. Perhaps the most popular of the 'twelve apostles' was St Brendan the Navigator (d. *c.* 577). As with other famous saints, it is difficult to disentangle historical fact from the wealth of legends about him. The family name of Brendan, moccu Alti, indicates that he belonged to the Altraige, a tribe who lived in Kerry. Brendan was educated by Bishop Erc of Kerry, and is said to have been fostered by St Ita, although their dates make this unlikely.

Brendan made his principal foundation in about 550 at Clonfert on the west bank of the Shannon, not far from Clonmacnoise on the opposite bank. He established another monastery near the Shannon's mouth, at Ardfert; it became the chief church of north Kerry. Fragments of Celtic crosses were found here, and early monks' graves, but the only surviving Celtic remains are the base of an eleventh-century round tower and a twelfth-century chapel. The door of its romanesque cathedral was modelled on Cormac's chapel at Cashel.

Brendan also established a community at Annaghdown in Galway, and an island chapel on Inisglora is dedicated to him (see map 3). Besides dedications to him in western Ireland, there are a number in western Scotland. Columba's biographer, Adomnán, wrote that Brendan and Columba met at Hinba. Brandon Mountain at the western end of the Dingle peninsula is also dedicated to Brendan. Each July, pilgrims climb the mountain to visit the shrine at its summit, where there are remains of cells, a chapel and a holy well. The pilgrimage is a revival of an earlier tradition which may have replaced a pre-Christian custom of gathering annually at the top of Brandon Mountain to celebrate the god Lug, whose festival was at the end of July.[7]

At the foot of the mountain is Brandon Creek, a narrow, sheltered cove from which Brendan is said to have set sail. Curraghs are still moored in the creek, where in 1976 Tim Severin launched a replica of Brendan's oxhide curragh, to re-create his most famous voyage in search of the Promised Land. The legend of Brendan's voyage is set in the context of real expeditions which were probably undertaken by various monks. Irishmen travelled far in their light curraghs: they settled in the Orkneys and Shetlands, where islands named 'Papa' recall the monks who lived and prayed on them. There were Irish monks on the Faroes in about 720; Norse sagas relate that Vikings found their books, bells and croziers in Iceland, which the Irishman Dicuil described as an island named Thule with a frozen sea to the north.

Making use of winds and currents, Tim Severin sailed north from Ireland to the Hebrides, the Faroes and Iceland; he then followed the currents westwards to Greenland and on to Newfoundland. This is one of the shortest routes between Europe and North America. With islands forming stepping stones, it was a route used by Vikings and more recently by early aviators. On his voyage, Severin passed sights described by Brendan: the Island of Sheep (probably in the Faroes), the volcanoes of southern Iceland (where the monks were pelted with hot rocks), and icebergs off Iceland, described in the book as pillars of crystal floating in the sea.[8]

At first, the story of Brendan's voyage would not have been read; it would have been recited as live entertainment. In his novel *Credo*, Melvyn Bragg has created such a scene: 'Muiredach was not a tall man nor was he imposing. But when he threw his bardic cloak around his shoulders and took in his hand a candle to represent the ship in which St Brendan and his followers wandered through the wildest reaches of the sea, he became majestic.... When the gryphon flew towards Brendan and his monks on the boat, extending its claws, to take up the monks and devour them, Muiredach flung open his arms, let his bony hands slide through the sleeves and swooped down on the children at his feet. Their screams hid the terrors felt by some of their drunken elders, now in fear of the fate of Brendan....

'And then, with all his powers, Muiredach described the attack of the killer whale, the defending whale of God, the turmoil and blood of the sea, the fury of it, the victory, his words and actions roaring and spuming through the great hall like a hurricane. The battle roared on and goblets and fists hammered on the table. When Brendan returned safely home, the men stood and cheered Muiredach and Cathal (the chieftain) took off one of his best rings and threw it to him.'[9]

Another monk who studied at Clonard was Congal (*c*. 515–*c*. 601). After some years as a hermit, he founded Bangor on the northeast coast of Ireland in about 555. Its name, meaning 'pointed arrangement', is thought to refer to the sharp sticks of the wattle fence that surrounded the monastic enclosure. Bangor in Wales and Banchory in Scotland have the same meaning. Congal's became the largest monastery in Ireland, with several daughter houses. Their total population, including families of the clan, was said to be three thousand. Missionaries went from Bangor to Scotland and to mainland Europe. Congal visited Columba on Iona, and may have accompanied him on journeys into northern Scotland.

A story relates how Congal's spiritual director or soul-friend (*anamchara* in Gaelic) died. Congal told his monks that he now felt like a man without a head and that, since he was their abbot, they too were now headless. When he asked their advice on how to find a new soul-friend, a student suggested that he fetch the gospels and kneel to pray until a new soul-friend was revealed to him. Congal sent the student to fetch the gospels and said 'Since it is in your hand, you shall be my soul-friend'.[10] The tradition of having a soul-friend came from the east, where a monk grew in wisdom and holiness by sharing his thoughts with someone of greater experience.

A small handbell has survived from Congal's monastery, and the seventh-century *Antiphonary of Bangor*. This is one of the earliest surviving Irish manuscripts, and contains a variety of Celtic hymns and prayers. It was taken to Bobbio in Italy by Irish refugees fleeing from Viking raids, and was later brought to Milan. Monks travelled to Europe not only as refugees, but also as missionaries; they took their learning and artistic skills, and contributed greatly to the development of life and culture in early medieval Europe.

Chief among these missionaries was a student of Congal named Columbanus (*c*. 540–615). He was born in Leinster, probably of a noble family, and was well educated. He stayed with Congal until he was about fifty, when he sailed to Gaul with twelve companions. He landed in Burgundy, where the king gave him a ruined Roman fort for a monastery at Annegray in the Vosges mountains. The community grew, and Columbanus then established Fontaines and Luxeuil, which became one of the leading monasteries in Europe, sending monks as far as Bavaria.

His monks followed Celtic customs and calculated the date of Easter according to the Celtic calendar. A lengthy letter to Pope Gregory the Great survives, in which Columbanus explains his position. The Roman bishops of Gaul summoned Columbanus to a Council, where he defended his views. He also challenged the royal family by refusing to bless the illegitimate sons of the new king, and in 610, together with his monks, he was taken under armed escort to Nantes, to be deported back to Ireland. While waiting to set sail, he wrote a touching letter to the new monks he had left behind, urging them to make foundations, encouraging their new abbot, and telling them of his sorrow at leaving them.

A storm prevented the ship from setting out, so with some of his monks from Luxeuil, Columbanus rowed up the Rhine, hoping to settle beside Lake Constance, but he encountered opposition and decided to cross the Alps into Italy. His companion Gall (d. *c.* 630), who had come from Bangor with him, remained in Switzerland, living as a hermit. A century later a community was established on the site of Gall's hermitage, and the town of St Gall grew round it. Meanwhile in about 613 Columbanus settled at Bobbio in northern Italy, where he and his followers built a monastery on the site of a ruined church. He died two years later; he was buried in Bobbio, while his pastoral staff was taken back across the Alps to his friend Gall in Switzerland.

Many Irishmen came to St Gall, and it accumulated a priceless collection of early manuscripts. Some have Irish poetry written in the margins, like this poem from a ninth-century Latin grammar book:

> 'A thicket hedge surrounds me;
> a blackbird sings to me:
> I will not hide such praise.
> Birds trill above my small, lined book.
>
> The grey-cloaked cuckoo sings its lovely song
> from the tops of the bushes.
> Indeed, may the Lord protect me,
> I write well beneath the forest trees.'[11]

Followers of Columbanus established the European monasteries of Faremoutiers in 627, Jouarre in 630 and Rebais in 636 (see map 4), and large numbers of Irish monks came to Europe in the next two centuries. Some found leading positions at the court of the Emperor Charlemagne at Aachen; others travelled as far as Taranto in southern Italy and Kiev in Russia. Irish penitentials (systems of penalties for wrongdoing) influenced the development of European civil law. Gradually, European monasteries replaced the rule of Columbanus with that of the Italian-born Benedict, but medieval Christian Europe was to a great extent shaped by the Irish.

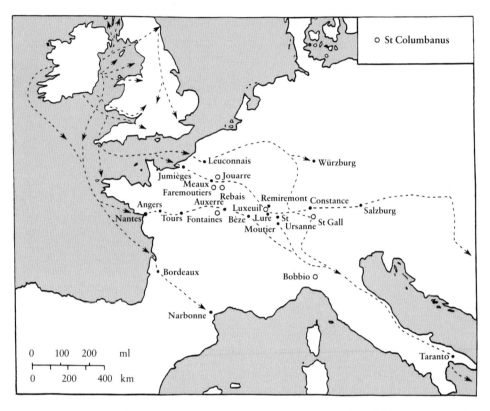

Map 4. Churches and monasteries in Europe which were founded by, or associated with, Celtic monks from Ireland.
Columbanus and other Irish missionaries travelled throughout Europe and beyond (after Fitzgerald).

There were also monks who travelled very little: Finbar (*c.* 560–*c.* 620), whose name means 'white crown' or 'white head', probably spent all his life in southwest Ireland. Finbar was said to be the son of a metalworker who married a slave girl. He studied under the bishop of Macroom, and became a hermit beside the lake of Gougane Barra (whose name means 'Finbar's rocky cave') in the Kerry mountains. Disciples gathered round him and he established a famous school on the east shore of the lake, which is the source of the River Lee.

Finbar later travelled downstream to the coast, where the Lee divides into channels separating twelve low-lying islands. Here, on a rocky outcrop he founded a community around which grew the city of Cork. Finbar's double monastery of monks and nuns lasted for a thousand years, but it was raided and burnt perhaps eleven times by Norsemen, who eventually settled. Finbar was buried in Cork, while Gougane Barra remained a centre of pilgrimage into modern times. Although Finbar travelled little, men of Cork did, and there are many places named after Finbar, particularly in Scotland, including, as we have seen, the island of Barra in the Hebrides.

Another monk who travelled little was St Kevin (d. *c.* 618). He was born in the early sixth century into a noble Leinster family ousted from kingship. He went to Glendalough ('glen of two lakes') in the Wicklow Mountains, and was said to have lived in a hollow tree while studying with three older monks. He later returned with a group of companions and settled there. Beside the upper lake at Glendalough there are the foundations of a circular stone hut, and a cave named 'St Kevin's Bed', originally a Bronze Age rock tomb. Nearby is a raised platform where other huts were probably built, and two chapels.

Near the lower lake, the gateway to the enclosure with its two granite arches is the only surviving monastery gateway in Ireland. The paving of the causeway through the monastery also survives, together with a round tower and six churches. One of these, St Kierán's church, may be dedicated to the young Ciarán of Clonmacnoise, whom Kevin is said to have visited when he lay dying of the plague; Ciarán is said to have given Kevin his handbell. Kevin himself died in old age. Clonmacnoise and Glendalough are the best preserved of Ireland's larger monasteries.

There are remains of smaller monasteries off the Irish west coast. The most complete is that of Skellig Michael, perched on a rocky island half a mile long, eight miles from the Kerry coast. On the island there are remains of at least six beehive huts, two square stone chapels and a ruined church, built on artificial terraces on the sloping rock. The windowless huts have walls two metres thick; most of their roofs are still intact. They have survived because of the mild climate here, with its lack of frost. There are carved crosses, grave-markers and two wells. The sixth-century monastery is reached by a flight of 1670 stone steps leading up from the sea. It is thought that the monks brought topsoil from the mainland to create small gardens in which they could grow vegetables. The monastery was raided by Vikings in the ninth century, and life on the rock was so harsh that eventually in the twelfth century the monks moved to Ballinskelligs on the mainland. In his novel *Sun Dancing: a Medieval Vision*, Geoffrey Moorhouse has reconstructed life in this remote monastery.[12]

Also in Kerry, at the western end of the Dingle peninsula, is Gallarus Oratory, in the foothills of Brandon Mountain. Its small monastery overlooks Smerwick Harbour, and was easily accessible by sea. A banked wall demarcates the monastery, and an internal wall separates the remains of the monks' huts from the chapel, which is perhaps eighth century. The rectangular oratory is eight metres long, and made of local gritstone. Its roof is formed by the gradual rise of its side walls from the base upwards (see overleaf). It is entered through a square-headed doorway in the west wall; inside are two projecting stones from which

Gallarus Oratory, Dingle peninsula, County Kerry. This is perhaps the only complete Celtic chapel to survive with its drystone walls and corbelled roof intact.

a leather or wooden door could be hung. A deeply splayed window in the east wall would shed morning light on the missal for the priest to celebrate Eucharist. Successive Viking and Norman invaders burned, robbed and destroyed settlements round Gallarus.

A mile north of Gallarus Oratory, on the pilgrim route to Brandon Mountain, is Kilmalkedar church, named after its founder, Maolcethair (d. 636). The present church is twelfth-century romanesque, with arcading modelled on Cormac's chapel at Cashel, but there are considerable earlier remains. At the churchyard entrance is a Celtic sundial, important for monks with an organized day of work and prayer. An early eighth-century pillar-stone has the Latin alphabet carved on it, and was used to teach literacy to students. To the west of the church, along its ancient causeway, is the monastery graveyard with a simple high cross, various grave-markers and an ogham-inscribed stone. The western end of the Dingle peninsula is a cult landscape, much of it dedicated to Brendan.

By the eighth century, communities varied widely in their degree of fidelity to the ideals of their founders, and there was a desire to return to the purity and austerity of early monastic life. A leading figure in this movement was Maelruáin (d. 792), who founded a monastery at Tallaght, on land given to him by the King of Leinster in 774. The reforming monks became known as Céli Dé ('Servants of God') or Culdees. Maelruáin's rule was severe: monks should stay in their monasteries instead of travelling freely, and should come together regularly for prayer, which consisted mainly of chanting the psalms.

Maelruáin wrote of the temptation that women posed to monks, and insisted on celibacy. He demanded abstinence from alcohol, and recommended penances such as night vigils standing in cold water. He emphasized spiritual direction and the confession of sin, and the importance of study and manual work. He encouraged devotion to Our Lady and to the Archangel Michael, the traditional guardian against evil. He taught that monks were entitled to collect tithes, a tenth of the produce of everyone else, and encouraged conformity to Roman practices.[13] The Culdees spread to Wales and Scotland, where they survived into medieval times.

The Culdees encouraged a return to solitude, and wrote poetry describing the attractive life of the monks of earlier days. The poems provide valuable descriptions of Celtic monastic life, even if their perspective is a little romantic. A tenth-century poem set in the seventh century takes the form of an imaginary dialogue in which a hermit named Marbhán explains to his brother Guaire, King of Connacht, why he has chosen to live in the woods rather than at court:

> 'I have a hut in the wood; no one knows it but my God.
> An ash grows in front, a hazel at the back.
>
> A great tree overhangs it;
> honeysuckle climbs round its lintel.
>
> My hut is small, but not too small.
> Brown-cloaked mother blackbird sings from the gable....
>
> An apple tree yields great bounty;
> watercress sprouts beside a pure spring.
>
> Tame swine lie down around it, goats, pigs,
> wild boar, tall deer, a badger's family....
>
> A clutch of eggs, honey: God has sent it.
> Sweet apples, blueberries,
> a patch of delicious strawberries.
>
> Haws, juniper berries, sloes, nuts,
> a cup of hazel mead....

> The lovely music of bright robin red-breast,
> the song of the thrush, the familiar cuckoo over my hut.
>
> Swarms of bees and beetles,
> the world's soft music, gently humming.
>
> Wild geese and ducks in autumn,
> the music of the dark river....
>
> The waterfall's cascade,
> the call of the swan: delightful music.
>
> A brave band entertains me without pay;
> in Christ's eyes, I fare no worse than you!
>
> These pleasures are greater than wealth can buy;
> I am grateful for what my good Christ gives me.
>
> Without an hour's fighting, with no noise of strife,
> grateful to the Prince who gives every good to me in my hut.'[14]

Another poem describes a small community of twelve monks, with their chapel, a spring for baptisms, their poultry and vegetables. It was written by a tenth-century poet, and put into the mouth of St Manchán, who died in about 750. Manchán had a hut near Dingle, Kerry, and the remains of his monastery can be seen at Lemanaghan, fifteen miles east of Clonmacnoise, where a tiny chapel and holy well are associated with his mother, St Mella. The unknown author writes:

> 'Son of the living God, ancient eternal King,
> I wish for a hut, hidden in the wilderness, as my dwelling.
>
> A lithe little grey lark beside it,
> a clear blue pool to wash away sins,
> through the Holy Spirit....
>
> Six pairs of men with me, continually at prayer
> to the King who moves the sun.
>
> A lovely church with a linen altar cloth,
> a home for the God of heaven,
> then shining candles above the holy, white Scriptures....
>
> This the housekeeping I would undertake,
> I would choose and will not conceal:
> fragrant leeks, hens, speckled salmon, bees.
>
> Enough food and clothing from the fair, famous King,
> as I sit for a while, praying to God in every place.'[15]

While the Culdees looked wistfully back to earlier times, the Irish monastic system gradually collapsed as the Church was reorganized into dioceses ruled by bishops. Religious Orders such as the Augustinians and the Cistercians were introduced from mainland Europe. In the late twelfth century the Anglo-Normans began to invade Ireland; they had conquered most of the country by the thirteenth century. In 1171 the Irish bishops convened a council at Cashel, presided over by the papal legate, at which they agreed to follow Roman customs for celebrating marriage, baptism and the Eucharist; they also passed decrees placing the clergy above Irish law. Bishops and abbots soon became feudal lords responsible to the English king. However in 1216 King John forbade Irishmen to become bishops, and the Celtic Church gradually merged into that of Rome, with its leaders now responsible to the Archbishop of Canterbury.

St Brigit's cross, made of rushes.

Chapter four
David and South Wales

BEFORE CHRISTIANITY reached Ireland, there were probably Christians in Wales. In Roman times, Wales had not yet emerged as an ethnic identity; it was simply part of mainland Britain, and Christianity reached it through the Roman army and administration. At this time, Wales was occupied by five main tribal groups of Iron Age peoples who did not yet use coinage. Between AD 48 and 78, most of the Roman offensive campaigns in Britain were directed against these tribes. In AD 75, Wales was brought under Roman control, and remained so for the next three hundred years.

Roman Wales was dominated by the two legionary fortresses of Chester in the north and Caerleon in the south, with twenty-four field forts placed at other strategic points. The Romans considered Wales to be a frontier zone on the edge of the empire; the only Roman towns were Carmarthen in the southwest and Caerwent in southeast Wales. As we saw in chapter 1, Julius and Aaron were two Christian soldiers who were tried at Caerwent and martyred at Caerleon in the mid-third century, but it is difficult to know how deeply Christianity took hold in later Roman Wales. It is probable that it spread mainly among the educated, for it appears that Christians spoke Latin rather than Welsh. Most inscriptions on early Christian tombstones are in Latin, and many early Welsh words describing Christian objects and ideas were borrowed from Latin.[1]

In the fifth and sixth centuries, Christians sailed from Gaul to northwest and southwest Wales, where tombstones are inscribed in Roman capitals, using a style that originated in Vienne in western Gaul and in Lyon to the southeast. After landing in south Wales, a number of these Gallic Christians travelled eastwards along what remained of the Roman roads into Brecon, where similar tombstones have been found. By this time monasteries were well established in Gaul, and among the Christians coming to Wales were monks and nuns with experience of both communal and solitary life.[2]

At the same time, after the Romans withdrew from Britain, Irish immigrants settled in southwest Wales. From the mid-third century onwards, Irish pirates had been raiding the southwest coast; Roman military policy at this time was directed at repelling the raiders. Irish families, too, had been migrating to southwest Wales in large numbers. Ireland's expanding population was organized into small kingdoms whose territory contained little pasture and much bog, mountain and forest. Since the Irish were largely cattle ranchers (they counted their wealth in heads of cattle), pasture was in demand, and families probably emigrated in search of land, but the influx of Irish settlers in south Wales caused new problems over land ownership.[3]

In the early fifth century, southern Irish families migrating to Wales brought with them their ogham writing, in which letters were notched on the edges of memorial stones to form a stroke alphabet. In Ireland, tombstones are inscribed in ogham alone, but in southwest Wales they are bilingual, inscribed in both ogham and Latin, as Irish settlers intermingled with Gallic Christians. The bilingual tombstones are found along the Roman roads of southeast Wales. Along the same Roman roads there are dedications to the fourth-century family of Magnus Maximus (see chapter 1). This suggests that his wife Helen and their children, particularly Peblig and Custennin, established some of the earliest Welsh churches.[4] Through her friendship with Martin of Tours, Helen brought to Wales an experience of monastic life in Gaul.

The early Welsh Church, like that of Ireland, was largely monastic, in contrast to the diocesan system that existed in Europe. By the early sixth century there were a number of Welsh monasteries, from which missionaries established other churches. Charters from Llandaff list thirty-six monasteries in southeast Wales alone.[5] The early monasteries contained both monks and non-monastic priests, and were presided over by an abbot who was often a bishop. Some monks left their community for a while and became hermits, in order to spend more time in prayer.

Bishops and abbots were normally married, and leadership was passed down within the family; monasteries were therefore tribal. This has resulted in a large number of very local saints, based on kinship patterns, where the family, the clan and its territory were of prime importance. Most Welsh saints have only one or two churches dedicated to them, in contrast to churches in mainland Europe and Norman re-dedications in Wales, which are mainly to Mary, to the apostles and to early Roman saints.[6]

Chief among the Irish adventurers who helped to shape the Church in south Wales was Brychan, who gave his name to Brecon. This small, ancient territory of southeast Wales is a landlocked upland region, encircled by mountains; it is centred on the upper Usk valley. We hear first of Brychan's grandfather, Tewdrig (or Theodoric), styled 'King of Gwent', who died in about 470. His dedications at Bedwas, Llandow, Merthyr Tydfil and Mathern indicate a sphere of influence in the coastal plain south of the Brecon Beacons. His church in the hamlet of Mathern was close to an important river crossing of the Severn, as it is today, with the Severn Bridge close by. In Roman times, most of these coastal flats were marshlands, but there was a harbour at Mathern.

According to the twelfth-century *Book of Llandaff*, Tewdrig handed over leadership to his son and became a hermit at Tintern, five miles

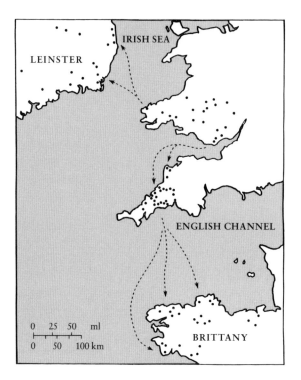

Map 5. *Dedications to the children of Brychan, who was a sixth-century ruler of Brecon in southeast Wales. Across the Celtic world, many churches are named after his children (after Bowen).*

north, in the Wye Valley. He was recalled to fight the Saxons, and defeated them, but was mortally injured. He asked to be buried on Flat Holm, an island twenty miles southwest in the Bristol Channel, but died at Mathern and was buried in the nearby church. Tradition relates that his wounds were washed in St Tewdrig's well, close by.

We hear of Tewdrig's daughter, Marcella, in a document dating from about 580 entitled *The Events of Brychan's Kingdom*, which was probably written by a priest in the royal household. It tells how Marcella was taken back to Ireland for a clan marriage to a prince named Amlech. Her journey took her from Brecon westwards along the ancient route-ways to Porth Mawr, the harbour of St David's, where her party embarked for Ireland. The journey took place during a severe winter, in which the night frosts killed many of the warriors who accompanied her. Tewdrig had a fur garment made for his daughter, to protect her from the cold which attacked the party 'like a wild boar'.[7]

Before returning to Wales, Marcella gave birth to Brychan (*c.* 490–*c.* 550), whose name means 'little badger'. The document describes how, after their return, Brychan was fostered and educated from the age of four by a local wise man, as was traditional at the time. When he was eleven, the young prince was placed as a resident hostage in the family of a neighbouring chieftain: this aristocratic custom prevented border skirmishes. The teenage Brychan raped the chieftain's daughter, who was named 'Broom Blossom', meaning 'golden-haired'. She bore him a son, Cynog, who was taken back to Brecon to be baptized; as a token of his royalty, Brychan gave him a precious bracelet.[8]

Brecon's elders refused to recognize Cynog as the heir apparent, perhaps because they considered his mother to come from an inferior family. Instead, Cynog became a 'holy man'; meanwhile, Brychan married formally, and had many children. Twelve sons are named, and twelve daughters. This ancient list may have been designed to be read aloud at the Eucharist, as benefactors for whom the congregation should pray.[9] No two accounts agree over the names or the total number of Brychan's children, but their dedications in southeast Wales, from Brecon westwards along the Roman roads, suggest that the family was instrumental in the spread of Christianity from Brecon in the fifth and sixth centuries.

One of Brychan's sons or grandsons named Cynon settled two thirds of the way along the route to Ireland from Brecon, in Carmarthenshire, beside the River Taf. Here, a church is dedicated to him at Llangynin, while his name appears on an inscribed stone at Newchurch, not far away. The gravestone of Cynon's daughter was found at nearby Eglwys Gymyn, inscribed in Latin and ogham: 'Avitoria, daughter of Cunignus (lies here)'. Since the Brychan family was half-Irish, it was considered appropriate to commemorate Avitoria in the Irish ogham script.[10]

Brychan and his family remained popular throughout medieval times. A fifteenth-century stained-glass window in St Neot's church at the foot of Bodmin Moor in east Cornwall portrays Brychan as a medieval monarch. He sits on a throne, wearing a golden crown and a blue robe trimmed with ermine, nursing eleven of his saintly children. Church dedications suggest that members of Brychan's clan migrated to Cornwall and Brittany, and also returned to Ireland (see map 5). In south Devon and east Cornwall, a cluster of adjacent parishes are named after members of Brychan's clan. Ogham-inscribed stones were found in this area.

There are another three tombstones inscribed in the Irish ogham script at Nevern church, near the north Pembrokeshire coast. Nevern is the chief church of Brynach Wyddel ('Brynach the Irishman'). According to Brynach's *Life*, he was Brychan's chaplain or soul-friend, and married one of his daughters. The thirteen churches dedicated to Brynach are along the ancient routes from Brecon to Ireland, concentrated at the western end, near the embarkation points for Ireland. Today's ferry-crossing from Fishguard to Rosslare follows a similar route. Brynach and his contemporaries made the crossing to Ireland by curragh; for river travel they used coracles. Illustrated overleaf is a traditional coracle from this area; they can still be seen on the River Teifi, not far from Nevern.

Brynach's church in Nevern is at the foot of a well-preserved hill-fort, whose chieftain gave Brynach land to enclose, with the Caman brook as

A coracle on the River Teifi, southeast Wales. Celtic missionaries used these craft for river travel and for fishing.

a boundary between them. In later life, Brynach is said to have become a hermit on the mountain above the fort, from where Ireland can be seen on a clear day. Nevern was an important church of Pembrokeshire, with a collection of carved crosses dating from around 400, during the time of the Roman occupation, and a great cross four metres high carved in the tenth or eleventh century, covered with elaborate knotwork panels.

The first Irishman associated with the southern Welsh monasteries was Tathan. According to his *Life* he was a prince who became a monk and sailed up the Severn estuary in search of a hermitage. He established a community on the coast at Llantathan in the mid-fifth century, and later travelled twenty-five miles east to Caerwent, where he obtained a grant of land from the local ruler and founded a monastery. As we saw in chapter 1, Julius and Aaron had been tried and condemned in Caerwent, two centuries earlier; Tathan's church is near the centre of the ruined Roman town. According to his *Life*, Tathan was known for his generosity, his hospitality and protection of the poor; people called him 'the Father of all Gwent'. Cadoc was said to have trained in Tathan's monastery at Caerwent, before founding his own.

We know considerably more about Dubricius (d. *c.* 550). His mother was a Welsh chieftain's daughter from the small territory of Erging in Herefordshire. His chief monastery was at Hentland, near Ross on Wye. Its name, *hen llan*, means 'the old, or former church', suggesting that it fell into disuse and was later re-dedicated. There is a cluster of churches named after Dubricius, some on Roman sites. One at Whitchurch (which means 'white' or 'stone' church) is built beside the River Wye, with an ancient landing stage in the churchyard to provide access by boat. The early *Life of Samson* describes Dubricius as having authority over Illtud's great monastery at Llanilltud Fawr, which will be described later in this chapter. Samson's *Life* relates how Dubricius visited Illtud's community on a Sunday to ordain Samson as deacon and two other men as priests. Early manuscripts describing the event call Dubricius *papa* or *episcopo*, so he seems to have been regarded as a Romano-British bishop.

Dubricius had jurisdiction over a community on Caldey Island in Carmarthen Bay; the monastery was a daughter house of Llanilltud Fawr in the Vale of Glamorgan, forty miles southeast, as the seagull flies. At this time, Caldey Island was named Ynys Pyr after its first abbot, Pyr. The *Life of Samson* describes Pyr's undignified death: walking back to his hut one night, the drunken abbot fell into the monastery's well, and was drowned. Dubricius appointed Samson as abbot to replace Pyr; under Samson the community was perhaps more peaceful, for Dubricius used to come to Caldey each Lent, for forty days of solitude. There are many caves around the island's coastline; the monks probably lived in these, and in wattle huts clustered around a chapel, near the spring which still supplies the island with abundant fresh water. A grave-slab found near the well is inscribed in ogham 'Magl Dubr...' or '(the stone of) the tonsured servant of Dubricius'.

Ynys Pyr was a foundation of some significance: a sixth-century fragment of red glazed pottery from the eastern Mediterranean was found here, and the base of a seventh-century jar from Gaul.[11] The tiny parish church of St David on Caldey may be built on sixth-century foundations; in earlier times this site was just above the high water mark. Linked with the monastery was a community of nuns on St Margaret's Island, which adjoins Caldey. At this time it was possible to walk across low-lying marsh to St Margaret's Island from the mainland at Penally.

In old age, Dubricius retired to Bardsey Island in north Wales, off the tip of the Lleyn peninsula, where he died and was buried. The followers of Dubricius played a part in the migration southwards of Welsh missionaries, for Porlock church on the Somerset coast is dedicated to Dubricius. Porlock is an easy day's sail from the southeast coast of Wales.

The most famous early Welsh monastery was founded by Illtud (*c.* 425–505). The early seventh-century *Life of Samson* tells us that Illtud was a Breton soldier of fortune who came to Wales to fight under a Glamorgan chieftain. Dissatisfied with a soldier's life, he became a monk and his wife became a nun. Illtud was ordained by Germanus, Bishop of Auxerre in about 445, and five years later he established a monastery at Llanilltud Fawr, meaning 'Illtud's great church' (in English, Llantwit Major). This was a channel port near the main route to Ireland, far enough up the Bristol Channel for a sheltered crossing to England and mainland Europe. It is not directly on the coast, but is hidden in a small river valley, out of sight of pirates. Nearby St Donats provided a natural harbour.

Illtud may have lived here first as a hermit before he attracted followers and built a church with a school and monastery. Dubricius prepared Illtud as a monk, and marked out the monastic enclosure. The author of Samson's *Life* describes how young Samson was taken by his parents to Illtud's famous school. He explains that Illtud combined Christian, classical and druidic learning: he was the most learned of all Britons in scripture and philosophy, poetry and rhetoric, grammar and arithmetic. He was of druid descent, most wise, and able to foretell the future. The writer adds a personal comment: 'I have been in his magnificent monastery'. Samson was later to succeed Illtud as abbot. A fine collection of early Celtic crosses at Llanilltud Fawr commemorates various monks and chieftains.

Illtud is said to have drained land for cultivation, and introduced an improved form of plough. He sailed back to Brittany with some ships of corn to relieve a famine. There are seven dedications to Illtud in Brittany. Monks set out from Llanilltud Fawr to preach: there are fourteen churches named after Illtud in southeast Wales. There is one dedication to Illtud in the north, on the coast two miles northwest of Dolgellau. It is named Llanelltyd, using the northern, Brittonic, spelling of his name, Elltyd, instead of the usual southern, Gaelic form. This is an ancient holy site, with a Celtic yew tree in its churchyard. Inside the tiny church is a stone with an inscription: 'The footprint of Kenrick is preserved at the top of this stone, and he was here himself before he went abroad'. It was carved in the ninth or tenth century, perhaps by a pilgrim on his way to Jerusalem, Rome or Bardsey Island, as a prayer for his safe return.

Famous monks and scholars studied at Illtud's monastery: Samson, Gildas and Paul Aurelian. Equally interesting are some of the less famous monks who came here. One of these was Gwyndaf from Brittany, who later studied at Caerleon. A Pembrokeshire tradition tells how Gwyndaf travelled westwards with Áedán, another monk, to St David's. When they were only two miles from their destination, they stopped to drink at a well, Ffynnon Tregroes ('well at the village crossroads'), in Whitchurch parish. Each wished to give his name to the well, so they fought, and Gwyndaf lost. Áedán dedicated the well to himself and continued to St David's.[12]

Beaten, Gwyndaf went off in a different direction, and established a settlement at Llanwnda, ten miles northeast, on a cliff top above present-day Fishguard, where a church and a holy well are named after him. There is another story of the hot-tempered monk: at the boundary stream of the settlement, his horse reared at a jumping fish. Gwyndaf fell off and cursed the water, which is why there are no fish in the stream that springs from his holy well. The two stories show a typically Celtic approach to blessing and cursing. There are remains of five interesting Celtic crosses in the outer wall of Gwyndaf's tiny church on its windswept cliff. Situated at a crossing point for Ireland, it became a significant monastery. Bishop Asser, counsellor to King Alfred the Great, is said to have trained at Llanwnda, and the historian Gerald of Wales worked here for a while in the twelfth century.

The first member of Brychan's clan to be associated with the great Welsh monasteries was Cadoc (*c.* 497–577). His mother was said to be Gwladys, one of Brychan's daughters, and his father a prince of Gwent, to whom Newport cathedral is dedicated. According to his eleventh-century *Life*, Cadoc studied at Tathan's monastery in Caerwent. As a young man he returned to Llangattock-nigh-Usk ('Cadoc's church near the Usk') in his father's territory to evangelize the inhabitants of the hill-fort above the river. He then travelled west and founded a monastery at Llancarfan, only four miles east of the community that Illtud had established, perhaps seventy years earlier, at Llanilltud Fawr.

Many of Cadoc's fellow-students from Caerwent came to join him at Llancarfan. Each lived alone in his hut, and they came together for worship. Cadoc valued classical learning and loved Virgil; Cadoc's *Life* notes his regret that as a Christian he would be unable to meet the pagan poet in heaven! Finnian of Clonard (see chapter 3) may have studied with Cadoc and taken back to Ireland his pattern of solitude, study and communal worship. Llancarfan is a small village, now some miles from the sea, which has receded. The Celtic monastery was probably in the field to the south of the medieval church; only its well survives.

There are fifteen dedications to Cadoc in Wales: a group around his monastery at Llancarfan, and another to the northwest in his father's territory of Gwent, centred around Llangattock-nigh-Usk. Cadoc also established a church in Caerleon, which he built in the courtyard of its ruined legionary headquarters, once familiar to Julius and Aaron, as we have seen. Part of a ninth-century high cross survives from Cadoc's church in Caerleon, decorated with bird-like angels. It stood outside the churchyard, beside the crossroads at the town centre. In between his travels, Cadoc spent much of his life at Llancarfan. In old age, he handed over the leadership of his community to a younger monk. His *Life* relates that he died while celebrating the Eucharist, when a Saxon horseman entered the church and killed him with a lance.

Cadoc or his monks travelled further afield. There are two dedications to Cadoc in Scotland, one at Cambuslang above the Clyde in Glasgow, and another at Kilmadock ('my Doc's church'), near Callander, twenty-five miles further north. In the opposite direction, Cadoc is honoured with an ancient ruined chapel and a holy well on Cadoc Farm in Harlyn Bay on the north Cornish coast, two miles west of Padstow. There are also twenty-three dedications to Cadoc in Brittany, spreading out from his monastery on the Ile de Cado ('Cadoc's island').

A scholar who may have trained in the great Welsh monasteries was the sixth-century historian, Gildas. His *Life* relates that he was a chieftain's son, born in Dumbarton on the Clyde. He married and had two sons before travelling southwards. He may have worked among the British of Strathclyde, together with Cadoc, to whom Cambuslang is dedicated, twelve miles further up the Clyde. Cadoc was said to be the soul-friend or chaplain of Gildas. There is a wide scattering of dedications to Gildas – the isle of St Kilda, far out to the northwest, may be named after him.[13] According to tradition, Gildas used to spend Lent on the island of Steep Holm in the Bristol Channel, while his friend Cadoc made his Lenten retreat on nearby Flat Holm, although both were attacked on these vulnerable islands by Pictish pirates from the Orkneys.

Gildas wrote a broadside against the British, which includes a denunciation of the British king, Maelgwyn Gwynedd, and other rulers of his day. Gildas blames their wrongdoings for the victory of the Anglo-Saxon invaders. The book combines powerful rhetoric with a knowledge of Virgil, the Scriptures and the Letters of Ignatius of Antioch (d. *c.* AD 107). The work was highly thought of by his contemporaries, and quoted by Bede. Gildas migrated to southern Brittany, where he founded the island monastery of St Gildas de Rhuys.

An eleventh-century monk from the community wrote a *Life of Gildas*, based on earlier material. He tells us that Gildas and his family were forced southwards from Dumbarton by the inroads of the Picts and Scots, and how Gildas came under the spell of monastic life in Illtud's monastery. The biographer situates Gildas within a clan who also accompanied him to Brittany, where they have widespread dedications. His *Life* relates that the last request of Gildas was to be placed in a coracle to drift out to sea. In Celtic tradition, the Isles of the Blessed lay beyond the setting sun, over the sea's rim.

Recent scholars, however, have outlined a different picture of Gildas. They suggest that he was a priest educated in the 470s not as a monk but as a rhetorician, in preparation for a career in government. His place of origin is questioned, but he is thought to have worked in the land of the Durotriges, corresponding to Somerset, Devon and east Wiltshire.[14]

 An early monk from southeast Wales who migrated westwards was Padarn. His seven known foundations follow the two Roman roads which run north and south, linking forts on either side of the Cambrian mountains. This implies that Padarn worked in the settlements around the ruined Roman garrisons; his name, Paternus, was a common Roman name. He may have preceded David and Teilo who also worked in this area of Wales, and will be discussed later in this chapter. Padarn persuaded the local chieftain to give him land between the Rivers Rheidol and Clarach, and built a monastery on a hillside in what is now a southern suburb of Aberystwyth. For the next twenty years, Padarn was bishop and abbot of his monastery of Llanbadarn Fawr, whose name means 'Padarn's great church'. The site is near Sarn Helen, an ancient trackway continuing the line of the Roman coastal road, named after Helen, the wife of Magnus Maximus.

Llanbadarn Fawr had close links with Ireland, and later it may have become a reformed Culdee community. Unlike other Welsh monasteries in the southwest, it became a centre of learning. By the eleventh century, under Abbot Sulien the Wise, its library was larger than those of Canterbury Cathedral or York Minster. Sulien was born in Llanbadarn Fawr and was twice bishop of St David's; his four sons also became monks at Llanbadarn. The eldest, Rhygyfarch, wrote a *Life of David*. Another, Ieuan, later archpriest of Llanbadarn, illustrated Rhygyfarch's Psalter, and wrote a poem about his father Sulien, wistfully recalling the former greatness of the monastery, which had perhaps been absorbed into the sphere of influence of St David's. A pre-Christian standing stone carved into a cross by Padarn's monks still survives at Llanbadarn Fawr, with a granite pillar cross, three metres high, carved in about 750, on which a worn figure with a crozier may represent St Padarn.

Another southern Welsh monastery was founded by Teilo in the sixth century at Llandeilo Fawr, near the main inland route to Ireland. Teilo was probably born at Penally on the coast, between Tenby and Caldey Island. In 1988 a Celtic chieftain's residence was excavated at Penally, on the Trefloyne Estate, whose name is thought to mean 'homestead of Teilo's grove' (*Tref Llwyn Teilo*). Pottery and coloured glass from Gaul and the eastern Mediterranean dating from the fifth to the seventh centuries was found here, together with fine metal work; animal bones provided evidence of feasting. Penally was therefore a place of some significance in Teilo's time.[15]

Writing in about 1130, Geoffrey of Llandaff says that Teilo was a student of Dubricius and Paul Aurelian. During the plague, Teilo went to Brittany for seven years, and stayed at Samson's monastery of Dol. He returned to Wales and established a community at Llandeilo Fawr above the River Towy, twenty miles from the sea. The extent of Teilo's monastery is outlined by the very large churchyard of three and a half acres; it is bisected by the town's main street, which may follow the line of a Roman road. A spring rises near the east end of the church, and flows into a large chamber beneath it. This is probably the site of a baptistery in which Teilo immersed converts. The spring provided the town with its water until the nineteenth century; today it bubbles into an alcove in the churchyard wall.

Teilo's monks travelled across south Wales and named thirty-three churches after their master. Teilo died and was buried at Llandeilo Fawr. Remains of two finely carved crosses from the late eighth century show the continuing importance of the community. A magnificent Irish or Mercian gospel book, illuminated around 730, was given to the monastery in about 820 'for the good of his soul' by a man named Gelhi, who had bought the book from a certain Guyal in exchange for his best horse. The gospel book contains stylized figures of the four evangelists: Luke holds a pastoral staff modelled on those carried by abbots of the Near East, and there are whole pages of intricate eastern-style 'carpet' decoration in which fish, dogs and pelicans are intertwined.

Monks at Llandeilo Fawr wrote entries in Welsh in the margins of the gospel book, recording gifts to the bishop of St Teilo. These records of land transactions and legal settlements are the earliest surviving examples of written Welsh. A gift of land at Brechfa, ten miles northwest of the monastery, is recorded: 'This writing shows that Rhys and Hirv (gave to God and St Teilo) Brechfa.... Its rent payment is sixty loaves, and a ram, and a quantity of butter.' Today, Brechfa's tiny church is dedicated to Teilo, and his well was across the road from the church, beside a tributary of the River Towy. The gospel book was perhaps paid as tribute to a Saxon king, for some time after 850 it was owned by St Chad's cathedral, Lichfield, where it still remains.

As with Patrick and Brigit, the life of David (d. *c.* 589) is overlaid with centuries of legend. We are fortunate that not long before his death, Professor Bowen presented the results of a lifelong study of David in a lecture to commemorate the eight hundredth anniversary of St David's. David's father was Sant, King of Ceredigion, a great-grandson of the chieftain Cunedda. According to tradition, David's mother was named Non, which means 'a nun'. Medieval pilgrims who flocked to St David's were shown his traditional birthplace on a cliff-top a mile south of the cathedral. The site is indeed ancient: a medieval chapel based on Celtic foundations, standing within a Bronze Age stone circle. Through the centuries, Non's holy well near her chapel has been one of the most famous in Wales, particularly known for healing eye diseases. Non may have travelled to Cornwall where several wells and churches are dedicated to her; she was buried in Brittany.

David was educated at the monastery of Henfynyw, just south of Aberaeron, on the coast road to Aberystwyth. The monastery had a reputation for learning, under its bishop Guistilianus. It stood on a cliff overlooking the sea, beside a steep-sided valley where boats could land. A block from a large pillar-stone built into the wall of the modern church is one of three inscribed to a seventh-century Welsh Christian, Tigeirnacus, who was evidently a well-known figure.

David rose to a position of leadership during the Synod of Brefi. This was a religious assembly called to stem the growing influence of the heretical teachings of Pelagius. This theologian taught that people make their first steps towards salvation or damnation by their own choices, a doctrine which had evident appeal to British tribal chieftains, who did not share the philosophical outlook of more fully Romanized peoples.

Brefi is a small village today, but it lies on a Roman road running the length of Wales from Carmarthen to Caernarvon, close to the Roman gold mines of Pumpsaint. The road was probably still in use in David's day, though partly overgrown. At the gathering, no one could make their voice heard over such a large crowd. David was a clear, convincing speaker, and was fetched from nearby to address the assembly.[16] He wore rough clothes, perhaps of animal skins, and carried a large branch rather than a crozier. He may have gone about bareheaded and barefoot, and he carried a bell which he named 'bangu' ('dear loud one'). A fine collection of gravestones from the Celtic monastery can be seen at Llanddewi Brefi church. An early seventh-century inscription on one, built into the outside wall, may be the first surviving reference to David. Before it was damaged, it was copied by the seventeenth-century antiquarian, Edward Lhuyd. It read: 'Here lies Idnert, the son of Jacob, who was killed while defending the church of holy David from pillage.'

Place-names suggest that David's cult spread eastwards from Henfynyw. His biographer relates that David returned south into the land from which his mother came, and established the monastery of St David's on a headland. Three companions worked with him, Áedán, Teilo and Ysmael, the first two of whom we have already met. St David's was not as remote as it appears today: it was an embarkation point for north Wales, southern Ireland, Cornwall, Brittany and the Bristol Channel. Major inland routes also led there. Dotted around the headland, within a few miles of the cathedral, are eight medieval chapels like that of Non, where travellers could climb up from the coast below and give thanks for a safe journey, for small boats were at the mercy of the winds, tides and tricky local currents.[17]

David chose a site in the narrow valley of the River Alun, hidden from sea-pirates by a bend in the river, for his small mud and timber church and monks' huts. They probably built a guardroom and store house, and erected a preaching cross inside an oval retaining wall, marking out a cemetery and fields beyond the enclosure. The land belonged to an Irish chieftain named Baia, who occupied an earlier hill-fort above the site. Baia and his wife noticed smoke rising from the monks' settlement, and challenged David in various ways, until Baia was killed by another Irish raider named Liski, who arrived in the night. The farm beneath the hill-fort is named after Baia (*Clegyr Boia*), while a nearby coastal inlet, Porth Lysky, is named after Liski.[18]

A little further round St David's headland, opposite Ramsey Island, is a chapel and well dedicated to a hermit called Justinian. He is said to have come from Brittany and settled on Ramsey, where a solitary named Honorius also lived; both men have early, Romanized names. David invited Justinian to visit him, and they became friends. Justinian's chapel beside the sea was restored by Bishop Vaughan in the early sixteenth century. The hermit's relics were placed in the same casket as David's, in the cathedral two miles east of Justinian's chapel.

There is an ancient church dedicated to Justinian in the valley of the River Cleddau at Llanstinan near Fishguard, ten miles northeast of St David's. The church is inside an early stone circle. Seven springs rise on the site, which was once a lakeshore. The village of Scleddau which surrounded the church has now disappeared, although rambler roses from cottage gardens still grow in the hedgerows. The church is built on Celtic foundations, and has a 'squinch' or small triangular room between the nave and the chancel, on the site where a hermit's cell adjoined the church. By living in a hut built against the church wall, a medieval hermit could retain his privacy, yet also be present at church services. A squinch is a feature of many early Pembrokeshire churches.

Most of our knowledge of David comes from Rhygyfarch's *Life of David* written in Latin around 1095 and preserved in a copy of about 1200. While this is a late text, it preserves earlier information, since Rhygyfarch's father, Sulien, was Bishop of St David's for ten years, and therefore well acquainted with the traditions about him. Sulien was instrumental in organizing a meeting between two of the most powerful Welsh princes and William the Conqueror in 1081 at St David's, at which Rhygyfarch was present. The Welsh princes probably appealed to the English king to uphold the Welsh Church against the increasing power of Rome. Rhygyfarch wrote his *Life* at this time, perhaps for this occasion. It is therefore not only a historical account, but also a political statement about the independence of the Welsh Church.[19]

Rhygyfarch's *Life of David* became a model for later works in this genre. Every *Life* followed a set pattern, based partly on the life of Jesus as portrayed in the gospels. The saint is therefore given a royal ancestry, and a miracle attests his birth. He is educated by famous teachers and guided by angels. He must perform miracles, including raising someone from the dead. He visits the pope, who consecrates him to high office. A divine visitor warns him of his approaching death.

Rhygyfarch also introduced elements from his own familiar world, and gave David's monastery an eleventh-century structure. It has a scriptorium for copying manuscripts, and provision for hospitality and care of the sick. There is an established rule and organized agriculture. These are elements found in the eleventh-century Benedictine and Cistercian monasteries of Rhygyfarch's day. There is also Irish influence on the *Life*: Irish place-names, a meeting with St Brendan afloat on a sea monster, recalling the *Voyage of Brendan*, and St Barre miraculously riding David's horse home across the Irish Sea.[20]

Another feature of Rhygyfarch's *Life* is its archaic Welsh flavour. It was traditionally held that a victorious bard could silence his opponents.

In the same way, David silenced lesser preachers while still in the womb, and at the Synod of Brefi, only he could quieten the crowd and convince them of the errors of Pelagius. The *Life* incorporates an early Welsh legend in which a girl with ritually dressed hair is sacrificed in a hazel wood. It sits uneasily in the *Life*, and has become attached to the struggle between David and Baia, whom Rhygyfarch describes as a druid: Baia's wife invites her step-daughter Dunawd to go nut-gathering with her. The step-mother sits down and asks the girl to lay her head in her lap for her hair to be dressed, but when Dunawd does so, her step-mother cuts her throat. A healing spring rises from the spot where Dunawd's blood touched the ground.[21]

Nine paragraphs of the *Life* describe how David and his followers lived, providing us with a vivid and authentic description of life in an early Celtic monastery. The monks were to grow all their food, working hard with mattocks, hoes and axes. They were to plough the fields themselves, instead of using oxen, and spend the remainder of each day reading, writing and praying. In the evening, the chapel bell summoned them to sing vespers, chanting the psalms 'with heart and voice in complete harmony'. They then prayed silently until nightfall, when at last they were allowed to eat together, but only 'bread and herbs seasoned with salt' taken in moderation, and washed down with ale. Guests, the sick and the elderly might have more appetizing food.

The monks then returned to chapel for silent prayer, 'trying not to make a noise by yawning, sneezing or spitting'. They remained 'in vigils, prayers and genuflections for about three hours'. After a short night's sleep, they woke at cock-crow to sing matins and to 'spend the rest of the night until morning without sleep'. They wore simple clothes, mostly of animal skins. There was little emphasis on study, in contrast to the value placed on learning in the monasteries of Illtud and Cadoc. Monks must keep silence and 'work so hard that they desire only to love each other'. They were to own nothing, giving away all their possessions before being allowed to join the community, and so enter the monastery 'naked, as if escaping from a shipwreck'.[22]

There is an interesting reference to David in a *Life of Paul Aurelian* written by a monk named Gourmonoc in the abbey of Landévennec in Brittany in 884. Gourmonoc tells us that David was nicknamed 'Aquaticus' ('water-drinker') because he lived on bread, vegetables and water alone. The austerity of David and his monks over several centuries suggests that in time St David's became one of the centres of the Irish Culdees, who were a powerful reforming force in the Irish Church from the mid-eighth century onwards. They emphasized a strict observance of the rhythms of monastic life, and a penitential spirit.

There is archaeological evidence of a Culdee community in south Wales at Burry Holms, an island off the western tip of the Gower peninsula, and penitential poems in *The Black Book of Carmarthen* resemble Irish Culdee poetry. Rhygyfarch's father Sulien studied in Ireland, where he could have encountered these reforming monks, before he became bishop of St David's in 1073. If St David's was a Culdee community, this might explain its continued ascetic lifestyle, so different from the southeastern monasteries established by Illtud and Cadoc.[23]

Dedications suggest that David's early followers may have worked in southern Ireland, Cornwall and Brittany. A Cornish church and holy well are dedicated to David on the edge of Bodmin Moor at Davidstow, only five miles from Altarnun, named after St Non. There are another eight ancient dedications to David in Cornwall, and seven more in Brittany. In the mid-ninth century, Viking raids on Wales began; in 984 St David's, Llanilltud Fawr and Llancarfan were sacked. St David's was attacked several times, and its bishop Morgenau was killed in 999. Small numbers of Vikings settled around the Welsh coast: Ramsey, Caldey and Fishguard are Norse names. As Vikings began to settle, they became Christian; by the eleventh century they were providing soldiers for the Welsh kings in their struggle against the English.[24]

After 1066, Norman warlords began to move across the Welsh border. In 1107 Llandaff Cathedral was given its first Norman bishop, Urban, who paid allegiance to Canterbury. More Welsh bishops were replaced by Englishmen, monasteries were suppressed and dedications to Celtic saints replaced by those in the Roman calendar. Illtud's monastery was closed down and its possessions given to Tewkesbury Abbey. Political uprisings continued as the Welsh struggled to retain independence, but in 1535, during the reign of King Henry VIII, an Act of Annexation declared England's intention to 'utterly extirp' Welsh culture and language.[25] The native church had already disappeared.

Chapter five
Celtic North Wales

A LL THE SIGNIFICANT early Welsh saints such as Dubricius, Illtud and Cadoc were born in south Wales. There was no similar development in north Wales, where the only major native saint, Beuno, was rather later. His work will be examined in the following chapter. North Wales was also relatively unaffected by the Irish Church. There are a few stones inscribed in Irish ogham in northwest Wales, but most are in the south. However, there are about fifty tombstones carved in Roman Gallic style in north Wales, including four of the earliest. This suggests that Christianity in north Wales from the fifth to the seventh centuries was influenced by the Church of Gaul. Twelve churches dedicated to the family of Magnus Maximus in north Wales tell a similar story. Most of these are near the coast, suggesting that Gallic Christians were among those who reached north Wales by sea.

North Wales also differs from the south in that there was considerable movement of people from northern England and southern Scotland into north Wales from the second century BC to the seventh century AD. Towards the end of the Roman occupation, in the late fourth century, the Romans reorganized the northern frontier of Britain and deported tribesmen from Northumbria and the Firth of Forth to north Wales, perhaps to protect British territory against Irish raiders. Ancient genealogists called these northerners the Sons of Cunedda, after an ancestral chieftain. The immigrants may have been evangelized by Ninian (see chapter 7) in the fifth century before they left home, or they may have encountered Christianity in north Wales; either way, a number of north Welsh saints are described as descendants of Cunedda.

Cunedda's people made their headquarters at Aberffraw, on the southwest coast of Anglesey, which remained the nominal centre of their kingdom until the thirteenth century. Other northerners migrated southwards and settled among the people of Cunedda. Among them was Maelgwyn Gwynedd, whose name means 'Princely Hound'. Maelgwyn was a Christian prince of Strathclyde who left home, possibly for political reasons, and carved out a territory in the land annexed by the Sons of Cunedda who, like Maelgwyn, spoke Brittonic, the language of the northern British Celts. In the sixth century, Maelgwyn ruled from Aberffraw; two miles to the east, Llangadwaladr was the royal burial-ground. The Catamus Stone, dating from 625, was found here: it is dedicated to one of Cunedda's family. The inscription on the stone is phrased in the style of the imperial court at Constantinople, and the lettering is in the latest European fashion of the day.

Llangadwaladr is named after another Cuneddan prince, St Cadwaladr (d. 664), a prayerful peace-loving man, the son of King Cadwallon. He was nicknamed 'the Battleshunner', but despite this, Cadwaladr, together with King Penda of Mercia, defeated and killed King Edwin of Northumbria in 633. He later led his people against the army of the King of Wessex and suffered a terrible defeat at Peonne in Somerset in 658. Two other churches in Denbighshire and Monmouthshire are dedicated to St Cadwaladr. Another of Cunedda's descendants was the monk Eurgain, whose splendid late medieval church dominates the small town of Llaneurgain (Northop in English), three miles south of the Dee estuary. Yet another of Cunedda's family was St Edern, with churches in the Lleyn peninsula and on Anglesey.

Einion, Prince of Lleyn, also of Cunedda's line, was a royal benefactor of churches in the sixth century. He was buried in the church of Llanengan, named after him, near the tip of the Lleyn peninsula. After his death, cures took place at his tomb. Einion founded a monastery at Penmon, near the eastern tip of Anglesey, and appointed his nephew, Seiriol, as head of the community. Here can be found the most complete monk's hermitage to survive in Wales. As with many Celtic sites, the isolation of its idyllic setting is misleading, for the monastery is surrounded by four clusters of hut circles, the remains of a large Celtic village of at least three hundred inhabitants. Between the groups of homes, terraces survive to show that farming was practised.[1]

The circular stone wall of Seiriol's hut rests snugly against a sheltering cliff. Beside its remains are the sixth-century foundations of his well and its antechamber, with stone seats along either side where a few people could gather for instruction as they prepared to be baptized in the square pool (see opposite). The brickwork over the well is eighteenth century; the red bricks do not blend with the solid Celtic stones that surround the pool below. The well was revered through the centuries, and the well-keeper lived in a house nearby until relatively recently.

The present church was built by Celtic monks in the twelfth century to replace a wooden one burnt by the Danes in 971. Two fine tenth-century carved crosses are preserved inside the church. From the monastery there is a magnificent view across the Menai Strait towards the mountains on the mainland, where Seiriol was said to have had a hermitage at Penmaenmawr. At that time it was apparently possible to cross the sands on foot at low tide.

Another group of monks lived on Ynys Seiriol (now Puffin Island), half a mile offshore. The monastic cemetery was also on the island, and many monks and rulers were buried here, including Seiriol and his cousin, King Maelgwyn Gwynedd. The island was not always a safe haven: in 632 King Cadwallon took refuge here while King Edwin of Northumbria laid siege to the tiny island, before capturing Anglesey. Norse settlers named the island 'Priestholm' after the priests and monks

St Seiriol's holy well and the stone foundations of his sixth-century circular hut beneath a sheltering cliff, Penmon, Anglesey.

who lived there. In medieval times, Seiriol's body was brought back from Priestholm to Penmon, and buried in a shrine in the church crypt, beneath the chancel. Pilgrims descended a stone staircase to visit it.

Writing in the twelfth century, Gerald of Wales informs us that Penmon was one of three reformed Culdee monasteries in north Wales. This suggests that the later monks of Penmon were strongly committed to the ideals of earlier days. The community on Priestholm must also have flourished, for in 1237 King Lliwelyn the Great granted the monastery of Penmon to the prior of Priestholm. Later in the century, Penmon became an Augustinian friary. Dominating the site today is the friars' thirteenth-century refectory, with a dormitory above and cellars below. The men ate in silence while one of them read aloud. There is a corner seat beside a window, where the reader could take advantage of natural light. The friars' main source of protein was fish: their fishpond survives, fed from Seiriol's well.[2]

The Augustinians were responsible for a fine stained-glass window above Seiriol's shrine in the church. Only two fragments of the great east window remain: they depict saints Christopher and Seiriol, and are now combined in a small window in the south transept. Seiriol is dressed as a medieval friar in brown and white robes, with a cap and a curly beard. Seiriol appears to have worked within a fairly small area: he has no dedications beyond Anglesey.

At Clorach, a mile east of Llanerchymedd, nearer the centre of Anglesey, twin wells on either side of the road were named after Seiriol and Cybi who, according to tradition, used to meet here. For both men, the journey was about ten miles each way. Since Cybi faced the sun both in the morning and the evening, he was nicknamed 'the Tanned' while Seiriol was nicknamed 'the Pale'. Both wells were visited for healing; Seiriol's is still contained within a surrounding stone wall, but Cybi's was destroyed when the present bridge was built. In the mid-nineteenth century, people went to Seiriol's well 'at dead of night' to collect water and take it to their sick relatives.[3]

If Seiriol spoke with a northern, Scottish accent, Cybi's was southern, for he was probably Cornish. Unlike Seiriol, Cybi was a missionary who travelled by sea until he settled at Caergybi (in English, Holyhead), where he founded a monastery. There would have been plenty for Seiriol and Cybi to discuss when they met at Clorach, for until these two men established communities in the mid-sixth century, there had been no monasteries on Anglesey. According to his *Life*, Cybi began his work in Cornwall, where the church and well of Tregony on the south coast are named after him. A grave-marker dating from the sixth or seventh century is built into the outside wall of the south aisle of the church. The River Fal at Tregony has now silted up, but in Celtic times this was a significant port on a tidal estuary.

There is another Cornish church dedicated to Cybi at Duloe, sixteen miles northeast of Tregony. Duloe was already a holy place: on the edge of the village is Cornwall's smallest stone circle, consisting of eight large white quartz stones. It may encircle a chieftain's burial mound, since a Late Bronze Age burial urn was found at the base of one of the stones and a golden torc, or spiral neck ornament, was found here.

Cybi's church stands on high ground, perhaps inside an Iron Age fort, three hundred metres southwest of the stone circle. A massive stone font inside the church may date from Cybi's time. It is decorated with a gryphon on one side and a fish on the other, to symbolize evil and the Christian's rebirth into goodness, for the fish was an early Christian symbol for Christ. Cybi's well is further down the hill, beside the road to Looe. Ancient steps lead down into the pool inside the well's inner chamber, suggesting that it was used for baptism.

Cybi's thirteenth-century *Life* sends him to Jerusalem and then to Ireland for training, but it is more likely that he proceeded northwards to Wales with a group of followers. The church at Llangibby-on-Usk is dedicated to him. He may have first taught the people here as they gathered at their holy place, a neolithic standing stone now called 'Cybi's Stone' in the field below the church. Cybi's holy well used to flow beside the churchyard wall.

According to his *Life*, Cybi attended the Synod of Brefi which took place at Llanddewi Brefi, ten miles northeast of Lampeter. Local tradition affirms that Cybi worked in this area, since the village of Llangybi, four miles southwest of Llanddewi Brefi, is named after him. Cybi's church is beside an ancient yew tree, above a tributary of the River Teifi. A quarter of a mile south is Cybi's well by the roadside, near an ancient stone named *Lech Cybi*, the remains of a cromlech. Cybi is said to have lived for a while near the well, whose water possesses mineral properties and relieved tuberculosis, scurvy and rheumatism. Until 1913 the well was roofed and its water flowed into a stone bath with seats on each side for bathers; its foundations still remain today. In the late seventeenth century, Edward Lhuyd describes patients washing at the well on the Eve of Ascension Day and being laid down to sleep beneath the cromlech, 'an arrow's flight away from the well'. If they sleep, he writes, they will recover; if not, they will die.[4]

Cybi's *Life* tells how he continued northwards to the Lleyn peninsula, where Maelgwyn Gwynedd granted him land for a settlement, which is also named Llangybi. Here, in a valley on the edge of a wood, five hundred metres from the church, is the most complete Celtic well-house in Wales. A small rectangular room built round the well adjoins a larger room enclosing a pool fed by the spring. The pool is surrounded by a paved walk; its dry stone walls, six metres high, and its corbelled vaulting are similar in style to those of early Irish cells. Some of its giant stones are likely to date from Cybi's time; the well-house has stood untouched since at least the twelfth century.

To approach the well, pilgrims used two ancient stone causeways across the damp field. A large sacred eel lived in the well, where the patient stood barelegged. If the eel coiled itself round the patient's legs, it was believed that a cure would follow. The spring water possesses mineral properties, and cured a wide variety of illnesses. A register of cures made in 1766 describes how a man who had been blind for thirty years bathed his eyes for three consecutive weeks and recovered his sight.

In the eighteenth century, seven people were cured of blindness caused by smallpox. The lame came to Llangybi on crutches or were wheeled to the well in barrows. When they were cured, they gratefully left their crutches and barrows around the well, where they were noted by an observer in the early eighteenth century. Water was carried away in casks and bottles for use as medicine. A party of smugglers returning from a night's work with casks of spirits explained when challenged by an excise officer that the casks contained water from Ffynnon Gybi![5] Until the eighteenth century the church contained a chest, Cyff Gybi, for thank-offerings from pilgrims cured at the well.

Cybi continued to Anglesey, where Ynys Gybi (Holy Island) is named after him. At Caergybi (Holyhead), Maelgwyn Gwynedd gave him permission to build a church inside the Roman fort. In the *Lives* of Patrick and other Irish saints, a Celtic chieftain, on conversion to Christianity, often handed over his *dun* or fortified homestead to the Church. The monks sometimes built a monastery in one part of the fort, while the chieftain retained the rest. The monks then set out to preach in his territory. Maelgwyn gave Cybi a late third-century Roman coastal fort, and his church sits neatly inside it, well protected by its Roman enclosure wall with towers at each corner. Cybi died and was buried here; inside the south corner of the fort, a chapel is built over his grave.

Other southerners worked in north Wales, both before and after Cybi. One of the first was Garmon (*c.* 410–*c.* 475), who was perhaps born in Brittany, and may have studied under Patrick in Ireland and Illtud in south Wales. There is a scattering of churches and holy wells named after Garmon in Denbigh, Montgomery, Radnor and Flint. The large churchyard of Llanarmon-yn-Iâl ('Garmon's church in the hills') in the Denbighshire uplands is the site of his monastery. The Tudor historian, John Leland, describes an annual pilgrimage to Llanarmon-yn-Iâl, when offerings were made in the presence of a statue of Garmon dressed in priestly vestments. The church was given a double nave to accommodate the large number of pilgrims.

A number of Breton monks preached in north Wales. Ancient genealogists describe a chieftain named Emyr Llydaw (which means 'Emyr the Breton') whose grandson, a monk named Cadfan, sailed to Wales in the fifth century with a band of missionaries. There are Breton churches dedicated to Cadfan, as well as a group in Wales. Place-names suggest that Cadfan's followers first settled near the shore and later travelled inland, where they have dedications in the uplands. Cadfan's own churches show this pattern: he came ashore on the west coast at Towyn, and place-names may trace his journey inland over the mountains to Llangadfan in Montgomery.[6] The twelfth-century *Book of Llandaff* describes how Cadfan and twelve monks arrived in curraghs and settled beside a spring on the shore. They built a monastery within its palisade, grew their own food and drew others to join them in a simple life of prayer, study and hospitality.

The present church of Towyn is southeast of the well on the sea shore. An eighth-century inscribed stone in the church is one of the earliest examples of written Welsh. The texts are carved low down, to be read by someone kneeling at the grave. They commemorate two women, 'Tengrui, legal wife of Adgan...' and 'Cun, wife of Celen; loss and grief remain'. Until this time, leading families inscribed their monuments in Latin, so the pillar-stone marks a step towards a new cultural identity.

Until the early seventeenth century there was a chapel in Towyn churchyard dedicated to Cadfan; it may have marked his grave. Towyn became the mother church of the area. Two successive wooden churches were burnt by the Vikings before the impressive Norman church was built. Pilgrims came to Cadfan's well long after the Reformation: it was known for curing rheumatism, tuberculosis and skin complaints.

Twenty miles to the east, Cadfan is honoured at Llangadfan; its single-chambered church is situated high above the River Banwy. A mile away at Foel, on the opposite side of the valley, stands the church of one of Cadfan's followers, Tydecho, on a hillock encircled by ancient yew trees. Cadfan was later given land by Einion, Prince of Lleyn, to build a monastery on Bardsey Island. It flourished and became well known. Dubricius retired with some companions to Bardsey, and was buried there.

Bardsey Island is two miles off the tip of the Lleyn peninsula. It is named Ynys Enlli (Island of the Currents) because of the strong seas which flow between it and the mainland. Pilgrims sailing to Bardsey from Brach-y-Pwll filled their water bottles with fresh water from Ffynnon Fair (St Mary's Well), a spring on the rocky beach, visible at low tide. The rectangular outline of the pilgrims' chapel at Brach-y-Pwll can be seen in the turf on the headland. Today the earliest remains on Bardsey Island are of a thirteenth-century Augustinian priory. These friars liked to restore ancient shrines, as they revived Seiriol's at Penmon.

A Welshman who joined Cadfan's monastery on Bardsey Island was Henwyn, who trained first under Illtud in south Wales. Henwyn became bursar and later abbot of Bardsey, and was buried there. His church on the mainland at Aberdaron owed allegiance to that on Bardsey. In Aberdaron's church are two early tombstones; they come from the cemetery of another daughter house of Bardsey at Anelog, two miles to the west. They read: 'Veracius the priest lies here' and 'Senacius the priest lies here with many brothers'.

Like other Celtic churches, Aberdaron's was a *clas* church, or a monastery without a rule, whose headship was hereditary. Each *clas* church was formed of a group of monks and priests who worked in co-operation under an abbot. The Norman English destroyed the *clas* system, disliking its independence, for a *clas* church was beyond the control of Rome and outside the power of the English king. Aberdaron was so remote, however, that the Normans failed to reach it, and St Henwyn's remained a *clas* church until the Reformation in the sixteenth century. By the twelfth century it had a sanctuary seat, a stone chair of refuge, where a person escaping from the law could claim the Church's protection.

Aberdaron's church is beautifully located beside the sea, but the lower half of the building is buried beneath the sand. In the fifteenth century it was doubled in size to accommodate pilgrims who came to Aberdaron for their last overnight stop on the journey to Bardsey Island. In the middle of the village is a pilgrims' hall, built in about 1300, where travellers rested before the rough sea crossing. The low stone building is brightly whitewashed and is named *Y Gegin Fawr* (The Great Kitchen), for here pilgrims bought their food and drink.

Two of Cadfan's followers worked among the people of central Anglesey, which was then mainly marshland. One was Cristiolus, whose church is still visible from the busy main road to Holyhead. The single-chambered church is on a ridge outside the village of Llangristiolus, with a view over the low-lying fields. It has a tenth-century tub-shaped font, carved with geometric designs by local Celtic craftsmen. These sculptors moved around in the course of their work; there is a similar font at Beuno's church in Trefdraeth, two miles southwest, and a more elaborate example in Beuno's church at Pistyll on the Lleyn peninsula.

Another follower of Cadfan was Tegai, a fifth-century hermit who began his religious life on Anglesey. He first built a chapel in the marsh named 'Cors Degai', and later crossed to the mainland where he built a church at Llandygai, a mile south of Bangor, inside a Neolithic and Bronze Age burial-ground. We assume that such churches served only a small population, but in 1967, sixty rows of Christian graves were found here, arranged around a pit surrounded by wooden props which contained Tegai's tomb. Christians had buried their dead around his shrine for generations. Later another church dedicated to Tegai was built half a mile away, around which the present village grew.[7]

Tegai's brother Trillo became a priest on Bardsey Island. He appears to have sailed north and landed at Llandrillo-yn-Rhos ('church of Trillo on the promontory'), near Colwyn Bay. The foundations of his circular stone hut can still be seen on the beach, beside a tiny chapel built over his freshwater spring. The present chapel of thick stones, built into the cliff, is probably thirteenth century. The parish church in the town is also dedicated to Trillo. For baptisms, water was brought from Trillo's well on the beach. Trillo is also honoured in the village of Llandrillo, thirty miles inland over the moors, on a tributary of the River Dee, where his church is built beside an ancient yew tree. Across the river, at the foot of an oak, is Trillo's holy well, which cured rheumatism; it flowed until a hundred years ago.

Four miles west of Trillo's inland settlement at Llandrillo is Llandderfel, named after another of Cadfan's missionary group. Like Cadfan, Derfel was said to be a grandson of Emyr Llydaw of Brittany. According to his *Life*, Derfel Gadarn ('the Mighty') was a soldier before he became a monk on Bardsey Island, where he was later abbot. He became a hermit and retired to Llandderfel, near the headwaters of the Dee, and died there in the sixth century. He was known for his skill in curing sick animals, and after his death, pilgrims came to Llandderfel with their animals, to pray for a blessing from Derfel.

Until the Reformation there was an ancient wooden statue in the church of Derfel mounted on a horse, or possibly a red deer stag. Thomas Cromwell, whom King Henry VIII made responsible for the confiscation of Church property, sent agents throughout Britain to seize goods and 'abolish Popish practices'. There is a record of Cromwell's agent in Wales writing to his master in 1538 for instructions about Derfel's statue, because 'the people have so much trust in him that they come daily on pilgrimage to him with cows or horses or money, to the number of five or six hundred on April 5th' (Derfel's feast day). Cromwell had the statue of the seated rider brought to London to be burnt at Smithfield, but Derfel's wooden mount can still be seen in the church porch. It stood in the chancel beside the communion table until 1730, when the rural dean removed it and sawed off half of the animal's head.

The wooden horse was still brought out each Easter Tuesday, around the time of Derfel's feast, and carried in procession to the Wake Field, where it was fixed to a pole for children to ride. Despite its damage through the centuries, the recumbent beast retains considerable character, with its deep eye-sockets, and most of a head half-turned over its right shoulder. The small church has a magnificent oak rood screen carved in about 1500. Llandderfel was sufficiently remote to remain a centre for Catholic worship; the last Mass in north Wales until recent times was celebrated here. Derfel's holy well flows from the hillside above the village, although its stone bath is now silted up.

Another of Cadfan's followers was Sulien, who has dedications in Brittany and two churches in Cornwall at Tresilian and Luxulyan. In Wales he is commemorated together with a monk named Mael at the village of Cwm, which hugs the slopes of the Clwyd Range. Their holy well is built into the churchyard wall: its water cured eye diseases. Sixteen miles inland, Corwen is also dedicated to Mael and Sulien. Its Welsh name, literally 'white choir', means 'stone church'.

Corwen was an ancient settlement built between the Berwyn Mountains and the fast-flowing River Dee, on a main route inland used through the centuries by travellers and by Welsh drovers taking their cattle eastwards. The church of Mael and Sulien is on a pre-Christian holy site, beside a standing stone two metres high, named in Welsh 'the pointed stone in the icy corner'. When the church was enlarged, the medieval porch was built around the ancient stone. East of the church is a large flat Bronze Age stone with seven small cup-marks carved into it. Later it was surmounted by a tall Celtic cross.[8]

Many of the great Irish monasteries were ruled by dynasties of abbots. The only comparable family in north Wales was that of Dunawd and Deiniol. They were said to be descendants of a tribe from Ayrshire in southwest Scotland, whose chieftain is named Coel Godebog ('Hawk-beak') in genealogies. Also known as Coel Hen ('the Aged'), he may be the Old King Cole of the nursery rhyme. The first of Coel Hawk-beak's dynasty to arrive in Wales was King Pabo, who fled south with his wife after being defeated in battle by pagan Picts. He was called Pabo Post Pryden, meaning 'Pabo, Pillar of the Britons' (or Pritani).

The couple were well received by King Cyngen of Powys, who gave them land. A royal intermarriage was arranged: Cyngen's eldest son married Pabo's daughter. Pabo and his wife settled in Anglesey, where they were said to have founded Llanbabo church above Lake Alaw. Pabo died in about 510 and may have been buried here: the church contains a fourteenth-century tombstone of Pabo dressed as a king, with crown and sceptre. The church now stands alone beside the ruins of a few stone cottages.

Pabo's son Dunawd became a monk and founded a great monastery beside the River Dee at Bangor-is-y-Coed ('Bangor below the woods'), four miles southeast of Wrexham. The Dee could be crossed only by coracle at this point, until the thirteenth century when a packhorse bridge was built – it is still in use. King Cyngen and his eldest son Brochwel endowed the monastery generously, and Dunawd's three sons assisted him. The monastery expanded rapidly: in 731 Bede drew on earlier sources to describe its organization into seven groups, each containing three hundred monks.

Among the monks who were said to have entered Dunawd's monastery were seven sons of a prince of Ceredigion, whose territory was engulfed by the sea. One of the seven brothers, Vendesetl, was perhaps among the first monks to work in the Lleyn peninsula. His church of Llangwnnadl near the tip of the peninsula is on the pilgrim route to Bardsey Island. In medieval times it was given three naves to accommodate the flocks of pilgrims, and south of the church is a large hospice field where they could spend the night before they continued to Aberdaron. A sixth-century bronze handbell from the church is now in the National Museum of Wales at Cardiff; it is likely to have belonged to Vendesetl. His tombstone is at Llanbedrog, six miles east of Llangwnnadl, on the opposite coast: it is one of the very few inscribed with the name of a known Celtic saint.

One of Vendesetl's six brothers was said to be Tudno, to whom a church is dedicated on the headland of the Great Orme (Old Norse for 'Great Worm', or sea-serpent) above the modern town of Llandudno. A limestone cave containing a freshwater spring on the shore below the church is named after Tudno, and there is another ancient well near his church. The Great Orme was well known in Celtic times: copper was mined here from the Bronze Age until the nineteenth century. Tudno also attracted bardic legend: one of the thirteen treasures of Britain was said to be Tudno's whetstone, which sharpened the sword of a hero but blunted that of a coward! A stone church was built here in the twelfth century; the carved bowl of its font survives. In medieval times, Llandudno was still a cluster of farms around Tudno's church, until a holiday resort grew along the strand in the nineteenth century. A flock of feral goats has been reintroduced onto the Great Orme. They roamed wild in Celtic times, and feature in the lives of the monks.

Unfortunately, Dunawd's great monastery was overtaken by political events. In 577 the West Saxons defeated the southern Britons, burnt Gloucester and Bath, and occupied land up to the Bristol Channel, separating the Cornish Britons from the Welsh. Six years later, Anglians from Denmark, led by the pagan King Aethelfrith of Northumbria, defeated the Britons and Scottish Gaels in Dumfriesshire. Meanwhile, the family of Cyngen of Powys had weakened their position. The poet Taliesin recounts how Cyngen's grandson had fought against and defeated his fellow Britons of Anglesey, south Wales, Brecon and Cornwall.

When King Aethelfrith attacked Powys in about 615, Cyngen's great-grandson was forced to fight the Northumbrians on his own, for no other native king would join him. He assembled his army near Bangor-is-y-Coed. Following druidic tradition, the monks from Dunawd's monastery climbed a hill above the battlefield to curse the Anglians and pray for victory. The Anglian commander declared: 'Whether or not they bear arms, they fight against us when they pray to their God'. He ordered his soldiers to massacre the monks, and two thirds of the community were killed.[9] The king of Powys was defeated and also killed.

Through his victory at the Battle of Chester, as it came to be known, King Aethelfrith drove a wedge between the Cumbrians and the Welsh. The country of the Britons no longer existed: there were now three Celtic regions separated by Anglo-Saxon territory. The remaining nine hundred monks from Dunawd's monastery fled westwards, some to a community established by Dunawd's son, Deiniol, at Bangor on the Menai Strait, and others to Cadfan's monastery on Bardsey Island, staying in the hospice churches along the route. Dunawd's community had lasted no more than a century, and by the twelfth century the monastery was a large ruin.

As a descendant of Coel Godebog, Deiniol (or Daniel in English) was of noble birth. He perhaps studied under Cadoc in south Wales, and became a monk in his father Dunawd's monastery. He may also have worked in the area around Bangor-is-y-Coed, for there is a cluster of dedications to him in Denbighshire and Flintshire. In about 546,

Maelgwyn Gwynedd gave him land overlooking the Menai Strait and Deiniol built a monastery, again naming it Bangor, after the wattle fence enclosing it. His church was to become a cathedral, and its territory grew into an early medieval diocese.

According to Rhygyfarch's *Life of David*, Deiniol and Dubricius were the two bishops who persuaded David to take part with them in the Synod of Brefi (see chapter 4). Deiniol died in about 572 and may be buried on Bardsey Island. He was succeeded as Abbot of Bangor by his son Deiniol Fab ('the Younger'). The village of Llanddaniel Fab on Anglesey, eight miles southwest of Bangor, is named after him. There are remains of some ninth-century crosses from Deiniol's monastery in Bangor, but the church was destroyed in 1073 by Vikings. The present cathedral is fourteenth century.

There were other members of Pabo's family who continued the line of prince-monks. A cousin of Deiniol was Asaph, whose mother was a daughter of Pabo. According to Kentigern's twelfth-century biographer, Jocelyn of Furness, the young Asaph was sent to Kentigern's monastery, later known as St Asaph, beside the River Elwy. Kentigern had fled south from Strathclyde as a political exile, and travelled through Cumbria to north Wales. The monastery grew rapidly and Asaph became Kentigern's most able student. After the defeat of the pagan forces near Carlisle in 573, Kentigern was invited back north. He appointed Asaph abbot in his place and returned to Glasgow, taking a large group of monks with him. Two were perhaps Nidan and Ffinnan, who have churches both in Anglesey near the Menai Strait and also in the east Grampian valleys, far to the north. Kentigern's life is examined further in chapter 7.

Five miles northeast of St Asaph, in a sheltered valley not far from the coast, the church at Llanasa is dedicated to Asaph and Cynderyn (Welsh for Kentigern). It has a quaint, asymmetrical fifteenth-century bell turret, and richly painted stained-glass windows brought from Basingwerk Abbey, two of which depict Beuno as a bishop and his niece, Winifred, with a scar round her throat; their story is told in chapter 6. There are several holy wells dedicated to Asaph in Denbighshire and Flintshire, including one in Cwm parish which was enclosed in a polygonal building. Its water used to ebb and flow, and cured rheumatism and nervous complaints.[10]

The last great prince-monk of Pabo's line was Tysilio, Prince of Powys, who was born in Shrewsbury and lived a generation after Deiniol. Tysilio was a son of King Brochwel of Powys, who had married Pabo's daughter, and ruled a kingdom in mid-Wales. Brochwel's chief fort was at Shrewsbury; he had another at Dinas Bran overlooking Llangollen, and two more farther south, near Welshpool and Meifod. Tysilio's name means 'dear little Sunday-child', so he was probably born on a Sunday.[11] As a younger son, he was sent to study at a monastery in Meifod, under a hermit named Gwyddfarch, who was one of Cadfan's followers from Brittany.

Gwyddfarch built his monastery in about 550 in a valley clearing beside a navigable river. The valley slopes were thickly forested, and several of the surrounding hilltops were fortified. The monks lived in small wooden houses, and probably built their church on an oak frame, filled with wicker and clay, thatching it with reeds. Today's churchyard of nine acres indicates the extent of Gwyddfarch's monastery, which in time contained three churches, one named after its founder (its remains were still visible in the seventeenth century), another named after Tysilio, and a third which was a pre-Norman dedication to Our Lady. The monastery became the mother church of Powys, and the burial place of its kings. A fine Celtic tombstone in the church may mark a royal burial.

Around the time of the Battle of Chester which brought disgrace on his family, Tysilio left the monastery of Meifod. He travelled westward and became a hermit on a tiny island in the Menai Strait. Llandysilio Island is now linked to the mainland by a causeway, and can be reached through the woods at the Anglesey end of the Menai Bridge. Oystercatchers and curlews forage round the rocks beside the church, and a colony of terns nests nearby.

According to his *Life*, Tysilio returned to Meifod and became abbot in place of the now elderly Gwyddfarch. When he died, Gwyddfarch was buried outside the village, at the top of Allt-yr-Ancr ('Anchorite's Hill'). Tysilio rebuilt the monastery church, and the poet Cynddelw described his achievement:

> 'He raised a church with fostering hand:
> A church brightly lit, with a chancel for Mass;
> A church over the streams, by the glassy waters....
> A church of Powys, fairest paradise.'[12]

There are other dedications to Tysilio in Powys: Llantysilio Mountain, northwest of Llangollen, is named after him. Where the River Dee flows past the mountain, there is a church named Llantysilio, while on the other side of the mountain is Bryn Eglwys ('Hill Church'), also dedicated to him. Boulders from its first Celtic stone church are built into its west wall.

The Battle of Chester caused the dispersal of many monks from Powys. One of Tysilio's companions was Llôlan, who travelled northeast to the Scottish Borders and settled for a while at Broughton, eight miles southwest of Peebles. Here, his chapel, alongside the present village church, was excavated and roofed in the 1920s. Llôlan continued north into Pictish territory, preaching at Culross and Kinkardine, where his church overlooks the Firth of Forth. The Earls of Perth at Kinkardine preserved his handbell and staff until the seventeenth century.

Although there must have been frequent and close contact between Ireland and Wales, there is little evidence of Irish monks working in north Wales. There were Irish settlers in Anglesey until about 500 when Cunedda's grandson, Cadwallon, defeated the Irish near Trefdraeth. A number of ogham-inscribed stones on the island indicate Irish Christian burials. At Penrhos Llugwy in the east of Anglesey is a sixth-century memorial stone to an Irish chieftain. Since *Gwyddel* means 'Irish', the village names of Gwyddelwern and Llanwyddelan indicate that there were other Irish settlers in Denbighshire and Powys.

An Irish monk named Mullins (d. 697) gave his name to Llanfyllin, four miles north of Meifod. His holy well flows from the hillside three hundred metres above Llanfyllin church. Its large well-chamber enabled Mullins or his unknown disciple to baptize converts by immersion in the pool. An account of 1894 describes how people tied rags to branches beside the spring as prayers for healing. On Trinity Sunday they came to drink sugared water at the well. The water was drawn by the girls, after which the lads paid for cakes and ale at the inn. This was a survival from a medieval pilgrimage to the well, around the time of Mullins' feast in June.[13] Mullins was a Leinster man who became a monk at Glendalough. He founded a community at St Mullins and later became bishop of Ferns, another monastery in Leinster. A ninth-century gospel book called the *Book of Mulling* contains a plan of his monastery. It can be seen in a beautiful jewelled shrine in the library of Trinity College, Dublin.

Saeran, another Irish-born monk, is honoured at the church of Llanynys in the Vale of Clwyd, eight miles south of St Asaph. Saeran's monastery became the mother church of the area. An early medieval hexagonal stone in the church may come from Saeran's shrine. It depicts a mitred bishop, crozier in hand, standing on a muzzled bear. Saeran's holy well, Ffynnon Sarah, is six miles farther south, on an ancient pilgrim route above Derwen. The waters healed rheumatism and cancer; pilgrims made offerings of pins before descending the three steps into the pool. Pins were thrown into wells throughout Britain, and represent offerings to the pre-Christian spirit of the well. The pins were generally bent, to show that they were no longer for use by mortals. Sufferers came to Ffynnon Sarah into Victorian times, and left their sticks and crutches as thank-offerings at a nearby cottage.[14]

There are a few surviving dedications to Celtic women in north Wales. There were probably many more before the arrival of the Normans, who had less respect for women than the Celts whom they conquered. Traditions survive about some of the Celtic women missionaries:

Melangell's story was told in chapter 1, and Winifred's life will be examined in the following chapter.

A nun named Marcella worked in north Wales in the sixth century. She lived in the Vale of Clwyd just east of Denbigh, where she was said to have built a hermitage at Whitchurch, beside a healing well. Whitchurch became the mother church of Denbigh. Marcella's two brothers, Deifor and Teyrnog, founded settlements on the other side of the River Clwyd. There is another church dedicated to Marcella at Marchwiel, two miles southeast of Wrexham. In her brother's church at Llandyrnog is a magnificent late fourteenth-century stained-glass window, locally made, in which Marcella and Teyrnog, Asaph and Deiniol are portrayed. Marcella wears an elegant cloak trimmed with ermine and carries a gospel book. She probably bears little resemblance to the original Marcella, born six hundred years earlier.

There is a church founded by a Welsh princess in late Celtic times in the remote hamlet of Bettws Gwerfil Goch, three miles northwest of Corwen. Its name means 'Prayer house of Gwerfil the Redhead', and it lies in a steep-sided valley on the ancient pilgrims' trackway across mid-Wales, not far from Ffynnon Sarah. The prayer house is at the centre of the village, and was built for pilgrims in the twelfth century by Princess Gwerfil of Merioneth, the red-haired daughter of King Owain Gwynedd of north Wales.[15] However, the church is set in an ancient raised, oval churchyard, and earlier saints came this way. A holy well in the village is dedicated to Beuno, who established a community at nearby Gwyddelwern. It is to the work of Beuno that we will now turn.

Chapter six
Beuno and Winifred

IN CELTIC TIMES, when travel by sea was easier than travel overland, north Wales had a culture quite distinct from the south, for the two regions were separated by mountains and forests. While David and his followers worked in the south, much of the north was evangelized by Beuno (pronounced 'Beyno' in Welsh). Beuno was born of a princely family in mid-Wales in the second half of the sixth century. His *Life* was written quite late: it survives in a fourteenth-century Welsh version, perhaps of a lost Latin original, but many of its details are corroborated by surviving place-name dedications.

Beuno's *Life* follows the traditional medieval pattern by presenting him as a model Christian who carried out the works of mercy described in Matthew's Gospel: 'He gave food and drink to the hungry and thirsty, clothes to the naked and lodging to the stranger, visiting the sick and those in prison'.[1] Oliver Davies notes a specific Welsh flavour to the *Life*, for Beuno is also presented as a powerful druid. Four times he kills people by cursing them; three times, individuals are decapitated, then healed by his magic powers.

Trees also possess supernatural properties: the *Life* tells how Beuno plants an oak tree over his father's grave which kills Englishmen but lets Welshmen pass beneath its branches unharmed! For pre-Christian Celts, springs were gateways to the underworld, and lakes were also considered holy; a sacred spring appears in Winifred's story and her attacker 'melts away into a lake'. Beuno is one of the Welsh saints whose story hints at the absorption of druidic tradition into Christianity. Saints may be described as 'magician', 'seer' or druid', a title also applied to God.[2]

Beuno seems to have been a zealous missionary, unlike the more settled scholars of south Wales, but his *Life* relates that he prepared for the priesthood in the south. His chapel at Llanfeuno ('church of Beuno') under Clodock in the Black Mountains is perhaps a memory of his early work in the southeast. His *Life* then recounts that on the death of Beuno's father, the son of Brochwel, a local prince, gave Beuno a site for his first monastery, the small settlement of Berriew in mid-Wales. As its name implies, Berriew is beside the River Rhiw, a tributary of the Severn, near the Roman road from Wroxeter. Strongly built for Roman troops to travel along, the road was still a highway through mid-Wales in the sixth century.

A pointed Bronze Age standing stone in Dyffryn Lane, a mile from Beuno's church in Berriew, perhaps marked the settlement's ancient holy place. According to tradition, Beuno preached to the people beside the monolith, which is still known as *Maen Beuno* ('Beuno's Stone'). Five miles southwest, the church of Bettws Cedewain is also dedicated to Beuno. Since *bettws* means a prayer house or hermitage, Beuno or one of his monks may have established a chapel on the hill at the top of the village, where the circular boundary of the Celtic site is marked out by a thorn hedge surrounding the church.

Beuno seems to have remained in Powys for several years before he left the Severn valley and crossed the Berwyn Mountains into the valley of the River Dee. Beuno's *Life* relates that in Berriew he was frightened by the sight of a Saxon warrior patrolling the far bank of the river, and so he moved westwards to the coast. This implies that Beuno decided to retreat before the advancing English. It is comforting to know that even saints are frightened sometimes! Near Corwen in the Dee valley, Beuno has a small cluster of dedications around Gwyddelwern, on another Roman road, where he has a church and a somewhat neglected holy well.

Beuno moved northwards again until he reached the Flint coast. There were already Romanized Celtic Christians in the area, for the church at Whitford on the coast contains a sixth-century gravestone inscribed in Latin, 'Here lies Bona, wife of Nobilis'. It dates from Beuno's time and comes from nearby Caerwys, a Roman garrison town. The tombstone is of a type found in Roman Gaul, where St Martin of Tours had been preaching Christianity two centuries earlier. The families of Roman soldiers drafted from Europe to north Wales brought their faith with them. Whitford church is dedicated to St Mary and St Beuno; Mary's name was often added to church dedications in Norman times.

On the coast a few miles southeast of Whitford is Holywell, where Beuno probably built his cell on the site of the present parish church. Across the road, on top of Castle Hill, Beuno's well is almost inaccessible beneath undergrowth. Beside the parish church is Winifred's well. The twelfth-century *Life of Winifred* describes her as Beuno's niece, but we know little about her. Her *Life* recounts that she was born of noble parents, from whom Beuno obtained land on which to build a church. Winifred's name, Gwenfrewi in Welsh, means 'radiant Freda', for *gwen* means white, shining or holy.

According to her *Life*, Caradoc, the son of a neighbouring prince, tried to marry her. When she refused, he pursued her and cut off her head; a fountain sprang forth where it touched the ground. Beuno raised her from the dead, and she established a convent at Holywell. The story is influenced by the ancient Celtic tradition that the severed head contains supernatural powers. In his practical way, the great antiquarian Sabine Baring-Gould suggests that in the original story Winifred was wounded in the throat, and nursed back to health by Beuno and her mother![3]

Winifred's well has never ceased to be a place of pilgrimage. In the fifteenth century, King Henry V walked the fifty miles from Shrewsbury to Holywell. When King Edward IV made a similar pilgrimage in 1480, Tudur Aled wrote: 'Garlands on garlands decked the way; thousands trampled down the greensward.' He noted how the king reverently sprinkled soil from the shrine on his crown. Lady Margaret Beaufort, King Henry VII's mother, built the present chapel with its star-shaped pool in 1483, to replace the earlier Norman chapel. A carving on a corner roof-corbel shows a pilgrim carrying an invalid on his back; the sick are still carried through the bathing pool in this way.

Jesuits and other priests lived at Holywell throughout penal times, when Catholics could be fined or imprisoned for worshipping openly. The well became a centre of resistance to the 'new religion' of Protestantism. Daniel Defoe wrote that priests were 'very numerous' here, but had to appear in disguise. In May 1719, hearing that Catholics intended to celebrate St Winifred's day, the authorities sent dragoons who seized the priest during the Eucharist, together with the church plate and richly decorated statues. In 1722 the church was confiscated and became a day school; 'however, to supply the loss of this chapel, the Roman Catholics have chapels erected in almost every inn, for the devotion of the pilgrims that flock thither from all the popish parts of England'.[4]

In the eighteenth century, Lancashire pilgrims visiting Holywell crossed the Mersey by boat, walked across the Wirral and the often treacherous sands of the Dee estuary at low tide, and climbed the narrow valley to Winifred's well. They travelled in groups, and lit beacons on the Wirral to signal for a boat on their way home.[5] In 1795 Thomas Pennard wrote: 'In the summer, still a few are to be seen in the water in deep devotion up to their chins for hours, sending up their prayers.'

In the following century, opposition to visiting the well waned, and the town council became aware of its possibilities. A hospice for pilgrims was opened in 1870 and at a meeting of the town council in 1896 the chairman stated: 'In the past year, 1,710 pilgrims, many sick and pitifully afflicted, were housed at the hospice.... Of these, upwards of five hundred were examined and registered by the medical attendant, and I am assured by him that a great many remarkable cures were obtained.'

Beuno was too much a missionary to remain at Holywell. When he moved westwards round the coast to the Lleyn peninsula, Winifred's *Life* recounts that she too left Holywell with a group of nuns and travelled ten miles inland to Bodfari, then to Henllan five miles farther on, and finally to a small monastery at Gwytherin, fifteen miles into the mountains. Winifred's journey can still be traced. Bodfari ('Dwelling of

Deifor') is named after St Deifor, who is mentioned in Winifred's *Life*. His church, which the Normans dedicated to St Stephen, is set on a hillside above a Roman outpost on the ancient road running westwards from Chester to Caerhun on the River Conwy. Massive buttresses anchor Deifor's church into the steep hillside.

Deifor has a holy well in Bodfari, a hundred metres down the road from the church, on the left verge, opposite the site of the old Roman station. Even after the Reformation, according to Bishop Maddox's manuscript, villagers went in procession from the church down to the well, where the litany, the ten commandments, the epistle and gospel were read. The poorest person in the parish offered a chicken after going nine times round the well: a cock for a boy or a pullet for a girl. Presumably this was a fertility ritual. Children were also 'dipped to the neck at three of its corners, to prevent their crying at night'.

Winifred continued inland to Henllan, whose name means 'old, or former, church', suggesting a period of disuse. It is set on a hillside where three roads meet. The foundations of the early church were too insecure to bear the weight of a stone tower, so in the fourteenth century a tower was built on a rocky outcrop farther up the hill. The church is dedicated to Sadwrn who, like Beuno, was brought up in the Romano-Celtic church of south Wales. He was said to be a brother of Illtud, and was nicknamed 'Sadwrn Farchog' (or 'Sadwrn the Knight').

He married a kinswoman, a Breton princess, named Canna. They may have come to Wales from Brittany as part of Cadfan's missionary band (see chapter 5). Churches dedicated to Sadwrn and Canna in south Wales may trace their work. Canna has a healing well at Llangan ('church of Canna') in Pembrokeshire, and a fine Celtic wheel cross with a Byzantine-style crucifixion carved upon it in her church of Llangan in the Vale of Glamorgan.

Sadwrn and Canna ended their days on Anglesey, where Sadwrn founded a church at Llansadwrn near Beaumaris. His church is half a mile southwest of the present village, and is still surrounded by its oval Celtic boundary bank. His tombstone, dating from about 530, is set in the chancel wall. Written in Latin and carved in Roman capitals by his immediate followers, it is translated: 'Here lies buried blessed Saturninus and his saintly wife. Peace be with you both.' This is one of the very few surviving memorials to a known Celtic saint.

According to her *Life*, Winifred left Henllan at Sadwrn's suggestion and travelled a final fifteen miles to the remote mountain settlement of Gwytherin. From the road to Gwytherin, Mount Snowdon's peak is visible, often glistening with snow. Set in a sheltered valley, Gwytherin had already been a sacred site for centuries. A pair of yew trees over two thousand years old were planted east and west of a burial mound, aligned with the rising and setting sun. Seventy such ancient yews survive, dating from Celtic times; many of them are in Wales. They are

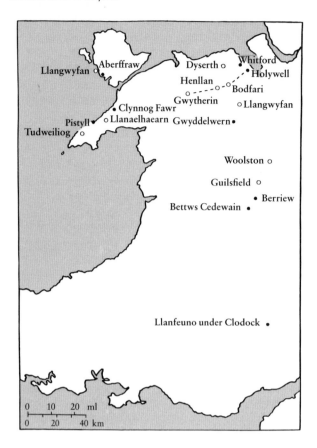

Map 6. *St Beuno's sphere of influence.*
- *Dedications to Beuno.*
o *Dedications to Beuno's followers.*
---*St Winifred's last journey. Other chapels and wells are also dedicated to these saints.*

in line with the axis of the church, although they would have been planted before the church was built.[6] Between the giant yews, a row of four pre-Christian standing stones marks the grave of an ancient chieftain. In the fifth or sixth century, one of these was selected by a Christian family as a tombstone, for inscribed on it in Latin is: '(The stone of) Vinnemaglus, son of Senemaglus'.

Beside this holy place a monk named Eleri established a small double monastery of monks and nuns, and his mother Theonia became its first leader. Winifred joined the community, and in time succeeded Theonia as its abbess. She died here, and was buried in the churchyard. In the eighth century her bones were enshrined in a house-shaped wooden reliquary decorated with ornamental metalwork. The antiquarian Edward Lhuyd sketched it in about 1696; part of its gable was recently found in Holywell. A Celtic cross-slab carved around the same time is built into the chancel step at Gwytherin.

Winifred's relics were taken to Shrewsbury Abbey by Norman monks in 1138. The journey took several days, and on the last night before their arrival in Shrewsbury the monks may have rested with their casket in the small village of Woolston, four miles southeast of Oswestry, near a holy well which was perhaps then renamed in St Winifred's honour. Its water was good for healing wounds, bruises and broken bones, and the stone troughs through which the water flows could be dammed to form pools for bathing. Another spring lower down was good for the eyes. A half-timbered sixteenth-century cottage, originally a courthouse, stands over the well. It was probably built in this secluded spot because from early times, gatherings to enact laws and hold fairs were held at holy places such as a mound or a spring, an oak tree or a group of standing stones.[7] Winifred's well at Holywell is rarely without visitors, but her well beneath the courthouse is seldom found.

When Winifred travelled inland from Holywell, her uncle Beuno set off in a different direction to begin a new chapter of his missionary work in the Lleyn peninsula (see map 6). His *Life* relates how he asked King Cadwallon of Caernarvon for a gift of land on which to build a church, but Cadwallon offered him land that belonged to someone else. When Beuno discovered this he angrily cursed Cadwallon, whose cousin Gwyddaint then offered his own township of Clynnog to Beuno. It is said that the grant of land was ratified over the stone marked with a cross now in Beuno's chapel at Clynnog, but this stone was probably carved two hundred years later, as was the sundial in the churchyard. This is one of only two known Celtic sundials in Britain. It is carved on the southern face of a pillar-stone, pierced with a hole into which the gnomon was inserted to cast its shadow.

Beuno probably built his tiny church in about 616 where the free-standing chapel in Clynnog churchyard now stands. He is said to have died on the Sunday after Easter in 642, and was buried beneath the chapel. Pilgrims came to his tomb to be cured until the late eighteenth century. The magnificent early sixteenth-century church was enlarged just before the Reformation to accommodate the vast numbers of pilgrims who gathered here to begin the Saints' Way to Bardsey Island, one of the most popular pilgrim routes in northern Europe. Building ceased with the Reformation; square holes for scaffolding on the internal walls were never filled in.

Inside Clynnog church is 'Beuno's Chest', hollowed out from a single tree trunk; there is another at Winifred's church in Gwytherin. People put offerings into Beuno's chest to atone for crimes; they also offered money from the sale of animals that they considered to belong to Beuno. At birth, some Welsh calves and lambs have a slit in their ears known as 'Beuno's mark' (*Nôd Beuno*), as do Jersey cattle. Until the late eighteenth century, farmers brought these animals to the church wardens on the Sunday after Whitsun; they were sold, and the money was placed in the chest. Two hundred metres beyond the church, in the left bank beside the Pwhlleli road, is Beuno's well. Its square pool of clear water is surrounded by an open-roofed stone well-house.

Clynnog Fawr is at the neck of the Lleyn peninsula, an area probably already Christianized by Irish settlers. Professor Charles Thomas suggests that 'Lleyn' comes from the Irish *Laigin* meaning 'Leinstermen'. The Lleyn peninsula is as near to Leinster by sea as it is to south Wales. Irish families and small bands of farmers and shepherds gradually settled here, as Dalriada Scots emigrated from northern Ireland to Argyll, and as Irish families from Ulster sailed across to the Isle of Man and to Galloway, only twelve miles from the northeastern tip of Ireland.[8]

Beuno and his followers established other churches along the Saints' Way to Bardsey Island. Two miles northeast of Morfa Nefyn is the tiny hamlet of Pistyll (Welsh for 'cataract' or 'water spout'). A track leads steeply down to Beuno's small church near the sea (see opposite). Beside it is a large pool, fed by the cataract which gave Pistyll its name, in which the crowds of pilgrims could bathe. Pistyll was a hospice church where pilgrims could rest at the nearby monastery, farm or inn, or in shelters in the adjoining hospice field. They could buy food and fuel from the villagers. At the farm, pilgrims could ask for shelter, bread and cheese; in return, tenant-farmers were excused from paying rent to their monastic landowners.

The great boulder which was the cornerstone of the Celtic church is still in place. Sometimes a church was simply built onto a boulder where it lay in the earth; or a foundation stone might be dragged for miles until the builder found a suitable location for a settlement. The twelfth-century font with its circular interwoven patterns was carved by local Celtic craftsmen. The church roof was thatched until 150 years ago, and ancient fruit bushes, gooseberry and daneberry, sloes, hops and medicinal herbs still grow in the oval Celtic churchyard. In 1969 parishioners revived the ancient custom of strewing the floor with rushes and sweet-smelling herbs. They are renewed three times a year, at Christmas, Easter and Lammas Day in early August. As you cross the threshold (a word meaning 'the rush-hold', a raised stone to hold in the rushes), the pungent smell invites you to step back in time.

Beuno also used to travel to Anglesey, not across the Menai Strait but further south, landing in the shallow mud flats of Llanddwyn Island near Newborough. His preaching tours gave rise to a charming story that once while crossing to Anglesey he dropped his homilies into the water, but a curlew picked them up with its long beak and placed them on a stone above reach of the tide. In return, Beuno prayed for the protection of curlews, which is why their nests are so hard to find. The story was perhaps invented by a hungry medieval forager in search of curlews' eggs, for it is unlikely that Beuno wrote down his homilies.

In Beuno's time, Anglesey was part of the kingdom of Maelgwyn Gwynedd, a descendant of Cunedda, whom we have already met.

St Beuno's church in its oval Celtic churchyard beside the sea at Pistyll in the Lleyn peninsula, north Wales, on the pilgrim route to Bardsey Island.

Maelgwyn established a Welsh dynasty in the sixth century; his family claimed some superiority among the British kings, and his line continued until the early ninth century. In his sixth-century *History of the Britons*, Gildas describes him as 'a great king'; he died in 547. Maelgwyn's chief court was at Aberffraw on Anglesey. Like Cybi, Beuno came to Maelgwyn to ask for land to build a church, and was granted a plot in Aberffraw beside the royal court. The Vikings sacked Aberffraw in 968, but the medieval bridge over its tidal river still remains; older inhabitants remember a nearby well dedicated to Beuno. He is also honoured at a chapel in Llanidan, overlooking the Menai Strait, where the bronze bell with which he called people to prayer survived until the eighteenth century. Perhaps the new burnished bell gleamed in the sunlight, for it was known as Beuno's Yellow Bell (*Cloch Felen Beuno*).

Beuno's *Life* describes how during his missionary journeys he gathered a band of followers around him. They are mentioned by name, and many of them have dedications near to those of Beuno. One of his followers, Cwyfan, has a church on a tiny tidal island two miles northwest of Beuno's church at Aberffraw. The raised churchyard is only ¾ acres in size; it is connected to the mainland at low tide by a causeway (see overleaf). Until the mid-nineteenth century, services were held at

85

St Cwyfan's church on a tidal islet at Llangwyfan near Aberffraw, Anglesey. Cwyfan was a follower of Beuno.

Llangwyfan on alternate Sundays, tide and weather permitting. The priest claimed a tithe consisting of hay for his horse, two eggs, a penny loaf and half a pint of beer.

Another church is dedicated to Cwyfan on the Lleyn peninsula at Tudweiliog, six miles southwest of Pistyll, with a holy well where sore eyes, ague and warts were cured. He is also commemorated with a church at another Llangwyfan near Beuno's church at Gwyddelwern. Cwyfan's fourth church is beside a high waterfall at Dyserth, five miles west of Beuno's church at Whitford. As we have already seen, the name 'Dyserth' comes from the Latin *desertum* ('empty place'), and implies a monk's desire for a solitary place where he could pray. Dyserth church is in a magnificent location, within sound and sight of spray ceaselessly pouring over the rock face.

Dyserth's waterfall provided Cwyfan or his unknown follower with water for drinking and washing, and a pool in which he could immerse candidates for baptism. They arose out of the freezing water to symbolize rising into heavenly life. Watercress, valued as food by Celtic monks, grows thickly in the cold stream flowing past the church entrance. Inside are the remains of two finely carved Celtic crosses. Here, too, Cwyfan is commemorated with a well, half a mile north of the church, which contained trout until the 1940s. Fish in wells were regarded with awe and respect. Some were used for divining the future and others were regarded as health-giving.

Beuno's *Life* describes a disciple named Aelhaearn, one of three monk brothers. There was a chapel dedicated to Aelhaearn at Gwyddelwern, near those of Beuno and Cwyfan. He is also commemorated at a church in the Lleyn peninsula named Llanaelhaearn, halfway between Beuno's churches of Clynnog and Pistyll. A fifth-century grave-marker, inscribed with the name Melitus, stands between the churchyard gate and the west door of the church. Aelhaearn may have conducted the funeral of Melitus. Inside the church, set into the wall, is a sixth-century gravestone commemorating 'Aliortus, a man from Elmet'. Elmet was a distant Celtic kingdom around Leeds. A family from the Leeds area settling in the Lleyn peninsula must have been even more unusual in Celtic times than it would be today, causing this unique Celtic epitaph. The gravestone was found in a field beside the churchyard named 'the Garden of the Saints'.

With his two brothers, Aelhaearn belonged to a ruling Powys family, and all three endowed churches. Aelhaearn's chief church was at Guilsfield in Powys, in the neighbourhood where Beuno was born, not far from Berriew. The church at Guilsfield predates Aelhaearn, however, for a monk named Teon from Illtud's monastery in Glamorgan, who subsequently became bishop of London, is recorded as either being born in Guilsfield or taking refuge there from the Saxons. The imposing church in Guilsfield has a tenth-century font decorated with carved heads, another reminder of the ancient Celtic head-cult.

Beuno's work in north Wales was similar to that of David in the south. Perhaps intentionally, Beuno and David led missions in opposite directions. David began in the southwest and worked eastwards, while Beuno began in Powys, in mid-Wales, and then led a mission through much of the northwest. We cannot tell whether Beuno and David were contemporaries, or whether Beuno was born a generation later than David. We know, however, that Beuno and his friends contributed greatly to the growth of the church in north Wales.

Chapter seven

Ninian, Kentigern and Strathclyde

IN LATE ROMAN TIMES, Scotland was a patchwork of Celtic kingdoms, whose people were led by chieftains or kings. Those in the north and east were Picts, while south of the Antonine Wall were the Britons of Strathclyde. This was a kingdom which stretched from Dumbarton at the mouth of the River Clyde eastwards to the Scottish Borders, and into northern England and the Lake District. In 360 the political scene shifted: Gaels from Ireland raided the west coast of Scotland, while Picts attacked Strathclyde from the north. Seven years later, Angles attacked from the east. In 369 the Emperor Theodosius repelled the invaders, and Strathclyde enjoyed twenty years of peace, but in 410 the Romans withdrew, leaving the Britons to defend themselves.

In Roman Britain, bishops lived in the main centres of population, and in the north, each tribal area perhaps formed a diocese, led by a tribal bishop. By the fifth century, these kingdoms and their bishops were based within the major river basins: the Forth and the Tweed in the east, and the Clyde and the Solway Firth in the West. The kingdom of Rheged, which was probably centred upon the Roman town of Carlisle, stretched north of the Solway Firth into Galloway.[1]

It was in this kingdom that Ninian was born; we know little about him. Writing three hundred years later, Bede tells us that Ninian studied in Rome, before settling at Whithorn in Galloway, on the Solway coast. Here, according to Bede, he built a church at *Candida Casum*, or 'the white house'. Bede implies that the church was built of stone in the Roman style rather than the Celtic style. The settlement's modern name, Whithorn, comes from the Saxon *hwit aern* or 'white house'. The monastery became an important centre of religious life and learning; it was widely known, and remained so for a long period.

Artefacts indicate the presence of Romanized Britons on the Galloway coast from about 400; they were traders and fishermen who perhaps came from Carlisle. Whithorn was a sheltered site for a town, just inland, with a small port on the Isle of Whithorn. The rich and complex site has been excavated for many years, under the direction of Peter Hill, who has recently summarized seven years' work in his book entitled *Whithorn and St Ninian; the Excavation of a Monastic Town, 1984–91*.[2]

Small timber buildings dating from about 400, possibly constructed during Ninian's lifetime, have been excavated at Whithorn. A memorial stone was erected here in the early fifth century by Latinus, grandson of

St Ninian's cave, Whithorn, with early crosses incised in the rock face. If this was Ninian's quiet retreat, this would have been his view.

a man named Barrovadus, who appears to have been the local chieftain. The stone may mark his donation of the site to the Church; it commemorates Latinus and his four-year-old daughter. The style of the memorial suggests contact with Gaul, which may be supported by the presence of fragments of fifth-century pottery from the Tours region and from Aquitaine.

On the seashore three miles southwest of Whithorn is Ninian's cave, approached by an ancient path (see above). Ninian is said to have used the cave as a quiet retreat. Celtic and Northumbrian crosses are carved on its walls, indicating that the cave soon became a place of pilgrimage. Three miles from the town on the opposite shore lies the Isle of Whithorn, which is now joined to the mainland. It was probably associated with the monastery throughout its history. There are traces of a Celtic fort on the island, around the ruins of a thirteenth-century chapel in which pilgrims arriving by sea could give thanks for their safe arrival.

By 550 there were new monastic buildings at Whithorn, including five circular shrines and a graveyard. Many Irish monks came to Whithorn to study, one of whom may have been Finnian of Moville (d. 579). He worked in southwest Scotland and gave his name to Kilwinning ('cell of Finnian'), sixteen miles southwest of Glasgow, before returning to Ireland to found communities of his own. There was another very early monastery to the west of Whithorn, at Kirkmadrine on the next peninsula, which may have been founded from Ninian's community. There are two tombstones at Kirkmadrine dating from about 500. One is dedicated to Viventius and Mavorius, 'the holy and outstandingly excellent bishops'; the other describes another pair of monk bishops in the same style.

In about 730 the Anglo-Saxons established a bishopric at Whithorn. They built a church and a monastery, and propagated Ninian's cult to legitimize their control of the Britons in Galloway. One monk wrote a Latin poem about Ninian's life and miracles, and sent a copy to the scholar Alcuin (735–804) at Charlemagne's court. The Northumbrian thanked him and sent back a silk veil for Ninian's shrine. Alcuin preserved the poem, entitled *Miracula Nynie Episcopi*; it is the earliest surviving account of Ninian's life. His journey to Rome is described: he crossed the Alps, where clouds like 'milk white fleeces glide in the silent sky, and snowdrifts bury mountain peaks'.[3]

The poet tells how Ninian established Whithorn under the patronage of Martin of Tours: 'the holiness and splendour of the shrine comes from the merits of Martin'. The author relates that the local ruler, King Tudwal, was angered by his people's devotion to Ninian, and forced him into exile. As a result, the poem continues, Tudwal was struck with blindness, and was forced to seek healing from Ninian. The relationship between Tudwal and Ninian will be explored more fully in chapter 12.

Remains of a wooden Northumbrian church and two timber halls date from the time of the poem. The buildings would have had bowed walls and curved, ridged roofs, each shaped like an upturned boat; they were part of a large monastic complex. There were Anglian bishops at Whithorn until about 800, but this was the northwestern limit of their territory. The Norman chronicler, William of Malmesbury, wrote: 'Beyond these, I find no more anywhere'. He describes raids by the Picts and Gaels, until the Angles could no longer remain in control.[4]

In the twelfth century, King David I of Scotland encouraged religious orders to take over Celtic monasteries, and Whithorn became a priory of Premonstratensian monks. The king also replaced the Celtic system of abbots ruling territory from their monasteries; henceforth each area was to be governed by a bishop approved by the pope. This was part of a wider policy of bringing the Scottish Church more fully under the control of Rome. To sanction these changes in the minds of his people, King David I dedicated churches to Ninian, as if to invoke the saint's approval. Of the sixty surviving dedications to Ninian, many date from the twelfth century. In 1165, the Cistercian abbot Ailred of Rievaulx wrote a *Life of Ninian*. Ailred was born in Hexham, which was then in Scotland, and was educated at the court of King David I before he became a monk; he therefore understood David's policy towards the Scottish Church.

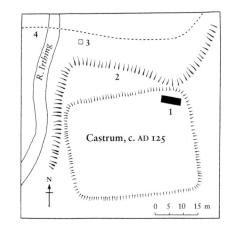

Map 7. *St Martin's church, Brampton.*
Key:
1. Church.
2. Escarpment.
3. Ninewells ('St Ninian's well').
Remains of a Roman cement
surround suggest that this was
previously a shrine to the local
water spirit.
4. Ancient track fording the River
Irthing.

Ailred had access to a lost British *Life of Ninian*, but admits that he despised its 'barbarous language'. He describes Ninian carrying out policies of which King David I would approve: 'Then (Ninian) began to ordain priests, consecrate bishops, distribute other clerical honours and divide the whole land into parishes'.[5] However, Ailred also travelled to Whithorn and collected stories about Ninian from the Galloway region, which then belonged to Ailred's own diocese of York.

At one point in his *Life of Ninian*, Ailred describes monks using coracles, which were apparently unknown in twelfth-century Yorkshire: 'Now it is traditional in that area to make a sort of cup-shaped boat out of light branches, large enough for three men to sit close together. They stretch an ox-hide over it, making it both buoyant and watertight.' The people of Galloway may have told Ailred stories of monks arriving in ocean-going curraghs, for he continues hesitantly: 'Perhaps they used to build much larger boats in the same way at that time'.[6]

We can best catch a glimpse of Ninian from the work he did in Strathclyde and the land of the southern Picts. Legends, place-names and archaeology offer clues about the extent and style of his work. At this time, the ecclesiastical centre of the kingdom was probably Carlisle, where Ninian may have been born. Carlisle was a large town inside the Roman frontier, at the western end of Hadrian's Wall, in a key position on the route north to Scotland. There were Christians in the Roman occupying army, and a church probably existed in Carlisle from late Roman times onwards, since fourth-century Christian artefacts have been found here.

One of the churches that Ninian may have founded is near Brampton, six miles northeast of Carlisle (see map 7). Here, beside the River Irthing, a Roman auxiliary unit built a small fort in about AD 125, to control the area before Hadrian's Wall was built. Amphorae for storing wine have been found within the camp, which was occupied for only twenty-five years. When Ninian or his followers reached the site, about three hundred years later, the fort was in ruins, and the monks built a church in the shelter of the camp's protecting wall.

Like Ninian's chapel at Whithorn, Brampton church is dedicated to Martin of Tours; there used to be an ancient holy tree here, named Martin's oak. The church was surrounded by an oval cemetery, and a spring emerges at the foot of the scarp on which the fort is built, beside an ancient track which fords the river. The well shows signs of a Roman concrete surround, so it may have been a shrine to the local water spirit. It was later renamed Ninewells ('Ninian's well'). The tiny church was rebuilt by the Normans, using some Roman stone from the ruined camp; only the chancel remains.[7]

Near Penrith, Brougham perhaps marks the southern limit of Ninian's sphere of influence. Brougham Castle is built on the site of a Roman fort named Brocavum, a Celtic name meaning 'home of the badgers'. The fort commanded the bridge over the River Eamont at a strategic Roman crossroads. The Emperor Hadrian came here to inspect his northern defences. There were Christian soldiers serving here, for built into the medieval castle wall is a fourth-century tombstone inscribed: 'Titus M ... lived thirty-two years more or less'. The Latin phrase 'plus minus' was used by Christians to show that their belief in resurrection made an exact record of age unimportant; your age at death hardly matters, they felt, when you expect to live for ever. In this, Christians were making a stand against a culture in which people normally kept a careful record of precise ages and dates.

Ninian is not associated with the Roman fort, however, but with the Roman civil settlement two miles east. This was the *vicus* or urban community normally found near a Roman military establishment, where local people provided for the soldiers' needs. At this point the River Eamont winds through fields, and beside it is Brougham Ninekirks, meaning 'Ninian's church at Brougham' (see map 8). It has an attractive setting, with the Pennine range visible ten miles to the east. The earliest material discovered here is eighth-century metalwork, and the medieval dedication of the church was to the Saxon, Wilfred, so it is impossible to know whether or not Ninian's followers worked here. In the present church, the fine wooden pulpit and screen are Jacobean. The fifteenth-century altar slab survives, but Stuart theology called for a communion table rather than an altar of sacrifice; the oak table now sits awkwardly on top of the earlier altar slab.

At the opposite end of the kingdom of Strathclyde, there is an early reference to a cemetery consecrated by Ninian either in Glasgow or at Cadder near Kirkintilloch. Ninian may have travelled from Kirkintilloch across the Campsie Fells to Stirling, using the ancient route which followed the Antonine Wall. In Stirling, the church and well of St Ninian's perhaps marks one of his foundations. Across the Firth of Forth, further into the territory of the southern Picts, there was a chapel dedicated to Ninian at Arbroath, where a cemetery dating from the sixth or seventh century has been found. On the western Scottish coast, Kilmartin in Glassary may be a dedication by Ninian's monks. Seven Celtic crosses were found here: four simple Latin crosses and three with ornate interwoven designs.

The Gaelic form of Ninian is Trinian; in northern Scotland there are several dedications to Trinian. Monks from Whithorn also settled on the Isle of Man, where St Trinian's chapel can be seen southeast of Greeba, beside the road from Douglas to Peel. To the right of its stone altar, paving stones form a simple cross within a circle, marking the shrine of its founder. The ruined chapel also contains a cross-slab dating from the sixth or seventh century. There are records of a twelfth-century grant of land near Greeba to Whithorn Priory, and the chapel was rebuilt at that time. Other keeills or chapels on the Isle of Man were dedicated by Ninian's monks to Martin of Tours: Keeill Martin, Ballakilmartin, and Ballavartin in Kirk Santan.

The political capital of Strathclyde was Dumbarton, in the northwest corner of the kingdom. A chieftain living on Dumbarton Rock, a twin-peaked lava plug, was ideally situated to fend off Picts from the northeast or Irish Gaels from the west. Dumbarton Rock dominates the Clyde estuary, and attackers would have had to sail past the Rock unscathed if they wished to penetrate inland. By AD 137, Dumbarton Rock was the site of a Roman military station, perhaps at the end of their northern frontier, the Antonine Wall. When the Romans withdrew from Scotland in 410, Dumbarton (or Dun Breatann, meaning 'fortress of the Britons') remained the tribal capital.

It was the Irish who named Dumbarton 'fortress of the Britons'; the British called it Alt Clut ('Rock of Clyde'). According to St Patrick's biographer, Muirchú, it was the stronghold of Coroticus, a British chieftain, from whom Patrick demanded the release of some of his Irish converts. Pottery and glass dating from the sixth century have been excavated on the Rock. As we have seen, Patrick may have been born within sight of the Rock, at Old Kilpatrick, and his follower Mochta worked not far away at Cardross. According to tradition, Gildas was born on the Rock around 500, and later travelled south to enter Illtud's monastery in Wales.

In 731 Bede described Alt Clut as 'a town of the Britons, strongly defended to the present day'. Within its ramparts of timber and rubble, the two fortified peaks were separated by a level area which probably contained halls, a church and a well. The Vikings attacked Alt Clut in

870: excavations showed that the rampart was destroyed by fire, and the pommel bar from a Viking sword was found nearby. It is said that the Britons surrendered after a four month siege, only when the well had run dry. Carved cross-slabs show that Christian Vikings buried their dead on the Rock, and there was a medieval chapel of St Patrick. The fourteenth-century portcullis guarding the entrance to the citadel can still be seen. By this time, a separate town of Dumbarton was growing at the foot of the Rock.

There were British settlements all along the Clyde, and a number of missionaries worked here (see map 10). The name of Paisley, on a tributary of the Clyde, comes from the Latin for 'basilica', and may indicate the presence of a church from Roman times. Here, beside the White Cart River, a pre-Christian cemetery is overlaid by the graves of Christians buried facing east. In about 560 an Irish monk named Mirrin founded a community here. As a boy, Mirrin had been taken by his mother to Congal, the abbot of Bangor monastery, at the head of Belfast Loch in northern Ireland. After training as a monk, Mirrin became prior of Bangor and later came to Scotland, possibly as one of the twelve followers of Columba.

Mirrin may have spent time on Inchmurrin ('Mirrin's Isle') in Loch Lomond. Here, on the largest island in the loch, a ruined chapel is dedicated to Mirrin. Fifteen miles south is Paisley, where he built a hut of clay and wattle. Mirrin's monks may have travelled east on preaching tours: a well is dedicated to him in the Campsie Fells above Kilsyth. The monastery at Paisley was later rebuilt – excavations revealed a stone chapel and enclosure wall dating from the seventh or eighth century.

Pilgrims continued to visit Mirrin's shrine, and in the twelfth century, Benedictine monks from a daughter house of Cluny were brought to Paisley from Much Wenlock in Shropshire. A fifteenth-century stone frieze in their abbey church illustrates scenes from Mirrin's life: a panel portrays him as prior of Bangor, and another shows him reviving a monk who had died of heat stroke, working in the fields. A third section depicts Mirrin praying in his cell at night, illumined by a ray of heavenly light.

Four miles east of Paisley, on the south bank of the River Clyde, is Govan, now engulfed by the city of Glasgow. Excavations here have revealed an early stone church with a surrounding enclosure wall and ditch. It is dedicated to Constantine, a king turned monk who founded a monastery here in the late sixth century. He may be the king to whom two Cornish churches are dedicated, and the Constantine who was martyred at Kintyre in 576. An impressive ninth-century stone sarcophagus at Govan perhaps formed part of his shrine. It portrays a stag hunt and various other decorative animals.

The monastery at Govan had a fine school of sculptors: in the church are a large number of carved crosses and a magnificent collection of tenth-century Viking hogback tombstones, each representing a house with a curved roof, wooden shingles, and mythical beasts clasping the gable ends. Another Viking slab portrays a cross surmounted by a sun in splendour, each ray ending in an animal's head. On the reverse side, a piper on horseback skirls the bagpipes as he perhaps leads troops into battle. This must have been a cemetery where Viking chieftains were buried. Around the time of Mirrin and Constantine, a church was dedicated to the Welshman Cadoc at nearby Cambuslang, on a tributary of the River Clyde, as we have already seen. It is interesting that monks who worked within ten miles of one another should come from as far afield as Ireland, Cornwall and Wales.

A generation later, a young Briton named Kentigern came to Glasgow as its bishop. Since he was a Briton, Kentigern is not mentioned by Bede or by Adomnán, the biographer of Columba. In their eyes, Kentigern belonged to an unorthodox and inferior race, and so did not merit consideration. The twelfth-century monk, Jocelyn of Furness, wrote a largely legendary *Life of Kentigern*, at a time when King David I of Scotland revived the popularity of both Ninian and Kentigern. We at least know that Kentigern existed, since he is mentioned in early pedigrees of British saints, and by ninth-century Irish writers. In addition, genuine traditions about Kentigern survive in the areas where he worked.

Kentigern, whose name means 'chief prince', was said to be the illegitimate son of a British princess. He trained as a monk in Serf's community at Culross on the Fife coast; the monastery is described in chapter 9. Beside the shore at Culross, a sixteenth-century chapel commemorates the supposed spot where, having been set adrift in a coracle, his disgraced mother floated ashore and gave birth to her son. After training as a monk, Kentigern travelled twenty miles southwest and established a base in Glasgow, where the thirteenth-century cathedral is dedicated to him under his nickname Mungo ('my little one'). All that remains from his time is the monastery's well, built into the wall of the crypt.

When an anti-Christian party came to power, Kentigern fled south through Cumbria and sought refuge among his kinsmen who had settled in north Wales as followers of Cunedda. Jocelyn of Furness describes how Kentigern interrupted his journey and stayed for a time in Cumbria: 'When he came to Carlisle, he heard that many people living in the mountains were pagan, and did not know God's law. So he turned aside and converted many to Christianity, and corrected the errors of others who were already Christian'.[8] Since Jocelyn came from Cumbria, his account of Kentigern's work there may be closer to the truth than other portions of his *Life*.

In Kentigern's time, Strathclyde, Cumbria and Wales were still a single Celtic kingdom. The people of Cumbria spoke a language similar to Welsh, Cornish and Breton until the twelfth century. Jocelyn describes how Kentigern came to the head of Derwentwater in about 553 and established a base at Crosthwaite, a mile northwest of Keswick. Kentigern 'spent some time in a forested area, strengthening the faith of those who lived there. He set up a cross there as a sign of faith, and so the place is named Crosthwaite'.[9] 'Thwaite' is Norse for a clearing in a forest; Kentigern evidently spent time teaching, converting and baptizing the inhabitants of the forest clearing.

The large church at Crosthwaite dates from 1523. The church is unique in possessing a complete set of consecration crosses: twelve are carved round its inside walls to dedicate the building to God. The church was blessed according to the English rite rather than the Roman one, and so a further twelve crosses were carved on its outside walls. Jocelyn only mentions Kentigern's work at Crosthwaite, but tradition describes Kentigern making a circuit of north Cumbria, beginning at Carlisle, Cumbria's capital, where he could gather information about the region. He then travelled south through Caldbeck and Mungrisdale before continuing to Crosthwaite, the farthest south of his Cumbrian dedications.

It is possible that there were already Christians in the region as a result of Ninian's preaching, and Irish monks may have worked here too, since there are early dedications to Patrick at Heysham and Preston Patrick in north Lancashire. Eight miles southeast of Crosthwaite is Patterdale, whose name comes from Old Norse and means 'St Patrick's Dale'. A church and well beside the lakeshore here are dedicated to the Irish saint (see map 8).

Overlooking the moors at Castle Sowerby, eight miles south of Carlisle, is an isolated church dedicated to Kentigern, with a well for christenings beside the churchyard wall. It is difficult to locate the low, whitewashed stone church since it is not marked on most maps, but it may be a foundation from Kentigern's time. At nearby Caldbeck, Kentigern is said to have baptized converts at the spring in the riverbank, beside the medieval packhorse bridge. In summer, babies are still christened here, while adults gather on the bridge to watch. There used to be a hospice for distressed travellers here; it would have been easy to lose one's way in the isolated moorland. Five miles south is another dedication to Kentigern, named Mungrisdale (or 'valley of Mungo's pigs'), where the porch of the tiny church is still paved with cobbles.

After leaving Crosthwaite, Kentigern perhaps headed northwest for Aspatria, an ancient settlement three miles from the sea. An incised tomb slab carved with a swastika was found here; it dates from about 430, over a century before Kentigern's time. The church and its well are dedicated to him: the well is now dry, but until recently it was fed from

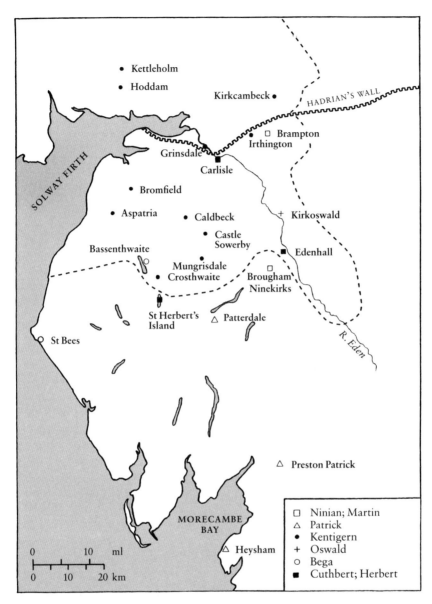

Map 8. *Celtic Cumbria and the northwest.*
Brampton and Brougham Ninekirks were possibly founded by Ninian's followers in the fifth century.
A broken line indicates the area reoccupied by Britons in the tenth century. Some of Kentigern's dedications date from this time; others may be earlier foundations by Kentigern's followers.

an underground spring and used for baptisms. Aspatria suffered from Norse-Irish coastal raids, and the remains of a Viking hogback tombstone, shaped to represent a house for the dead, indicate a wealthy Norseman's burial.

These Vikings came from Ireland and the Isle of Man; they had been Christian for three or four generations. Their ancestors came from western Norway, where the harsh climate had led them to adopt transhumance farming: in winter they stayed in the sheltered valleys, while each summer they led their flocks of sheep up to higher pastures. Today, Cumbrian farmers can still be seen leading their flocks up the fellsides in summer. The Irish-Norse remained in the uplands, while different kingdoms vied for control of the lowlands. By the late eighth century, Angles from Northumbria had colonized Cumbria. Two centuries later, the British princes of Strathclyde recaptured their former territory and held it from 900 to 1092 against both Northumbrian Angles and the Irish-Norse.

The Britons of Strathclyde, proud of their saintly bishop, Kentigern, built churches at places where he was said to have preached, with new dedications at Bromfield, five miles northeast of Aspatria, and at Kirkcambeck, two miles north of Hadrian's Wall, where only a ruined east window remains. On the mud flats where the River Eden flows into the Solway Firth is another tiny church perhaps dedicated to Kentigern at this time, in Grinsdale. Kentigern may have sailed from here to Wales, where we saw in chapter 5 that he established a monastery at St Asaph, at the junction of the Rivers Elwy and Clwyd. He remained here until about 573, when King Rhydderch Hael, a Romanized Christian from Lanark, invited Kentigern back to Strathclyde.

Rhydderch Hael (or 'Roderick the Generous') emerged as a leader after a savage battle of British war-lords north of Carlisle in 573. He gained a foothold on the Scottish west coast north of the Solway Firth at Hoddam, and made Dumbarton Rock his fortress capital. In about 590, together with three other British kings, Roderick almost drove the Northumbrian Saxons into the sea at Lindisfarne on England's northeast coast. Columba's biographer, Adomnán, relates how Rhydderch Hael sought advice, perhaps before this great battle, and Columba assured the king that he would survive. Adomnán writes: 'As (Roderick) was a friend of the saint, he sent (a monk) to him on a secret mission, wishing to know whether or not he was to be slain by his enemies.... The saint then declared, "He will never be delivered into the hands of his enemies, but will die in his own home on his own feather pillow".' Roderick died peacefully in 601.[10] It is nice to know that even sixth-century war-lords liked feather pillows!

Throughout this time, boundaries between the Britons, Picts, Gaels and Angles were not rigid: there was migration and intermarriage. Warriors of several nations would fight under a powerful chieftain, and there were shifting alliances between clans. Rhydderch Hael's fort at Hoddam was beside the River Annan, near Kinmount Hill where, according to tradition, the king invited Kentigern to address his people. The monk built a church close to the bridge over the River Annan; only its cemetery remains, with the foundations of a small chapel. Pieces of three elaborate Northumbrian crosses were found here. Kentigern's monks probably preached in nearby settlements: the adjacent parish of Kettleholm is dedicated to Kentigern under his nickname, Mungo.

Kentigern also journeyed northeast into the Scottish Borders and the area south of Edinburgh. He may have been born here in the Lothians, where there are eleven dedications to Kentigern and his followers including, as we have seen in chapter 5, Nidan and Ffinnan from north Wales. Eight miles south of Edinburgh, a church is named after Mungo at Penicuik, which means 'hill of the cuckoo'. Further south near Peebles is the hamlet of Stobo, where the chapel built by Kentigern's followers became the mother church of the Upper Tweed valley. Stobo Kirk is mainly Norman; until the Reformation it was linked with Kentigern's cathedral in Glasgow.

Following the River Tweed upstream for five miles, one reaches the village of Drumelzier, where a large boulder at the roadside opposite Altarstone Farm is said to be the place where Kentigern baptized a Celtic bard named Merlin of the Woods, who lived here in exile after Rhydderch defeated his chieftain in 573.[11] A standing stone in a nearby field is said to mark the bard's grave. There is no authentication for the story, but such incidents could not have been unusual. When King Rhydderch established his fortress on Dumbarton Rock, Kentigern returned to Glasgow as its bishop. He died in his monastery and is buried in the cathedral crypt; arcading from his thirteenth-century shrine survives. King David I presided over the dedication of the first stone cathedral of St Mungo in 1136.

It is only eighteen miles from Strathclyde to northern Ireland, and many Irish monks sailed back and forth to study or preach. One of the earliest Irish monks to settle in Strathclyde was Kessóg (d. c. 520), who lived in the period between Ninian's death and Kentigern's birth. Kessóg was born at Cashel in southern Ireland, of the royal family of Munster. He travelled to Scotland, where he became a monk and later, bishop of the ancient earldom of Lennox. Kessóg built a monastery on a small island in Loch Lomond which is named Inchtavannach, or 'Isle of the Monks'. Older people call it in Gaelic 'Isle of the two bells', referring to the bells which summoned the monks to prayer.

Kessóg built a church on the mainland a mile to the northwest beside Luss Water, around which grew the small town of Luss. Two sixth-century grave-markers, each carved with a simple Latin cross, and a more elaborate cross from the next century indicate that monks continued to work here. Kessóg was known as a zealous preacher and was said to heal the sick with a herb named *Lus* in Gaelic (similar to *fleur-de-lys* in French), which may be the yellow flag that grows near the mouth of Luss Water, giving the settlement its name. Kessóg's followers worked on the island of Great Cumbrae, twenty-five miles southwest of Glasgow, and also travelled in the opposite direction to Strathblane at the western end of the Campsie Fells, where they built a church at an ancient burial site marked by a Bronze Age standing stone.

Kessóg travelled north to Callander in the Trossach Hills, where he founded a church beside the River Teith. Today, only the graveyard remains, close to a small hill known in Gaelic as Kessóg's Mound, where the monk is said to have preached. In 520 Kessóg was murdered by assassins at Bandry, a mile south of Luss, within sight of his island monastery. A cairn marked the place where he died, and a chapel was built beside it. In his *Life of Columba*, Adomnán describes people building a cairn of stones on the spot where a Christian leader has just died.[12] The cairn at Bandry was destroyed when the road was made in 1761, and a carved stone head, perhaps representing Kessóg, was found at the site. It can be seen in Luss church, where Kessóg's relics were revered well after the Reformation.

At the mouth of the Clyde estuary, Bute was an attractive island to Celtic monks. It was low-lying and fertile, and at the centre of routes from northern Ireland and southwest Scotland, with Iona to the northwest and Dumbarton to the northeast (see map 9). The island is sheltered from the ocean, and since it is five miles by fifteen, it could support a considerable population. It is so close to the mainland that sheep and cattle could safely swim across. One of the earliest locations on Bute to be chosen by monks was a tiny rocky promontory named St Ninian's Point. This was first a pagan cemetery; Neolithic flints were found in two hearths below the chapel walls and nearby, two small Bronze Age standing stones perhaps mark a chieftain's burial. In late Roman times there was a Christian cemetery here, and in the sixth century a chapel was built of rubble, plaster and clay. Its inner wall was lined with clay, and its altar had a cavity for relics. The chapel was abandoned after Viking raids, but was used again in medieval times.

A mile west of St Ninian's Point is the tiny island of Inchmarnock, which means 'Isle of my little Ernán'. Ernán, as we have seen, is a diminutive of Marnoc. For centuries, Christians ferried their dead to Inchmarnock: Scottish people preferred to bury their dead on islands, where their bones would not be disturbed by prowling wolves. Hermits, too, chose to live on islands, where they could be safe from the bears, wildcats and boar which lived in the northern forests.[13] On Inchmarnock

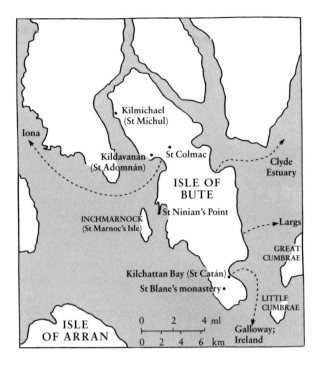

Map 9. *The Isle of Bute,
southwest Scotland.
Bute was a useful stopping
place between Iona and the
Scottish mainland. Various
missionaries made use of
its sheltered harbours.*

there are remains of carved crosses from the eighth century onwards, and
foundations of a twelfth-century chapel with red sandstone pillars.
There were twenty-two St Marnocs, and it is unclear which of these
monks gave his name to the island. It is likely to be the Marnoc who
founded Kilmarnock, sixteen miles south of Glasgow.

Other monks stayed for a while at the northern end of Bute. One of
the three hundred St Colmáns created a preaching cross by carving
a cross on a pre-Christian standing stone, near the ruined church of
St Colmac. The chapel of Kilmichael is dedicated not to the archangel
Michael but to an unknown monk called Michul. Kildavanan Point is
named after Adomnán, the abbot of Iona who wrote Columba's
biography. Kildavanan is the nearest bay in which monks from Iona
could land, after carrying their craft across the Crinan isthmus and
rowing down Loch Fyne. Having rested a while, they would cross Bute,
which is only two miles wide at this point, row up the Clyde, and
continue overland to Lindisfarne.[14] On the hill above Kildavanan Point
stood Adomnán's chapel; his life will be described in chapter 9.

At this time, the southern end of Bute was the most populous. There
was a fort, and a monastery of some fifty monks, with a surrounding
settlement. The monastery was founded by Catán, after whom
Kilchattan Bay, a mile to the north, is named. We know almost nothing
of Catán, who apparently arrived from Ireland in the late sixth century
with his sister Ertha, later to become the mother of St Blane. Sources

differ as to whether Catán was Blane's uncle or his tutor; as abbot, Catán could well have been both. He was probably a missionary, since there are ten churches dedicated to him, most of them in the highlands and islands of Argyll, with one to the far north in the Hebrides, and another in the land of the southern Picts, at Aberuthven in Perthshire.

Catán's monastery on Bute, now dedicated to Blane, is in a lovely spot in a sheltered valley near the shore. It is still surrounded by its original enclosure wall, within which are remains of a circular fort, a well, and the ruins of monks' huts set against a sheltering cliff. In the cemetery are the remains of a small chapel, surrounded by a few early crosses. There is a stone bowl for washing pilgrims' feet, a traditional ceremony of welcome in the early Celtic Church. Adomnán describes Columba ordering his monks to receive unexpected guests in this way: 'Prepare the guest house quickly, and draw water for the visitors' feet!'[15]

Catán sent Blane to northern Ireland for several years, to be trained by Abbot Congal of Bangor, where the young monk may have studied alongside Mirrin, whom we met earlier in this chapter. After returning to Bute, Blane succeeded Catán as bishop and abbot. In time, Blane moved eastwards to the Scottish mainland, and we hear of various monk bishops who succeeded him, some of whom met violent deaths at the hands of Norsemen. The monastery was a centre of culture and craftsmanship; a tiny ninth-century crucible for casting bronze brooches was found here, and there are designs engraved on slate which were preparatory sketches made by craftsmen. Norse Christians were buried here: there is a hogback tombstone in the churchyard. A Viking's gold ring was found, and a gold fillet for binding a lady's hair. By medieval times the monks had created an inner cemetery for themselves and an outer one for lay people. There are remains of the medieval church at the centre of the site.

Blane left Bute and headed east to the Campsie Fells, where he is said to have preached for a while at Strathblane, a settlement in which Kessóg had worked a century earlier. Blane then journeyed northwards into the land of the southern Picts above the Firth of Forth. He was given the *dun* or fort of Dunblane, built to defend the main route to the north. In about 602, Blane and his monks built a cluster of beehive huts inside the fort, to the east of the present cathedral, set high above the fast-flowing Allan Water. Blane is said to have returned to the Isle of Bute to die, but his relics were brought back to Dunblane, perhaps to preserve them from Viking raids down the coast in the ninth and tenth centuries. Blane's handbell is preserved in the cathedral, together with a large tenth-century Pictish cross-slab. The twelfth-century belfry was originally separate from the church, and was built for defence as well as for housing bells. It was erected during the reign of King David I, who endowed the bishopric.

Blane was one of the last native missionaries to work in Strathclyde. By this time, Kentigern had died in Glasgow; the Irish missionary,

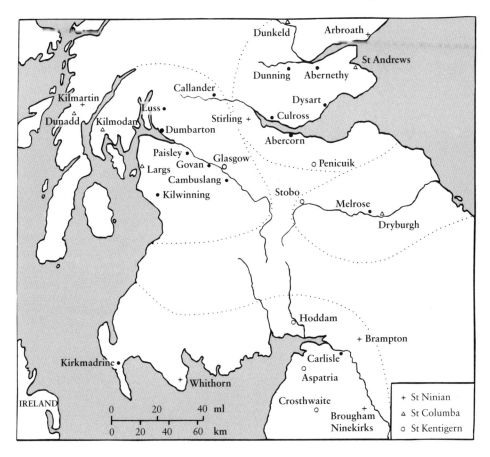

Map 10. Celtic churches of southern Scotland in the sixth century.
Possible fifth-century dioceses of north Britain are indicated by dotted lines.
They follow rivers: the Tweed, Clyde, Forth, Tay and the Solway Firth. Some sites
associated with Ninian, Columba, Kentigern and other missionaries are indicated.
Included with Columba are two of his followers, Kenneth and Modan.

Columba, had died fifteen years before Kentigern. Bute was a home to
both Strathclyde Britons and Irish Gaels, and monks of both races
worked alongside each other on the mainland. Map 10 illustrates how
the followers of Ninian, Kentigern and Columba did not remain in
separate areas, but travelled throughout southern Scotland and beyond.
It would be interesting to know how closely British and Irish monks
worked together. Many of them studied together at Whithorn and in the
Irish monasteries. Having looked at the contribution of the Strathclyde
British, in the next chapter we will examine the work of Columba and
the Irish monks who made western Scotland their home.

Chapter eight
Columba and Argyll

COLUMBA (521–597) was perhaps the most outstanding of the Celtic monks. We are fortunate in that we can glimpse Columba as he lived and worked in his island monastery, thanks to his biographer, Adomnán, who was abbot of Iona only a century later. Columba was a warrior and politician, a scholar, priest and poet, who played an important role in both Irish and Scottish history. He was born into the royal family of the Northern Uí Néill, at Gartan in Donegal. This was a powerful northern clan descended from Niall of the Nine Hostages, who reigned as High King at Tara in the late fourth century. He was a war-lord whose title indicates his authority: by holding nine hostages, who were usually kings' sons, he compelled nine powerful clans to pay tribute to him.

Columba's birthname was Crimtháinn, which means 'fox'. He studied under a Christian bard named Gemman, in his mother's country of Leinster. Bards were highly respected in Celtic Ireland, for a tribe's history was preserved through their heroic sagas and war poems. He became a monk at an early age, and was given the Latin name Columba, meaning 'dove'. Before he was twenty he was ordained as a deacon in the monastery of Finnian of Moville. Later he was ordained a priest by his cousin, Bishop Etchan, and founded his first monastery in his family's territory at Derry on land given to him by his tribe in about 556. Since its name means 'oak grove', it was probably an ancient holy site; its oaks survived for several hundred years.

Columba founded the monastery of Durrow, whose name means 'oak plain', in central Ireland. He had a mountain retreat at Glencolumkille in Donegal; and is also reputed to have made foundations at Swords near Dublin, at Drumcliffe in Sligo, at Moone in Kildare, and on Tory Island off the Donegal coast. Irish accounts of Columba relate how on a visit to his former abbot, Finnian of Moville, Columba borrowed a book from the library and secretly copied it at night. He was discovered when he had almost finished, and Finnian demanded the copy. This first recorded breach of copyright was brought to trial before the High King, who ruled in Finnian's favour.

A psalter known as *The Cathach of St Columba*, which dates from the sixth century, is said to be part of the copy Columba made. The *Cathach* is now in the Royal Irish Academy Library, Dublin. Its text is that of Jerome's Vulgate, written at speed by a skilled scribe, veering occasionally into the Old Latin version of the psalms. A footnote to the magnificent seventh-century illuminated gospel book of Durrow claims that it was written in twelve days by Columba. This would have been impossible, but a practised scribe like Columba could have copied the psalms and the gospels in twelve days, and the *Cathach* may well be the exemplar on which the *Book of Durrow* was based.[1] *Cathach* means 'battle reliquary'; the book acquired this name because Columba's clansmen used to carry it into battle as a symbol of the saint's blessing on their enterprise.

Columba appears to have kept his book in defiance of the court's decision, which probably soured relations with the High King. In 561, the High King invaded Connaght after the slaying of a royal hostage who was under the protection of Abbot Columba. Fog surrounded the army of Connaght and Columba's clan of the northern Uí Néill, and the High King advanced blindly into an ambush, suffering a disastrous defeat. Clergy fought in battle at this time, and it is perhaps at this point that Columba was wounded, which might account for the scar which his servant on Iona later noticed as a 'blueish mark on his side, that lasted for the rest of his life'. The scar was later explained, however, as the result of being whipped by an angel! After the battle, the throne of Tara passed to Columba's clan.[2]

Columba sailed to Scotland as a 'pilgrim for Christ'. He did not select his destination at random, however: as a successful warrior-prince, politician and abbot, Columba was probably invited by Conall, the new king of Argyll, to help him repel the Picts. The Irish Gaels, or Scots, had begun migrating to Argyll in about AD 300, and at that time they had fought alongside the Picts against the Romans in north Britain. The Gaels called their territory Dalriada after the Irish kingdom from which they came. Dalriada lay north of the powerful British kingdom of Strathclyde and west of the Picts who lived on the far side of the Grampian Mountains, which were then referred to as 'the Spine of Britain'.

Conall's father had established a hilltop fortress at Dunadd, where his warships commanded the sea route to Ireland and his army was poised to attack the Picts. Meanwhile, a powerful Pictish ruler emerged named Brude, whose father was Maelgwyn of north Wales and whose mother was a Pict. By 560, Brude had conquered the lesser Pictish kingdoms, attacked Argyll, killed Conall's father and driven the Gaels westwards to the sea. In response to this dangerous situation, Columba, then aged forty-two, set sail from Ireland with twelve companions; Kintyre was only a day's journey from Derry.

There is a tradition that Columba sailed up Loch Caolisport in Knapdale and landed at Ellary. Here, he found shelter in a large, airy cave, where there is an altar built of flat stones and a cross carved into the rock wall above, dating from early times. There is a stream with a waterfall nearby, and from the cave Columba could have watched seals playing around the islet at the head of the loch. There are remains of a medieval chapel beside the cave. By the eighth century there was a monastery a mile away, probably founded from Iona, at a place named *Cladh a Bhile*, or 'burial ground of the holy tree'. We can glimpse the monks baking bread and conducting funerals, for many early gravestones and querns for grinding corn were found here.

Columba is said to have continued northward to Dunadd, whose rocky outcrop had been fortified only sixty years earlier. Rising from flat, boggy land beside the River Add, it made an excellent fortress. A surprise attack was impossible: its main entrance is a natural gully through massive walls of rock, which was closed by great gates with a timber superstructure. Dunadd was at the centre of Dalriada; the king and his retinue stayed here on royal progress between his other forts.

A small peak was used as an inner citadel, and carved into the bedrock in front of it are a ceremonial basin and the impression of a foot, dating from the seventh or eighth century. These may have been used for royal inaugurations, in a ceremony in which the king was anointed and symbolically stepped into the shoes of his predecessor, or perhaps claimed the land on which he stood, since Dalriada can be surveyed in all directions from this spot. Beside the ceremonial footprint is an Irish ogham inscription and a Pictish carving of a boar, possibly relating to a marriage alliance between Gaels and Picts. Dunadd's chieftains lived in style: a red garnet set in gold filigree from Anglo-Saxon England was found here, and pottery from Gaul. Dunadd's craftsmen made jewelry, iron tools and weapons. A lump of yellow pigment used to illuminate manuscripts was also discovered here. The fortress was occupied until 1000.

The sixth-century *Annals of Ulster* record that King Conall gave Iona to Columba; but the island was on the frontier between Dalriada and the territory of the Picts, and King Brude considered Iona to be in his kingdom. Columba therefore journeyed north to King Brude's royal stronghold near Inverness, beyond 'the Spine of Britain'. He would have travelled by curragh, sailing up the Great Glen, through Loch Lynnhe, Loch Lochy and Loch Ness, where Adomnán relates that one of Columba's companions was almost swallowed by the monster! This is the earliest recorded reference to the existence of this shadowy creature. It is likely that, as Conall's ambassador, Columba's chief task was to negotiate peace with Dalriada; he also asked permission to settle on Iona.

Columba spoke Irish Gaelic, which the Picts did not understand, so he took with him Abbot Congal of Bangor and Kenneth of Aghaboe, both monks from Irish Pictish families, who spoke a language similar to that of King Brude. Columba's diplomacy was successful, for there was peace between Dalriada and the Picts for the next eighty years. Fifteen years after this expedition, the ageing Columba embarked on a second diplomatic mission to King Brude, during which he

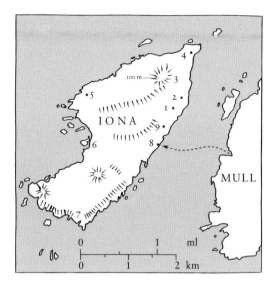

Map 11. *Columba's monastery on the Isle of Iona, which lies west of Mull and the Scottish mainland. Columba's monastery is sheltered by a low ridge of hills.*
Key:
1. *Columba's monastery.*
2. *Celtic hermitage.*
3 and 5. *Pre-Christian forts.*
4. *Site of the monks' massacre by Norse invaders.*
6. *Flat plain where the monks grew food.*
7. *Curragh Bay, where Columba traditionally landed in AD 563.*
8. *Point where the dead were ferried from the mainland, along the route indicated, for burial in the monastic cemetery.*
9. *Medieval nuns' convent.*

negotiated the necessary safe conduct for Cormac, Abbot of Durrow, to sail to the Orkneys and preach there. Adomnán mentions that this was granted by King Brude in the presence of his hostage Orkney chieftain. The hostage prince might have lost his life if Cormac had come to harm. Columba's diplomatic missions to Brude were subsequently portrayed as large-scale preaching tours, but the gradual conversion of the Picts to Christianity was probably carried out later by monks from Iona and elsewhere.[3]

After his negotiations with King Brude, Columba settled on Iona. The island is 2½ miles long and lies west of the larger island of Mull (see map 11). It had been inhabited by Neolithic farmers, and contains the burial cairn of a Bronze Age chieftain, and an Iron Age fort inhabited until the third century AD.[4] Iona's Gaelic name, *Hy*, means 'yew island' and perhaps refers to the Celtic yew god. The Irish *Life of Columba* relates that he found druids on the island and expelled them.[5]

A century before Columba arrived on Iona, an Irish monk named Odhráin (d. 548) was living there. He came from Tipperary and has other dedications on the nearby islands of Mull, Tiree and Colonsay, where he probably worked among the Gaelic settlers. The oldest burial-ground on Iona is named Reilig Odhráin after him. The word *reilig*, meaning cemetery, comes from the Latin *reliquiae* or remains; similarly, the word 'relic' means the remains of a holy person. The Old Irish *Life of Columba* attaches to Odhráin a pre-Christian account of a person ritually buried alive beneath the building's foundations, as a blessing on the island:

'Then Columba said to his people, it would be good for us that our roots should pass into the earth here. He continued, "It is permitted that one of you go under the earth of this island, to consecrate it". Odhráin rose quickly and said: "If you accept me, I am ready to do this". Columba replied, "Odhráin, you shall receive the following reward: no request will be granted to anyone at my tomb, unless they ask it first of you". Odhráin then went to heaven; (Columba) then founded the church of Iona.'

When Adomnán wrote Columba's biography he translated the island's name, *Hy*, into Latin as *Ioua*, which a medieval scribe miscopied as Iona. The scribe had evidently studied Hebrew, for 'Iona' is the Hebrew for Columba's name, 'the dove'. Adomnán wrote the *Life* in about 690, probably to impress upon Abbot Ceolfrith of Jarrow and his fellow Northumbrian clergy the importance of Columba and the Celtic tradition. Adomnán divided his book into sections recounting Columba's prophecies, miracles and visions. These remarkable qualities may have impressed his early readers, but it is the background detail of the stories that provides a unique picture of monastic life on Iona. We are fortunate in that the earliest surviving copy of the *Life of Columba* dates from the author's lifetime or soon after his death. It was written in Iona on goatskin parchment in a heavy Irish hand by the man who succeeded Adomnán as abbot of the monastery.

It is a busy book: the author describes fifty-five separate voyages, half of them between Scotland and Ireland, undertaken in ocean-going curraghs which had oars and a sail. Visitors from the mainland crossed Mull, then shouted across the Sound to Iona for a monk to ferry them over. Guests had their hands and feet washed on arrival, a practical gesture of hospitality in a place with no running water, when guests could have been travelling for a long time. If you were a bard, at the end of your stay it was customary to ask you to sing a song of your own composition before your departure. If you were heading for an island like Tiree, twenty miles to the northwest, Columba might suggest that you set off at first light, with the offshore dawn wind behind you, but if you were leaving for Ireland, he would suggest waiting until 9am, when the warm sun caused the wind to turn southwards.

As you wandered through the monastery, you could distinguish Columba by his white hooded cloak, or cowl, for the other monks wore unbleached cowls. If you arrived in church early for the night office, you had to grope your way in through the darkness, until the brothers brought in lamps lit from the communal fire. When you joined the monks in chanting the psalms, you could recognize Columba's clear, penetrating voice. His hut was built on planks at the top of a small mound inside the monastery compound, where he could survey his domain, and notice visitors shouting across the Sound.

If you followed the monks on their daily round, you would find them putting on their shoes, and trudging a mile and a half westwards across the island to the sandy plain with light soil where they grew crops, using seaweed as fertilizer (see map 11). The brothers carried their heavy implements on their backs; the land was barren and required hard work. Columba liked to go round and encourage his monks as they toiled, and when he could no longer walk very far, he rode in a cart or wagon. It was not always possible for his monks to fill their barns: Columba inspected them not long before his death and, seeing two piles of grain, he congratulated the brothers on having enough corn to last them through the year.

As you walked along the road that led south from the monastery, you might meet the white horse that carried the milk churns from the cow pasture to the monastery; or you could watch the sheep, kept for their milk and their wool. You might go down to the shore and watch brothers fishing, or arriving in curraghs laden with a cargo of branches to build another wattle and daub hut for guests. Or there might be a bigger construction project under way, with monks in curraghs towing hewn logs of pine and oak to build a larger house or a longship, for there were few trees on Iona.

Columba acquired neighbouring islands to provide necessary resources for the monastery. The monks grew grain on the isles of Tiree and Coll. Columba's cousin, Báithene, was prior for a while of a group of monks on Tiree, 'barley island', where you could accompany the brothers for a more adventurous day and perhaps encounter a squall. There might be other excitement: Adomnán describes two monks sailing over to Mull and discovering a seal robber, who had arrived under cover of darkness and was hiding in the sand dunes beneath his upturned boat, which he had tried to camouflage by covering it with dry grass. His plan was to wait until darkness fell once more, and then raid the seals' breeding ground on an islet belonging to the monks.

In the long summer days you were able to watch the monks copying manuscripts. Columba loved this work, and continued writing until the day of his death. Monks asked one another to proof-read, and Columba reprimanded his nephew for wasting time by asking for someone to correct his book when only a single word was misspelt. Books were kept in wooden chests and carried in leather satchels. Since each book represented many hours' work, Columba was eager to prevent damage through carelessness. We hear him warning a brother not to carry a book under his arm, but in vain, as it slipped into a pitcher of water. Ink was precious and took time to prepare. We read of Columba busy writing when a tiresome guest arrived and eagerly embraced Columba, catching his inkhorn with the hem of his cloak and spilling the ink. These are the tiny details of everyday life in a monastery which we learn from Adomnán's biography of his master.

Columba lived on Iona for thirty-five years. To escape from life's pressures, he sailed southeast to the Isle of Jura for a period of solitary retreat. Columba's uncle, Ernán, was prior of a community here, and is buried on the island, while Columba's mother, Eithne, is said to have established a convent on Jura. A small island off Mull, visible from Columba's monastery on Iona, is called 'island of the women' in Gaelic, suggesting that a group of nuns lived there. By the early seventh century, soon after Columba's death, Princess Ebbe of Northumbria presided over a double monastery of monks and nuns who lived under Columba's rule at Coldingham, and Hilda was abbess of a similar double monastery at Whitby, both on the Northumbrian coast.

In 574 King Conall was killed by a tribe of Irish settlers in a naval battle. As a close relative, it was Columba who chose Conall's successor. Instead of appointing one of Conall's sons, Columba consecrated Áedán, a cousin of the dead king. It was a wise choice which reflected well on Columba: Áedán became a powerful king who consolidated Dalriada. The following year, Columba returned to Ireland after a twelve-year absence. His cousin Áed, King of the northern Irish Uí Néill clan, summoned an assembly at Druimm-Cete in Derry, which King Áedán of Dalriada attended, with Columba as his adviser.

A major subject for discussion was the political position of Dalriada. The kings decided that henceforth it should be independent from Ireland. Its people need no longer pay tribute to the Irish king; instead they were to be military allies, joining with them in 'hosting and expedition'. Columba probably used his negotiating skills to achieve this new recognition of King Áedán's authority.[6] The Irish bards were also discussed: they were demanding greater privileges, and their standing was questioned by the Christian Irish kings, who had three times threatened to expel them from the country. Columba, who had studied under a bard, spoke eloquently in their defence, and thereby earned their praise.

Columba returned to Ireland ten years later, in 585, to visit his monastery at Durrow and Ciarán's at Clonmacnoise. In the previous year, King Brude was killed by southern Pictish rebels, and was buried by Columba on Iona. There are many churches on the Scottish mainland dedicated to Columba, most of them later foundations from Iona, but a few may be earlier communities established by Columba or his immediate followers. He is said to have travelled to the Clyde area, following the traditional route from Iona through Crinan Water and across Bute, landing on the mainland at Largs, where he came ashore below the present church of St Columba.

Columba then headed inland, and is said to have met Kentigern, the local bishop, either in Glasgow or at Kilmacolm, twelve miles northeast of Largs. According to tradition, they met at the Gillburn, which flows past the churchyard; Kentigern named the settlement Kilmacolm, or 'cell of my Columba'. The chancel of the thirteenth-century church has been

Remains of a Celtic hermitage and burial ground on Iona, based on a drawing by Drummond, c. 1866. The massive stone lintel over the entrance to the burial-ground has now fallen.

incorporated into the large modern church on the site. Nearer to Durrow than to Iona, there was another Columban foundation at Andreas, at the northern end of the Isle of Man.

Adomnán gives a simple and moving account of Columba's last days. He describes Columba's final tour of the monastery, pulled in a cart, to bless the island and its inhabitants, the barns and the white horse. He returned to his hut, to work on a psalter which he was copying. Halfway through psalm thirty-three, he found he was unable to continue. As he laid down his quill, he indicated his wish for Báithene to succeed him by saying, 'I must stop here, at the end of this page. Let Báithene write the rest.' Báithene was his first cousin, and a close companion; he had been one of the twelve monks who originally accompanied Columba to Iona.

That June night was Whitsun Eve. When the bell rang for the midnight office, Columba went to the church ahead of the others, before the monks brought in the lamps. He felt his way to the altar, where he collapsed. His servant, Diormit, found him and raised him a little, sitting down beside him to support Columba's head in his lap. As he died, the monks filled the little church with cries of sorrow. They chanted the night office and carried Columba's body back to his hut, where they prayed around their father for three days before burying him. Columba was so famous that visitors would have flocked to his funeral, but gales prevented travel across the Sound, and the monks were left to grieve in peace.

A century later, Columba's bones were placed in a gold and silver shrine to be revered by pilgrims. Today, little remains of the Celtic monastery except a section of its large rectangular rampart and ditch, which enclosed an area of twenty acres. It was built of stones and earth, and formed the symbolic and legal boundary of the monastery. The wall was built around the time of Columba's death, and was strengthened by a hedge of holly and hawthorn. Three hundred metres northeast of the great enclosure wall are the remains of another Celtic cemetery and hermitage (*Cladh an Dìsirt*). A lesser wall surrounded the cemetery, which was entered through a gateway framed by two large stone pillars supporting a heavy lintel which has now collapsed (see previous page). Beside it was a hermitage, whose superior was named in a twelfth-century list of monastery officials. There are remains of a medieval stone chapel at the entrance to the cemetery.

An ancient road paved with large boulders, known as the Street of the Dead, also dates from Celtic times. It leads from the shore to the monastery, and is the path along which the overlords of three kingdoms were borne before being buried in Odhráin's cemetery. Beside the path, Odhráin's twelfth-century chapel is the earliest surviving building on the island. The Street of the Dead winds towards the monastery past a fine eighth-century high cross, while the replica of another great cross stands in front of the tiny chapel of Columba. This is built on the footings of a Celtic chapel which may have contained Columba's shrine.

In the thirteenth century a group of Benedictine monks was introduced by Reginald, son of Somerled, Lord of the Isles, to replace the Celtic monks, some of whom were absorbed into the new community. The Benedictines immediately began to build the present abbey church. South of the abbey, Reginald established a community of Augustinian nuns; his sister, Beatrice, was its first prioress. Reginald perhaps brought the first nucleus of nuns from Ireland, where there were many convents following the Rule of St Augustine. Much of Beatrice's convent survives, together with the remains of a massive medieval turf dyke which crosses the island from coast to coast, to separate the nuns' property from that of the monks.

From the time of Columba onwards, Iona was considered to be the centre of Celtic learning. Irish monks came to Iona to study and pray, as did Irish-trained monks from across Europe. Meanwhile brothers from Iona played a leading part in the spread of Christianity among the Picts of eastern Scotland and the Anglo-Saxons of Northumbria. The Columban monastery of Lindisfarne was founded by Aidan, a monk from Iona, and these two communities became focal points of the Columban family and its cultural traditions. Lindisfarne and Iona became centres for manuscript art; their monks produced such masterpieces as the *Book of Kells*.

This gospel book was created on Iona in about 800 by monks trained in the Irish style of calligraphy. Its text is a poor version of the Latin gospels; its scholarship does not match the skill lavished on its magnificent illustrations. These were created by brothers trained at Lindisfarne according to the latest Northumbrian style. The gospel book includes themes from Pictish art, suggesting that they were designed by monks who had worked east of 'the Spine of Britain'. The book is also influenced by Byzantine icons and eastern art.

There are records of a succession of Viking raids on Iona, beginning in 795, and the community decided to move to a safer location in Ireland. They acquired the monastery of Kells near Tara, in eastern Ireland, and when Norsemen slaughtered sixty-eight monks in a third attack on Iona in 806, most of remaining monks transferred to Kells. They arrived with some of Iona's most precious treasures, including the *Book of Kells*. The abbot of Kells was now called 'the successor of Columba'.

As we have seen, the name Kells means 'cells'. Traces of the monastery's circular surrounding wall can be seen in the layout of the modern streets. Beside the monastery's round tower, an unfinished high cross shows how sculptors planned their work: they carved the outlines of its panels first, and filled them with figures later. The monks must have been used to taking refuge in their round tower, for Kells suffered its share of attacks: it was plundered at least seven times before 1006, when its gospel book was stolen and buried for three months. It was retrieved, but had lost its jewel-encrusted golden cover.

Some of Iona's treasures remained in Scotland, including the tiny Monymusk reliquary, a portable house-shaped shrine containing a few of Columba's bones. It is only ten centimetres across, and was made of wood with gilt and silver ornamentation in the seventh or eighth century. During attacks on Iona by Norsemen, the shrine was taken to Dunkeld for safety by King Kenneth MacAlpin of Dalriada. Dunkeld had grown beside the fast-flowing River Tay as a frontier town to the Scottish Highlands, with mountains and wilderness to the north of the settlement. Culdee hermits had built a cluster of wattle huts at Dunkeld by 570, and Columba is said to have preached here. The monastery became a daughter house of Iona, and was a centre of the united kingdoms of the Picts and Scots.

In 848, King Kenneth MacAlpin rebuilt Dunkeld's church in stone, as a fitting resting place for Columba's relics. The monastery grew in importance as that of Iona dwindled; its abbot was usually a member of the royal family, and the office was hereditary. Abbot Crinian of Dunkeld was a son of the Lord of the Isles, and was the father of King Duncan, portrayed in Shakespeare's *Macbeth*. Dunkeld became the mother church of the region, and Columba's shrine was an important place of pilgrimage until the tenth century, when the Pictish King Constantine II became Abbot of St Andrews, and Columba's relics were removed from Dunkeld to Constantine's new church.

A number of Columba's followers worked among the Picts, and will be described in the next chapter. Adomnán was influential in Scotland,

Ireland and Northumbria, where we will meet him again. A few of Columba's monks turned southwards to work in Strathclyde and the Scottish Borders. One of these was Modan, a sixth-century disciple of Columba, who may have been born in Argyll. Modan is an affectionate name meaning 'my Aidan'; there were fifteen other Aidans, including the well-known monk from Iona, Aidan of Lindisfarne.[7] Modan perhaps began working around Loch Etive on the Scottish mainland opposite Mull, before journeying southeast, where he has dedications in Stirling and Falkirk.

Modan continued southwards into the Scottish Borders, and settled for a while beside the River Tweed at Dryburgh, at a bend in the river four miles southeast of Melrose; Dryburgh Abbey was later built on the site of Modan's chapel. Further northwest, he is commemorated in Strathclyde at Kilmodan in Cowal, on the mainland five miles north of the Isle of Bute (see map 10). Modan's chapel was on the hillside to the east of the present charming eighteenth-century church in the valley below, which is named Glendaruel, meaning 'Glen of the red river'. It received its name after bitter fighting in 1098 between the Scots and the Norse forces of Magnus Barelegs, which caused the river to run red with blood.

Eleven gravestones in Kilmodan churchyard were carved in the fourteenth and fifteenth centuries by craftsmen who had come from Ireland to work on the abbey buildings of Iona. When their task was completed, they crossed to the mainland, and travelled through Cowal and mid-Argyll, working wherever they were needed. They quarried most of their stone beside Loch Sween in the Knapdale peninsula, and since they worked from pattern books, their style can be easily recognized. They carved freestanding crosses in twelfth-century Romanesque style, and used traditional motifs for grave-slabs: men in armour, priests, mythical creatures and interlaced patterns. On simpler slabs, a sword or a pair of smithing tongs might show the occupation of the dead person. Another collection of gravestones carved by the Iona sculptors can be seen in Kilmartin churchyard, three miles north of Dunadd, and others can be found throughout the region.

Modan retired to Rosneath, on a sheltered peninsula opposite Greenock, in the mouth of the River Clyde. The Gaelic for Rosneath means 'headland of the sanctuary', so Modan probably settled at a pre-Christian sacred site. He died at Rosneath, and a Celtic cross is preserved in the church, where people came to his shrine. Local pastors took their name from him: a Michael Gilmodyn ('Michael of Modan's church') was a priest here in 1199, and we hear of Gilmothan, son of the sacristan, in 1294. The majority of Columba's followers, unlike Modan, chose to work in areas where Christianity was still unknown. We will now journey with them into mission territory, across 'the Spine of Britain'.

Chapter nine

The Pictish Church

Early chronicles refer to the peoples south of the Antonine Wall as Britons and to those north of the Wall as Picts. The Picts also inhabited the Scottish islands, where many of their circular stone-walled forts, or brochs, are found. These are tower-shaped houses with double walls which taper inwards, built prior to the second century AD. There are 145 in Orkney and Shetland, and on the mainland in the far north there are 150 in Caithness and 67 in Sutherland. In the Hebrides, further south, they built another 80 circular towers. Their brochs were probably pirate strongholds; there are only 22 on the mainland south of Sutherland, and the position of these suggests that they were bases from which the Picts could raid Britain and Ireland.[1]

From about 200 BC onwards there are records of expeditions against the *Orci* or 'Boar People' who lived in the Orkneys. Celtic tribes admired the boar for its strength and ferocity, and depicted the animal on their helmets and shields. There are frequent references to pirate raids by the 'Boar People'. They used the sea freely and boldly, and took raiding parties as far south as London in AD 388, although they were driven back north across the Antonine Wall again the following year.

We hear of Pictish robbers raiding monasteries in the sixth and seventh centuries. Columba knew the island Picts, and advised Donnán, one of his monks, not to settle among them. However, Donnán disregarded his abbot's warning and established a monastery on the Isle of Eigg, south of Skye. The local Pictish queen resented their settlement and wanted to recover her pasture rights. During Mass on Easter night in 618, the monks were attacked and herded into their refectory, where the Picts burned them alive.[2]

The Picts used an ogham alphabet, but none of their written records survive, apart from a few names on tombstones and a Gaelic list of their kings, which demonstrates a matrilineal succession. The Romans called them *Picti*, meaning 'Painted Ones', which may describe how their warriors painted or tattooed their bodies. The Picts were perhaps at their most powerful in the seventh century. By this time their leaders had established a stronghold on the mainland beside the northern shore of Loch Ness, at Castle Urquhart, a native Pictish word which means 'woodland'.

Although the Picts left few inscriptions, they carved symbols on their monuments; their regular combinations approach a form of writing. On earlier stones, which are generally unshaped boulders or natural slabs, groups of three or four symbols are depicted: human figures, animals, fantastic beasts, and bands of decoration. On later stones, figures are often centred around an elaborate knotwork cross, showing the influence of Christian sculptors from Northumbria; these stones are carefully shaped and dressed.[3]

Some fifty symbols appear on the stones. Native fauna are represented: salmon, snake and goose, eagle, wolf and boar, red deer and reindeer, horse and bull, and perhaps dolphin. They may represent clans and tribes such as the 'Horse People' or *Epidii* and the 'Boar People' or *Orci*. Other symbols represent artefacts: a mirror and comb, a hammer, anvil and tongs, a sword or a cauldron. These might be territorial markers, or they may commemorate the dead, indicating their rank and status, or the kinship of the person who commissioned the monument. A mirror and comb might represent a wife or a princess, while a hammer, anvil and tongs may indicate a smith: these craftsmen held an important place in a warrior society. The meaning of other symbols such as V- and Z-shaped rods is unknown.[4]

British, Irish and Columban monks worked among the Picts. In the fifth century, Ninian and his followers travelled northeast, preaching as they went: there are early dedications to Ninian in Stirling and further northeast at Arbroath on the coast of Angus. In chapter 3 we saw how one of Brigit's nuns became the leader of a community at Abernethy on the south side of the Firth of Tay, six miles southeast of Perth, in about 460. Columba's monks also began to establish small Christian settlements among the Picts in the late sixth and seventh centuries, but these were without royal support, and they had little influence on society.[5]

A native missionary who is said to have worked among the southern Picts in the district around Stirling was Serf, whose mother may have been a local princess. We do not know whether Serf lived in the fifth or in the eighth century, or whether there were two men with the same name working in this area. The 'early' Serf was said to have been ordained by Palladius, a deacon from Auxerre who accompanied Germanus on a mission to Ireland in 431 to combat the Pelagian heresy. Palladius continued to Scotland, where he is said to have died at Fordoun, twenty-one miles southwest of Aberdeen.

Serf established a community at Culross on the north shore of the Firth of Forth, twelve miles southeast of Stirling. The twelfth-century monk Jocelyn of Furness relates that the young Kentigern trained as a monk at this monastery. Its site can be found on the hill above the picturesque seventeenth-century merchant town with its cobbled streets. Beneath the ruins of a thirteenth-century Cistercian abbey are traces of a fifth-century church, with its altar below the present one. A reliquary in the ruined wall of the nave once contained Serf's bones. A few streets below, a deep well in Erskine Brae was the monastery's source of water; it was covered over in the nineteenth century. Coal is plentiful on both sides of the Firth of Forth, and the monks of Culross became the region's first coal miners. Culross owes its prosperity to this discovery: the coal lay near the surface and was easily transported by sea.

According to his *Life*, Serf's earliest and his favourite Christian settlement was at Dunning, on the old road from Perth to Stirling, eight miles southwest of Perth. There was an ancient village here, where three roads crossed. Serf is said to have slain a dragon at Dunning with his staff; part of the village is named Dray-gon. The story perhaps describes how Serf released the people from the grip of paganism, through the authority of his pastoral staff. Dunning's church has a late Celtic doorway, and a steeple built in about 1170.

Serf's *Life* describes him visiting Blairlogie, three miles northeast of Stirling. The village lies beneath the hill-fort of Dumyat, whose name means '*dun* (or fort) of the Maetae'. Serf may have been given land here by the chieftain of this early Pictish kingdom. Dumyat is situated on a shoulder of the Ochil Hills, and Serf or his followers travelled eastwards, visiting the settlements that lie south of the Ochil range. He is commemorated by churches at Alva, Tillicoultry and Tullibody. That of Alva is at an ancient holy place marked by a cromlech, two of whose stones survive in the churchyard. Serf's holy well, downhill from the church, has been filled in.

Further south in Clackmannan, Serf's church stands on high ground overlooking the Firth of Forth. Clackmannan takes its name from the *clach* or stone of the Manau, a local Celtic group. The whinstone boulder was their tribal stone: it marked a sacred place and assembly point for local clans, just south of the present town. In 1833 the boulder was placed on top of a monolith in the centre of the town, where it now perches. The Manau gave their name to the entire region around the Firth of Forth: early chroniclers called the region 'Manau Gododdin', meaning 'Manau of the Votadini tribe'.

As the Firth of Forth broadens, east of Edinburgh, Serf is honoured on the northern shore at Dysart, now a northeastern suburb of Kirkaldy. As we have seen, the name Dysart comes from the Latin word *desertum*, which means an empty place; Serf is said to have lived alone here in a cave beside the shore. It is now in the grounds of a Carmelite convent, near the fortified tower of Serf's church. This is one of a series of caves along the Fife coast which were inhabited by monks and hermits. A cave that looked out to sea provided solitude and encouraged prayer; it gave adequate shelter, and was no less comfortable than a typical Celtic home.

Three miles northeast of Dysart are the caves of East Wemyss: *weem* is Gaelic for 'cave'. These red sandstone caves have been inhabited for six thousand years. There were nine caves here, of which five survive. Three of them contain the largest collection of Bronze Age, Iron Age and early Christian rock carvings in Britain. Unfortunately, vandalism, coal-mining and erosion of the soft sandstone have blocked access to many of the carvings and obscured others.

A further fifteen miles northeast along the coast is St Fillan's cave at Pittenweem, a town whose name means 'place of the cave'. Here, according to tradition, the eighth-century missionary, Fillan, lived in a spacious cave containing several chambers. In one of these, a freshwater pool provides drinking water. The rock plug that contains the cave looks strangely out of place among the fishermen's cottages which now surround it on either side of the steep road down to the harbour below.

Two miles northeast are the caves of Caiplie. One can reach them by walking along the shore southeast from the hamlet of Barnsmuir, before reaching Anstruther. The two caves look across the open sea, and were used by monks and hermits from earliest Christian times until the sixteenth century. Early monks enlarged the caves, and in the larger one named 'Chapel Cave' they carved small crosses some time between 800 and 1000. Six miles southeast of Caiplie lies the Isle of May, on which an Irish missionary named Adrian built a monastery. He founded several churches on the east coast of Scotland, and used the caves of Caiplie as a retreat. In 875 the Vikings raided Adrian's monastery on the Isle of May and killed the entire community. His church and shrine on May have been excavated. In the twelfth century, King David I of Scotland built a monastery on the island, which became a centre for pilgrimage.

The martyrdom of Adrian and his monks took place near the end of the Celtic period, perhaps a hundred years after the 'later' Serf was granted an island in Loch Leven, seven miles west of Glenrothes, by one of the Pictish kings. Serf's biographer tells us that a certain King Brude (we are unsure which) 'gave the Isle of Loch Leven to God and St Serf and to the Culdee hermits who lived there'. This happened in about 700 or 840. We are told that Serf remained here for seven years with his Culdee monks; the community continued until the twelfth century. Its priests were well accepted, and some of them held office at St Peter's in York until 936. Canons at St Peter's were referred to as Culdees until the reign of King Henry II in the mid-twelfth century.[6]

North of the River Tay lies the territory of Angus, where a number of Irish missionaries worked. There was a close connection between the Pictish Church and that of Ireland. Pictish clergy went to Ireland for training, and Pictish nobles and monks learnt to speak Gaelic as well as their native language.[7] However, the Irish were not the first to evangelize this area: at Arbroath on the Angus coast, a cemetery dating from the sixth or seventh century has been found at the site of a chapel dedicated to Ninian.

A mile north of Arbroath lies the hamlet of St Vigeans, named after the Irish prince and abbot, Féchán: Vigeanus is a Latin form of his name. Féchán founded a number of Irish monasteries, and died of the plague in Ireland in the mid-seventh century. Since he did not visit Scotland, St Vigeans was probably established by his followers. The church stands on a hillock, and an important monastery grew around it, where a school of sculptors carved a large number of grave-slabs between the eighth and tenth centuries. Twenty-five stones survive, including one that depicts two monks carrying leather book satchels on straps round their necks, each with a staff in his hand. Another eighth-century cross-slab is the only known Pictish stone with an inscription. A later ninth-century mason commemorated 'Drostan, in the time of Ferat and Fergus'.

King Ferat reigned from AD 839 to 842, and St Drostan may be the St Drostan who founded a monastery at Deer, further north in Aberdeenshire, ten miles west of Peterhead. It became a missionary centre from which churches were built on both sides of the Moray Firth. Drostan died in the early seventh century. St Fergus, the third person named on the slab at St Vigeans, was probably a native Pict who trained in Ireland and returned to Angus. In about 715 he settled at Glamis between Forfar and Coupar Angus, beside a pre-Christian standing stone; the cup marks at its base indicate its ancient origin. In the time of Fergus, the great stone was elaborately decorated with carvings of a snake, salmon and mirror on one side, and an interlaced cross on the other, flanked by warriors fighting with hand-axes, and other symbols. Fergus lived here in a cave that collapsed a century ago, beside a holy well which flows into Glamis Burn.

Six years later, we read of Fergus in Rome, gathered in council with twenty-one other European bishops, under Pope Gregory II. They signed a document that condemned irregular marriages, sorcerers, and clergy who grew their hair long, perhaps in the traditional Celtic style. Fergus signed himself as 'Fergustus, episcopus Scotiae Pictus'. He returned to Scotland and worked in the far north, in Aberdeenshire and Caithness, where he is commemorated in the churches at Wick on the east coast of Caithness, at Banff on the north coast of Aberdeenshire, and at Dyce, further inland, four miles northwest of Aberdeen.

Fergus later returned to Angus, where he is honoured at the church of Eassie, three miles southwest of Glamis. At this time, a fine cross was carved at Eassie. On one side, stylized angels appear above a cross decorated with interlacing; beneath its arms, huntsmen and hounds chase a red deer stag. On the other side Adam is depicted, eating the apple of knowledge in the Garden of Eden. Fergus settled once more at Glamis, where he died in about 750. He was buried there, but his arm was enshrined in Aberdeen, and his head was taken to Scone where it too was placed in a shrine.

King Ferat, who is mentioned in the inscription on the stone at St Vigeans, was one of the last Pictish kings to reign before the Gaelic

King Kenneth MacAlpin of Dalriada took over the land of the Picts and gave its estates as rewards to his Scottish war-lords. King Ferat had a royal estate at Meigle, six miles west of Glamis, and there was an important Pictish monastery on the estate. We know the name of one of the monks who worked as a scribe in the royal villa at Meigle: he was called Thana.[8] Meigle was perhaps first evangelized by Ninian; in the eighth century its monastery was in contact with Iona and Northumbria.

Meigle was a very early holy site: cup and ring marks decorate two giant boulders here dating from 3000 to 2000 BC. By the late eighth century, the two great slabs flanked the east gate of the churchyard. Like the other twenty cross-slabs found at Meigle, they are formed of old red sandstone, a soft rock which is easy to carve. One of the two large slabs stands 2.5 metres high. One side is perhaps modelled on a much smaller, jewelled cross: its circular stone 'jewels' are carved in high relief, and its cross-shaft is decorated with lively animals.[9]

The reverse side features the Old Testament story of Daniel in the lions' den. This subject appealed to Celtic Christians: Daniel's struggle to tame ravenous lions reminded them of Christ who conquered the forces of death. Daniel's heroic feat also symbolized the battles in which Celtic warriors were often engaged. Daniel appears, pawed by two lions, on the eighth-century cross of St Martin at Iona. The lions are also carved on the lid of a purse in the seventh-century Sutton Hoo treasure from Suffolk: they gleam from golden plaques inlaid with red garnets and blue millefiori glass.

On the stone at Meigle, Daniel wears a long, pleated skirt or kilt. His arms are outstretched as he tames the lions; his gesture also reminds us of Christ on the cross. Two lions paw at his skirt, while another pair lick his face. Above Daniel are an angel and huntsmen with their hounds. Below him, a centaur chops down a tree and a wild beast eats an ox whose undevoured, horned head is still visible. The mighty slab may once have stood inside the church, for it has side tenons, designed to slot into cavities in the wall. The church was magnificently decorated. Part of a sculptured frieze survives which perhaps adorned the outside wall of the church, in which clawed beasts appear on either side of a mermaid with a twisty tail.[10]

On another slab, which was fortunately drawn before it was lost, a driver holds the reigns of two horses pulling a carriage (see opposite). Two passengers sit comfortably behind him under an awning, above the twelve-spoked chariot wheels. In his biography of Columba, Adomnán describes how linch pins were inserted into holes at each end of the axle to hold the wheels firm. If the linch pin was not secure, the wheel fell off. The stone panel formed part of a low screen inside the church which perhaps separated the chancel, where the priest presided at the Eucharist, from the nave, where the congregation stood.

Pictish chariot, from a stone screen in the monastery church of Meigle, Perthshire. Missionaries used such carts or chariots for travel.

Twelve miles west of Perth is the hamlet of Fowlis Wester. This, too, was an ancient religious site, with a Neolithic burial cairn dating from 3000 BC a mile south of the hamlet and standing stones nearby. Fowlis Wester lies on the old road to Perth; highlanders drove their cattle through the village to the markets, and also sold them here. The replica of a fine red sandstone Pictish cross stands at the roadside; the original is inside the church. The unusual protruding arms of the cross indicate Irish influence. It was erected by followers of St Bean, who evangelized this area. Bean was a native monk whose name means 'lively person'. He trained in Ireland, where he is mentioned in a chronicle dating from 800.

Bean preached as he travelled: he is honoured at a scattering of sites across Scotland from Dumbartonshire in the west through Stirling and Perthshire to Angus, Aberdeenshire and the area around Inverness. Three miles north of Fowlis Wester lies Buchanty, on the River Almond. St Mavane's Mill here means 'mill of my St Bean'. Nearby McBean's Bridge and McBean's Chapel also refer affectionately to 'my Bean' (*mo Beathan* in Gaelic). Further into the hills is 'My Bean's Seat', where he was said to sit and pray.[11] There are a number of similar 'seats' in the hills where other missionaries sought solitude, or rested on their journeys through the mountains.

Fifteen miles northeast of Meigle, between Forfar and Brechin, is Aberlemno, whose name means 'river confluence at the elm tree'. It lies southeast of the Pictish stronghold of Finavon. Ninian or his followers may have worked here in the fifth century, for nearby Nine Maidens recalls his name, as does Ninewell, below the fort. Three impressive carved symbol stones stand by the roadside, dating from the late sixth or early seventh century. These stones and some early graves indicate that there was a royal burial-ground here.[12] In the churchyard half a mile away, a magnificent early eighth-century royal cross-slab depicts a battle between the Picts and the Northumbrians which took place in 685 at Dunnichen, four miles south of Aberlemno. The Picts defeated the Northumbrians and recovered their territory.

Ironically, the other side of the grave-slab is decorated in the latest Northumbrian style with a fine knotwork cross flanked by intertwined beasts and sea-horses, for at this time the Pictish Church came under the influence of Northumbria. Nechtán, King of the Picts from 706 to 729, wanted his Christian subjects to abandon their Celtic customs and take on those of Rome, and so in 710 he wrote to Abbot Ceolfrith of Jarrow in Northumbria to seek his help. Bede was a monk in Jarrow at the time, and met the Pictish delegation.

Bede records how Nechtán's emissaries asked 'that architects be sent to him in order to build a stone church in the Roman style, promising ... that he and his people would follow the customs of the holy, apostolic, Roman Church as far as they could learn them, in view of their remoteness from the Roman people and language'.[13] Abbot Ceolfrith sent masons to King Nechtán, who built the first stone church in the land of the Picts at Aberlemno.

The present church of Aberlemno is modern, but a section of the tower at Restenneth Priory, four miles southwest of Aberlemno, may have been built by eighth-century Northumbrian masons. Its design incorporates a porch with a processional entrance archway through which the monks could walk with dignity down the length of the church. It resembles the archway beneath the tower of Jarrow's sister church at Monkwearmouth, through which Bede himself would have walked. King Nechtán named the stone church at Aberlemno 'Egglespether', or church of St Peter. The ancient churches of Meigle and Tealing were also rededicated to Peter, Prince of Rome.[14]

By 715, King Nechtán's reforms were almost complete. He imposed the Roman method of calculating the date of Easter, and expelled Columba's monks from Abernethy and also from Iona, where they refused to accept Roman customs. The Roman style of clerical haircut, or tonsure, was to shave the crown of the head, while Celtic monks shaved the front of their head from ear to ear and grew their hair long at the back. Bede records Nechtán's work with approval: 'All the priests and monks had their hair shorn, and the corrected people rejoiced that they were now devoted to Peter as new disciples, and placed under the protection of their patron, the most blessed Prince of Apostles'.[15] King Nechtán was helped in his reforms by Curitan, a Celtic monk who followed Roman practices. Curitan travelled widely among the Picts, and is commemorated as far north as Glen Urquhart, on the north shore of Loch Ness.

Five miles northeast of Aberlemno, King Nechtán's influence is evident in Brechin Cathedral, which has a fine Northumbrian cross with the Virgin and Child carved at its centre. However, later kings returned to Irish Celtic practices. In the tenth century, under King Kenneth II, Brechin became a Celtic Culdee church. A round tower was constructed in the Irish style, and a similar tower was built in Abernethy at this time.

The round tower at Brechin is thirty metres high, with a door above ground level for protection; the doorway is flanked by carvings of two bishops, each carrying a pastoral staff. Brechin became a cathedral only in the mid-twelfth century, under King David I of Scotland. Three magnificent stone fonts at Brechin, Aberlemno and Restenneth Priory are evidence of his royal patronage.

Although Columba does not seem to have spent much time preaching to the Picts, a number of his monks did. One of the earliest was Kenneth of Aghaboe who, together with Abbot Congal of Bangor, accompanied Columba on his first journey to visit King Brude in Glen Urquhart, to ask permission to build a monastery on Iona. Columba presumably invited Kenneth and Congal to accompany him because, as we saw in chapter 8, the two men could speak a language similar to that of King Brude, for Gaelic was quite unlike the Pictish languages.

Kenneth (*c.* 525–*c.* 600) was the son of a bard from Derry; he and Columba would have met in Ireland as young monks. When Kenneth's community at Glasnevin dispersed as a result of the plague in 544, he travelled to Cadoc's monastery at Llancarfan in south Wales. When the plague had abated, Kenneth returned to Ireland and founded a number of communities. He then moved to Scotland; he did not join Columba's foundation on Iona, but he was a friend of Columba, and often visited him. At other times he lived as a hermit.[16]

He settled on Inchkenneth ('Kenneth's island'), an islet off the coast of Mull, ten miles northeast of Iona. He copied books in solitude, including a manuscript of the four gospels, and was a fine preacher. A church and cemetery on Iona were named after Kenneth, and he has dedications at Kilchennich on Tiree and Kilchainie on South Uist, in the Western Isles. He travelled east through Stirling to Fife: Cambuskenneth Abbey on the River Forth, a mile northeast of Stirling, is named after him. Kenneth continued to St Andrews on the east coast of Fife, which became the centre of a mission among the southern Picts.

It seems that there were already Christians at St Andrews, for we hear of St Rule, a monk who lived in a cave by the shore (now known as Lady Buchan's Cave). The Celtic name for St Andrews was Kilrimont, or 'church of the king's mound', which suggests the presence of a royal fort. Its monastery is first recorded in 747, when Irish annals note the death of its abbot. Fifteen years earlier, in 732, Bishop Acca of Hexham was driven from his diocese and came to live at Kilrimont. He brought with him relics of St Andrew, which his predecessor, Wilfred, had obtained from Rome. The precious relics of the apostle enhanced the prestige of Kilrimont, which was later renamed St Andrews.[17]

Fine Pictish crosses were carved at this time by monastic stone masons, and a magnificent house-shaped shrine was created in about

800, perhaps to contain the bones of one of the Scottish kings, since scenes from the life of the Old Testament king, David, are carved on its panels: the young David pastures his father's sheep and breaks a lion's jaw with his bare hands. In 943, King Constantine II retired from office and became abbot of Kilrimont's Culdee community. The church of St Rule was built to serve its monks. When Norsemen began to raid Iona and the Scottish west coast in the late tenth century, leadership of the united kingdoms of the Scots and Picts was transferred to Kilrimont, which was in a safer location on the east coast.[18]

King Alexander I, who reigned from 1107 to 1124, attempted to convert the Celtic monks of Kilrimont to Roman ways. He tried to appoint a bishop who would help him to reform the Church, but the first two bishops he chose were unwilling to do so. The king achieved a measure of success with his third candidate, Robert, Prior of the Augustinian abbey of Scone. Bishop Robert determined to establish a community of Augustinian canons at Kilrimont, who would transform it into a model Roman cathedral chapter.

The Celtic clergy opposed their new bishop so fiercely, however, that Robert was unable to carry out his plans until 1144, over twenty years later. The Celtic clergy, consisting of about thirteen Culdee monks and some priests, all of them married, were invited to join the new community, but they declined. They were given a permanent home in the church of St Mary on the Rock, whose foundations can be seen outside the cathedral walls, close to the shore. In 1248 the Culdees were recognized as an independent college of diocesan priests.[19]

This was not an unusual arrangement: the Culdees had a strong sense of identity, and were used to living alongside, yet separate from, other monks. As we have seen, the Culdees originated in Ireland as a group of reforming monks who sought to return to earlier ideals. They established some monasteries of their own, like that of Tallaght, now a southern suburb of Dublin, but at other foundations such as Roscrea in central Ireland, they created a separate adjoining community. At Armagh in the north, the Culdees formed a group who lived within the monastic enclosure and followed a stricter lifestyle than the monks around them.[20]

 The ninth abbot of Iona was St Adomnán (624–704). Like Columba, Adomnán was a member of the family of the Northern Uí Néill. He was born in his father's homeland of Donegal; Adomnán was his monastic name, and means 'man of great dread'. Adomnán first trained as a monk under Columba's nephew, Ernán. We know little about him until he became abbot of Iona in 679 at the age of fifty-five. In his early years as abbot, a bishop from Gaul named Arculf visited Iona when he was shipwrecked off the British coast on his way home from a pilgrimage to Jerusalem. Adomnán welcomed him and wrote a book about the Holy

Places using information from Arculf and other sources. Bede knew and used this book. He wrote of Bishop Arculf. 'He was very gladly welcomed by Adomnán, who listened to him even more gladly. Adomnán was quick to write down everything of significance which Arculf said he had seen in the Holy Places. As I have said, he compiled a book which was valuable to many people.'[21] Adomnán's guidebook became widely used throughout Europe.

Before he was appointed abbot of Iona, Adomnán may have been counsellor and chaplain to King Finnachta of the southern Uí Néill, who became the High King of Tara. In 686, King Finnachta asked Adomnán, in his prestigious position as Columba's successor, to go on a mission to King Aldfrith of Northumbria and ask for the release of sixty Irish hostages who had been captured by Aldfrith's predecessor. King Aldfrith was himself half-Irish, and a lover of peace; as a young man he had been a pupil of Adomnán. His former tutor knew Aldfrith's tastes, and when he arrived in Northumbria, he presented the king with his book on the Holy Places. Adomnán left England laden with gifts, and brought the sixty captives back to Ireland.[22]

In the following year, Adomnán returned to Northumbria to visit the monastery at Jarrow, which was one of the great centres of learning in Western Europe. Its library and scriptorium were the finest in England; here, Bede researched and wrote the first history of Britain to be written by an Englishman. Adomnán spent at least a year at Jarrow, where he impressed the monks, and would have met Bede, who was then a teenager. Writing forty years later, Bede recalled: 'he was a good and wise man, with an excellent knowledge of the scriptures'.

There was disagreement, however, between Adomnán and Ceolfrith, Abbot of Jarrow, over the subject that had been debated at Whitby twenty years earlier. King Aldfrith's father had summoned the Council of Whitby to decide between Celtic and Roman practices, and Northumbria had agreed to follow Rome. By the time that Adomnán visited Jarrow, only the monasteries of northern Ireland, the home of Columba and Adomnán, clung to the Celtic tradition. Adomnán arrived in Jarrow as an important and well-respected Church leader, but he wore his hair long in the Celtic style, and shaved it at the front from ear to ear.[23]

Bede relates that Adomnán 'was earnestly admonished by many, who were more learned than himself, not to presume to live contrary to the universal custom of the Church ... considering the small number of his followers, situated in such a distant corner of the world; as a result of this, he changed his mind.... Returning home, he tried to bring his own people on the Isle of Iona and its dependencies into the way of truth.'[24] However, the monks of Iona refused to accept Roman practices. It seems that from then on, the abbot and his community celebrated Easter at different weekends, but it is not clear whether Adomnán was permanently resident at Iona after 692.

As a peace-loving diplomat who was responsible for the oversight of all the Columban monasteries, it is possible that by travelling extensively he avoided clashes with his own monks on Iona over Roman practices, particularly during the Easter season. On the Scottish west coast, Adomnán is honoured on North Uist in the Outer Hebrides, and had a chapel on the Isle of Bute at Kildavanan. Kirk Lonan on the east coast of the Isle of Man is also named after him; there are early grave-markers at the keeill, and an elaborate wheel cross decorated with knotwork. Adomnán spent much time among the Picts, east of 'the Spine of Britain'. He maintained a good relationship with the Pictish royal house, and is commemorated throughout Pictish lands, especially in Aberdeenshire, Banff and Forfar.

In the four years after his return to Iona from Northumbria, Adomnán worked on his *Life of Columba*. In 692 he returned to Ireland, where he challenged his former friend, King Finnachta, over an annual payment of cattle tribute. The Irish king now favoured the monasteries of Patrick, Finnian and Ciarán, rather than those of Columba. Adomnán cursed King Finnachta, who died three years later. As the ruler of Columba's monasteries in northern Ireland, Adomnán returned to Ireland in 697 to take part in the Synod of Birr. He proposed a law to exempt women, children and clergy from taking part in warfare. His new law applied also in Dalriada and the kingdom of the Picts. Penalties for transgressing it were to be paid to the Columban monasteries. He also pleaded for the acceptance of the Roman date of Easter, which was by now followed throughout the western world. Only his own monasteries refused to do so.

In his old age, Adomnán is said to have worked among the Picts in Glen Lyon, one of the highland routes leading eastwards towards Loch Tay (see map 12). As he arrived at the western end of the glen, he would have passed two Pictish brochs on the north bank of the river, at Cashlie. Their ruined walls stand a metre high. He followed the river as it flows northeast, where Milton Eonan ('mill town of Adomnán') beside the Bridge of Balgie probably records a mill which he built for the local people to grind their corn. The church at Innerwick, on the other side of the bridge, contains what is said to be his bronze bell; it has no tongue, but would have been struck. Three miles further east along the glen is a small hill named Camusvrachan, traditionally the place where, when plague struck, Adomnán prayed with the people and sent them up to their summer shielings, away from the polluted river. Adomnán returned to Iona, and died shortly after his final visit to Ireland.

Twelve miles further down Glen Lyon, where the valley broadens, lies Dull, whose name means 'meadow' or 'valley'. There was a Pictish monastery here, which attracted Adomnán's contemporaries, Cuthbert, and possibly Cedd and Chad. These monks will be discussed in chapter 13. Three sturdy Celtic crosses survive from Dull, one near the church,

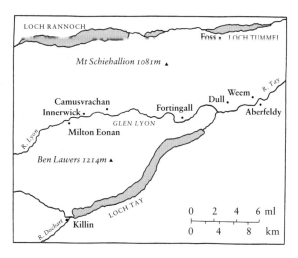

Map 12. Glen Lyon.
This highland glen, north of the Tay,
was well used by Celtic missionaries.

and two preserved in St Cuthbert's chapel at Weem, two miles further along the glen. Weem is named after its cave, which is in the rock face high above the church. While Cuthbert was a monk at Melrose in the Scottish Borders, he is said to have spent time preaching in the land of the Picts. Cuthbert's Irish *Life* describes him building a chapel beside a pool at Weem, and using the cave below as a retreat. The tiny pool is fed by water seeping from the overhanging rocks.

Still in Glen Lyon, four miles west of Dull, lies the ancient settlement of Fortingall. Until this century, a bonfire was lit here each November on a Bronze Age burial mound, to celebrate the pre-Christian Celtic feast of Samhain. This was the forerunner of All Souls' Day, when Christians remember their dead, on 2 November. Beside the churchyard are the remains of Britain's oldest yew tree. It is seventeen metres in girth, and has grown by producing saplings around its circumference; it has been dated to about 5000 BC.[25] The church is dedicated to Cedd (d. 664), a monk from Lindisfarne. The chapel of St Chad (d. 672) at Foss, ten miles to the north, near Loch Tummel, may honour his brother, who later became bishop of Lichfield, in Mercia.

A century after Adomnán, Fillan, the son of a Munster chieftain, became a monk and came to Scotland with his mother, Kentigerna, and her brother, Comgan, who had been driven out of Leinster by a coalition of neighbouring rulers. The extended family settled on the Scottish west coast, where churches recall their names. Comgan founded a small monastery at Lochalsh, which is the crossing point for the huge island of Skye, and Princess Kentigerna retired to an islet at the southern end of Loch Lomond, named Inchcailloch, or 'island of the old woman', in her honour. She died there in about 733; ruins of her church can be seen on the island.

Her son, Fillan, travelled eastwards: as we saw at the beginning of this chapter, he spent some time as a hermit in a cave at Pittenweem in Fife, and became abbot of a nearby monastery. Fillan is said to have retired to Glen Dochart, to the south of Glen Lyon, building a mill at Killin, at the head of Loch Tay (see map 12). There is still a mill on the site, beside the rushing waters of the Dochart Falls; here Fillan's eight healing stones, smoothed by the river, are preserved. People still come to hold them and pray for healing.

In his *Life of Columba*, Adomnán describes the abbot blessing a white pebble in the same way, in order to cure one of King Brude's druids: 'Columba came to the River Ness; he picked up a white stone from the river and said to his companions, "Through this white stone, the Lord will heal many of the sick among this pagan people".'[26] At Auchtertyre, two miles east of Tyndrum and fifteen miles west of Killin, people bathed in Fillan's Pool, a shallow stretch of the River Dochart, as a cure for madness. It was frequently visited for healing as late as the nineteenth century. Fillan died and was buried nearby. His handbell survives, and his staff, encased in a delicate medieval reliquary, is now in the Royal Museum of Scotland, Edinburgh.

Before his death, Fillan entrusted to guardians his bell and staff, his portable altar and the last manuscript that he was writing. In return for preserving Fillan's treasures, each received a farm croft. This was a widespread custom in Celtic times. The guardians or hereditary keepers were known as 'dewars'; Dewar is still a Scottish surname. Since saints were tribal, family people, a dewar was normally a relative. The saint's relics were handed down through the family, and never became church property, although they might be kept in a church. The guardian received a small salary, generated by ancestral land which could not be sold, because by law the land belonged to the holy object. In this way, the family, the saint's few possessions and the land were bound together, and have remained so until today, unless the family has died out, or given up its ownership.[27]

Another Irishman, Máelrubha (c. 642–722), worked among the northern Picts. He became a monk at Bangor in County Down, sailed to Scotland and established a flourishing monastery at Applecross, on the mainland opposite the Isle of Skye. He built a church on an island in Loch Maree, thirty-five miles west of Inverness, where his spring was famous for its healing properties. Máelrubha was killed by Norsemen at Skail, near the north coast of Sutherland. His body was brought back to his community at Applecross, but within a century the monastery was destroyed by Vikings. Their role, first as destroyers and later as Christian settlers, will be examined more fully in chapter 13. By the time of Fillan and Máelrubha, the Picts were gaining control over the whole of Scotland. During the next century, they merged so fully with the people they ruled that their identity as Picts was gradually lost.

Chapter ten

The Southwest: Somerset and Cornwall

IN THE SIXTH and seventh centuries, Devon, Somerset and the south-west were criss-crossed by monks travelling to and from Ireland, Wales and Brittany, before the Saxons drove the Celts westward into Cornwall, and obliterated much of their culture. The Saxons and their successors continued to honour Celtic saints, however. In Devon, seventeen churches are dedicated to Petroc, and others are named after Nectan, son of Brychan (Stoke and Welcombe) and the Cornish king Constantine (Dunsford). That of Bradstone, near the ancient route across the River Tamar into Cornwall, may be named after Non, the mother of David. Devon churches also honour Celtic monks named Breward (Braunton and Branscombe), Kea (Landkey) and Rumon (Romansleigh). All these settlements are on the coast, or close to rivers providing access to the sea.

Christianity reached southwest Britain quite early, and a number of Romano-Celtic cemeteries have been found in Somerset. In 1990, excavations beside the Fosse Way at Shepton Mallet, four miles east of Wells, uncovered a small Roman town which perhaps serviced an as yet undiscovered garrison. Within the town were three small cemeteries, the largest of which was used by the local Christian community. Here, seventeen bodies were buried facing east, mainly in wooden coffins set into rock-cut graves, within a ditched enclosure.[1]

One man wore a silver-alloy pendant in the form of a cross. At its centre was a disc on which the *chi-rho* monogram had been punched. A loop at the top of the pendant enabled its owner to hang it from a chain round his neck. It was made soon after AD 400, and may have been worn by a priest.[2] A replica of the pendant is worn by George Carey, Archbishop of Canterbury, to symbolize the continuity of Christianity in Britain over the last sixteen hundred years. Four miles to the west, the Anglo-Saxon chapel at Wells was built over a late Roman mausoleum, which suggests that Christians continued to worship here.[3]

At Cannington in Somerset, several thousand people were buried in a cemetery near the hillfort which lies to the north of the village. Cannington is two miles northwest of Bridgwater, near the River Parrett, which provides access to the Bristol Channel; its cemetery was in use from the second to the eighth centuries. A young woman whose grave was radiocarbon-dated to the early seventh century may have been a local Christian saint. Her grave was marked out by a low mound, and the use of imported stone suggests a memorial chapel over her tomb. There was evidence that her grave was frequently visited; her tomb provided a focus for many other burials.[4]

In the Somerset coastal plain, churches are named after Celtic missionaries: on the north Somerset coast, Dubricius is honoured at Porlock, and a cluster of nearby settlements are dedicated to Petroc (Timberscombe), Carantoc (Carhampton) and Decuman (Watchet). A charter dating from 712 describes a chapel dedicated to Martin of Tours on the Isle of Marchey, in marshland near Wedmore: its dedication suggests an early date. Monks named Kea, Fili, Rumon and Collen were honoured at Glastonbury, where there may have been a Celtic monastery, and where early hermits lived on the Tor above the settlement. Excavation on the Tor has revealed what may be the remains of monks' cells, cut into the rock below the summit, in the fifth or sixth century. However, many Somerset dedications to Celtic saints date from the eleventh century, when monks of Glastonbury Abbey created a new interest in the lives of their Celtic predecessors.

Three Celtic missionaries who are likely to have worked in Somerset are Congar, Kea and Indract. Congar is commemorated at Congresbury, six miles east of Weston-super-Mare. He probably lived in the hillfort to the north of Congresbury, and was later buried in the church, in the village below the fort; his shrine attracted medieval pilgrims. There was a church dedicated to Kea at an unknown location named *Lan to Cai* ('church of Kea') at Leigh in Street, two miles southwest of Glastonbury; it is mentioned in a late seventh-century charter. The third monk, Indract, is described in his tenth-century *Life* as an Irishman who was killed together with his companions by robbers in the marshes between Shapwick and the Somerset coast. Ine, King of Wessex (688–726), transferred his relics to Glastonbury, six miles to the east of Shapwick. In about 800, the Irish *Martyrology of Tallaght* described Indract as 'a martyr for the faith at Glastonbury'.[5]

The offshore islands of southwest Britain were visited by seafaring Celts. Some were useful stepping-stones: on a clear day, Lundy Island is visible from both south Wales and Devon. There are inscribed stones, a chapel and a burial cairn on Lundy. To the southwest, one of the smallest and most westerly of the Scilly Isles is named after Samson, whose travels will be described in chapter 11. To the south, Samson is also honoured in the northeast corner of Guernsey in the Channel Islands. In the west of Jersey, St Brelade is named after Breward and St Ouen, three miles away, perhaps commemorates Wenna, one of Brychan's daughters.

 Roman remains in Cornwall are few, and evidence of Roman Christianity is scanty. However, five Roman milestones have been found in Cornwall, on routes leading to Cornish harbours. They include a third-century milestone at Breage, at the north end of the Lizard peninsula, and two dating from the third and fourth centuries near Tintagel on the northeast coast; at both locations there were Christian settlements by the fifth century.

Thirteenth-century legends describe how Joseph of Arimathea, the disciple who buried Jesus in his family tomb, came to Glastonbury and built its first church. The story was probably created by the monks of Glastonbury to assert their superiority over other English monasteries, at a time when their church had burnt down and their authority was threatened. While there is no evidence that Joseph of Arimathea came to Somerset as a tin-trader, southwest Britain was on the ancient tin-traders' route. Tin streaming had taken place in Cornwall from Bronze Age times; after panning the river gravels for tin, metal workers produced ingots in stone moulds. Tin was used in bronze and pewter, and the Romans encouraged Cornish tin production in the third and fourth centuries.[6]

Many of Cornwall's farms, lanes and hedges, particularly in the southwest, date back to the Bronze Age and even earlier. The landscape has changed little since Celtic times. By the fourth century, Cornwall's population may have numbered forty thousand; Celtic place-names hint at how they lived. *Lis* meant a chieftain's hall or court, and appears in such names as Liskeard and Lizard. *Bod* meant a dwelling, as in Bodmin, and the frequent use of *tre*, meaning 'farmstead', as in Tregony and Trethevy, indicates the lifestyle of much of the population.[7] In the fifth century, the chief royal fort was probably on the rocky outcrop of Tintagel on the north Cornish coast.

Cornwall could not boast major monasteries like those founded by Illtud and Cadoc in southeast Wales; the earliest Cornish communities, like that of Landocco, were probably founded from Welsh monasteries. Many of Cornwall's nine or ten monasteries may have grown up around earlier churches with their cemeteries, as happened in Ireland and Wales, where monks enclosed a larger tract of land around the graveyard, in order to grow their food.[8]

In the fifth and sixth centuries, Cornwall may have been influenced by Christians arriving from Ireland, Wales, Gaul and the Mediterranean. At small monastic sites around the Cornish coast there is a scattering of Near Eastern pottery and fragments of wine vessels dating from this period. From the fifth century, Christian grave-markers were erected in churchyards and beside tracks and fords; their Irish, British and Latin names indicate a range of cultural influences.

We have only a sketchy knowledge of the history of Cornwall in Celtic times. Devon, Cornwall and Somerset formed the kingdom of Dumnonia, and we know the names of at least four of its kings: Cunomorus (meaning 'Hound of the sea') and his son Constantine in the sixth century, Gereint in the eighth century, and Doniert in the ninth. An elaborate cross shaft and base dating from this time were found at

St Cleer, two miles north of Liskeard, inscribed in Latin: 'Doniert has requested (prayers) for (?his) soul'; he was drowned in 878.

We also know that there was considerable migration to and from Armorica, which from the mid-sixth century was named Brittany, after its British inhabitants. Two of its regions were named Cornouaille and Dumnonia, and until the eighth century, Cornish and Breton folk spoke the same language. It was not only Cornish families who migrated to Brittany: many Welsh groups made the same journey. The five dioceses of north Brittany were all founded by monks from south Wales. Families who migrated to Brittany made settlements in forest clearings. Their priest, who was often a close relative of the head of the family, normally negotiated on their behalf to obtain permission for them to build homes and a church.

Families from south Wales and Brecon settled mainly in eastern Brittany, while migrants from Ireland more often colonized western Brittany. The Channel Islands formed convenient stepping stones on the journey to and from Cornwall. As Breton monasteries grew and flourished, their monks sailed north to preach and settle in Cornwall; by 600, many Cornish churches were foundations from Breton monasteries.

At this time there were perhaps six hundred Cornish villages with small Christian cemeteries, some with a chapel attached. Little is recorded of the Celtic missionaries who worked among the people: we know nothing of the monks who lived on the tidal island of St Michael's Mount near Penzance, or of the hermits who lived among the startling granite tors of Roche (French for 'rock'), five miles north of St Austell. However, the dedications of villages, churches and holy wells indicate a strong Christian presence. Many Cornish saints' wells are contained within medieval stone well-houses, each a miniature chapel, often with a tiled roof, an arched doorway and a niche on its inner wall for a statue of the saint. Few documents survive to throw light on Cornwall's Celtic saints, but clusters of dedications provide clues about the various groups of missionaries who preached in different parts of Cornwall. We will now trace some of these clues, beginning in the west.

 Legends tell how Irish Christians sailed to northwest Cornwall; their work was described in a group of *Lives* which were destroyed at the Reformation, but some information from them has survived in notes gathered by the antiquarian John Leland in the sixteenth century, and in Breton manuscripts. The missionaries arrived at Lelant in the estuary of the River Hayle in about 450. In Celtic times, Lelant (formerly Lananta, or 'Anta's church') was a port for voyagers to and from Ireland. In stark contrast to the way in which Christians were welcomed in Brittany, most of the missionaries were apparently killed by a local chieftain named Tewdrig.

Since the surviving sources describing the lives of these Irish martyrs are so fragmentary and written so much later, we cannot know whether these men and women existed, or whether legends arose merely to explain existing place-names. There is possibly a grain of truth in the stories that survive. They tell us that the group included Ia, with her brothers Euny and Erc; they were said to be the children of a Munster chieftain. In Cornwall, a local prince named Dinan became Ia's patron and gave her land at St Ives, where the church and its holy well are named after her. A Breton church is dedicated to Ia near Carhaix, about forty-five miles southeast of Brest.

In Celtic times the River Hayle was navigable upstream as far as the village of St Erth, which is named after Ia's brother Erc (*c.* 424–*c.* 514). Erc was said to have been baptized by Patrick, and to have become Bishop of Slane near Tara, the seat of the Irish high kings, in the Dublin hinterland. When Erc came to Cornwall, he was one of the few missionaries in the group who escaped being killed by King Tewdrig. Erc may have built a chapel and hut beside the River Hayle, on the site of the present village church. Another member of the Irish group who managed to escape martyrdom was said to be Breage; her settlement was described in chapter 3.

There are a number of churches in west Cornwall named after Euny, the brother of Ia and Erc. Lelant was rededicated to him, and became the mother church of St Ives. Euny is patron of Redruth, while at Sancreed in the far west, midway between Penzance and St Just, he is honoured with a chapel and a holy well which was famous for its cures even in the nineteenth century. Local people still tie rags, or clouties, to nearby branches, as prayers for healing. This custom is continued at a few other Cornish wells.

Legend relates that Piala and her brother Gwinear were another Irish couple who were killed by King Tewdrig. Like Erc, Gwinear was said to be a convert of Patrick's; he had spent time in Brittany as a hermit, and was the leader of the Cornish group. He may be buried in the church at Gwinear, three miles southwest of Camborne, an ancient settlement at the top of Herland Hill, where tin was streamed in the early Bronze Age. His sister, Piala, settled at nearby Phillack, close to the mouth of the River Hayle.

Phillack was an important post-Roman settlement. In the tenth century its name was Felec, a British name meaning a chieftain or governor; it perhaps refers to the original donor who gave the site to be used as a church. A large, coarse granite slab which now rests against the outer wall of the vestry reads: 'Clotuali Mobratti', or '(the stone of) Clotual, great in judgement'. The name Clotual itself means 'worthy of fame', and may commemorate someone important in the tribe. The early fifth-century *chi-rho* symbol of Christ which is now set in the church wall above the porch is carved in a style derived from models found in Gaul, south of the River Loire.[9] In the churchyard is a fine eleventh-century wheel-headed cross with a figure of Christ; it is decorated with elaborate plaitwork. Near the church was Piala's holy well.

On the south Cornish coast, a number of churches on the Lizard peninsula are Breton foundations. Four miles south of Helston is Cury, dedicated to an early monk named Corentin (d. 401). According to tradition, he was born in Britain of Christian parents, and went to Brittany, where he became a hermit. He was consecrated as first bishop of Cornouaille, where he has several churches. Later, he became bishop of Quimper, which is where he died, and a shrine was built in his memory: the town was known as Quimper-Corentin until the French Revolution. Blessed cakes are still given out in Quimper on Corentin's feast day.

To the east of the Lizard peninsula, other missionaries have dedications in the estuary of the River Fal. On the west bank is Mylor, above the main seaway, yet out of sight from pirates. The church is said to commemorate two Mylors, the first being a fifth-century Breton monk, whose followers landed in Mylor harbour and built a chapel close to a pre-Christian monolith, five metres high. It stands beside the present church, with a prehistoric sun-symbol consisting of three concentric circles carved at its top. The stone is taller than it appears, for it is planted two metres deep. It was later capped with a Christian cross. The farmhouse beside the vicarage is called Lawithick (Cornish for 'enclosure in the woods'), and probably recalls the monks' settlement. In the churchyard is a well whose water is still used for christenings. Mylor is remembered in Brittany as Meloir.

The later Mylor was said to be a son of King Melianus of Cornwall. According to legend, his uncle wanted to disinherit him and cut off the boy's right hand and left foot; in Celtic law, a maimed person was not allowed to rule. The boy was brought up in a monastery, and his destroyed limbs were replaced with metal ones. When he returned home as an active teenager, his infuriated uncle had him killed. Mylor is also remembered at Merther Myle ('martyr Mylor'), and has a holy well at Linkinhorne on the east side of Bodmin Moor. King Athelstan of Wessex gave Mylor's relics to Amesbury Abbey, near Salisbury. It later became one of Britain's most famous Benedictine abbeys.

Across the Fal estuary, two miles southeast of Mylor is St Mawes. According to their *Lives*, Budoc and his teacher, Mawes, arrived here from Wales, stopping for a while before they continued to Brittany. Budoc settled on the west side of the Fal estuary, where the church in the village of St Budoc became the mother church of Falmouth. Beside the River Tamar, St Budeaux, now a western suburb of Plymouth, is also named after Budoc. Mawes was honoured with a chapel and holy well at St Mawes on the east bank of the River Fal, in St Budoc parish. The well is in the main street, which descends steeply to the sea. The well-house is surmounted by a fifteenth-century stone arch.

Mawes and Budoc continued to northern Brittany, where Mawes settled on an island, Ile Modez ('Mawes Island') near Tréguier; there used to be a chapel on the island dedicated to Budoc, suggesting that followers of both monks may have lived here. Budoc became bishop of Dol in northwest Brittany. Mawes became known as a famous teacher and healer: people prayed to him if they suffered from headaches or worms, or were bitten by snakes. Some sixty Breton churches commemorate Mawes.

Back in Cornwall, two churches on the Lizard commemorate a student of Budoc named Gunwalloe. We are fortunate that an early *Life of Gunwalloe* survives, written by a ninth-century abbot of his monastery at Landévennec in Brittany. Gunwalloe's parents were among the Cornish migrants who arrived in Brittany in the fifth century. Cadfan (whom we met in chapter 5) was said to be Gunwalloe's half-brother; he led a group of monks from Brittany to Wales. The family lived at Saint-Brieuc on Brittany's north coast, and Gunwalloe was brought up by Budoc in a monastery on a nearby island called Laurea. The name comes from an early Christian monastic word, *lavra*, which is the Greek term for a group of hermits' cells. Budoc built his island monastery within the ruins of a fourth-century Roman villa.

After studying with Budoc, Gunwalloe became a hermit with a few other monks on the island of Tibidy, and then moved to the mainland, where the local king gave him land on the west coast of Brittany. Here, Gunwalloe established the great monastery of Landévennec in Cornouaille, on a river bank twelve miles southeast of Brest, in 485. Its name means *Lan to Winoc*, or 'Church of Gunwalloe'. His grave and the community's well can still be seen. The monks followed Gunwalloe's rule until 818, when they adopted that of St Benedict. The monastery was burnt and sacked by Vikings in 913, and the monks then abandoned it for thirty years. They returned, and remained until the foundation was suppressed during the French Revolution, when there were only four monks left. A new abbey church was built in 1965.

On the Lizard, Landewednack church is a daughter house of Gunwalloe's Breton monastery, founded in about 600; it is the most southerly parish in mainland Britain. There is another church named after Gunwalloe on the west coast of the Lizard, in picturesque Gunwalloe Cove. Its freestanding tower is built into the cliff, and its churchyard leads down to the beach. Gunwalloe was popular in medieval Britain. A Norwich weather rhyme describing the windy days of March links his feast (3 March) with that of David (1 March) and Chad (2 March):

'First comes David, then comes Chad,
Then comes Winnol, roaring like mad.'

Two miles south of Penzance, near the southwestern tip of Britain, is the parish of Paul, named after Paul Aurelian. A seventh-century monk of Landévennec wrote his *Life*, since Paul became well known in Brittany. The author conflated his story with that of one or possibly two other Pauls, but it seems that Paul Aurelian was born in about 490, the son of an important Romano-British family who lived near Llandovery in the valley of the River Towy, in south Wales. Six miles south of the town is the hamlet of Llanddeusant ('church of the two saints'), named after his two brothers. Another church commemorates Paul at Llangors in Brecon, where a chapel named in Welsh 'Llan of the twelve saints' refers to the twelve monks whom Paul took with him first to Cornwall and then to Brittany.

The Breton biographer tells us that when they reached Cornwall, the band of monks visited the court of King Mark, 'who is called Cunomorus', who probably resided at the fort of Castle Dore near Fowey. This chieftain is named on the so-called 'Tristan Stone', a stone pillar from near Castle Dore which was carved in the sixth or seventh century and inscribed: 'Here lies Drustanus, the son of Cunomorus'. The father and son may be King Mark and Sir Tristan in the later legend of King Arthur, in which Tristan appears as Mark's nephew. Paul continued westward through Cornwall with his companions and settled at Paul, close to Mousehole harbour, opposite the Breton coast. Here, he built a chapel at an ancient holy place, beside a Neolithic standing stone, dating from perhaps 2000 BC. The massive stone was built into the churchyard wall and Christianized by the addition of a Celtic cross-head (see opposite).

Other members of Paul's family travelled with him, including two of his sisters, one of whom, named Sidwell, settled with her companions near St Michael's Mount. Paul felt that the site was unsuitable, and acquired a new plot for the nuns beside Lake Gwavas at Newlyn, not far from the village of Paul. Sidwell is honoured with a church and a holy well in east Cornwall at Laneast, six miles west of Launceston. Sidwell is a modernization of her Old English name 'Side-fulle', which means 'full of light'. Her name, like those of Brigit and Winifred, therefore means 'radiant woman'. Sidwell became a popular medieval saint, and pilgrims visited the shrine where she was buried, outside Exeter's east gate.

An old Celtic legend became attached to Sidwell; it told how she was murdered when her stepmother incited reapers to kill her with their sickles. This story refers to the ancient harvest goddess who was said to die when reapers cut the last sheaf of corn. The scene was enacted in various ways on farms throughout medieval times. Sidwell is painted with her scythe on seven rood screens in Devonshire churches, and is

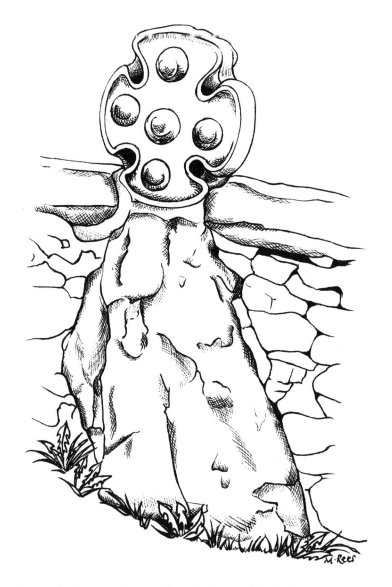

Celtic cross carved on a Neolithic standing stone, built into the churchyard wall at Paul, near Penzance, Cornwall. Paul Aurelian worked here in the sixth century.

depicted in stained-glass windows at Exeter Cathedral and All Souls College Chapel in Oxford.

Paul set sail with his companions, probably from Mousehole harbour in Paul parish, and reached the island of Ushant, off the west coast of Brittany. The voyage from Mousehole across the English Channel to Brittany is a lengthy journey of 120 miles, yet it was one that migrating parties frequently made in their light, hide-covered curraghs. Monks often established their first foundation on the island where they chanced to land. Later, they would move inland and evangelize the surrounding people. Paul moved eastward to the Ile de Batz off the north Breton coast, and eventually founded a church on the mainland opposite, at St Pol de Léon. This present-day village became the first bishopric of Lower Brittany. Paul's sixth-century handbell survives in its cathedral. He ordained two bishops, and died in old age on the Ile de Batz. Ten Breton parishes are named after him.

There are several interesting foundations in the far west of Cornwall, dedicated to missionaries about whom we know very little. Three miles southwest of Paul is St Buryan, whose name may derive from *hi beriana*, meaning 'the Irish lady'. Buryana was said to be the daughter of a Munster chieftain. The circular enclosure of her church stands within an earthwork which indicates a fortified Celtic farmstead. In the eighth century, the son of King Gereint of Dumnonia was cured of paralysis when he prayed to Buryana.

In 930, the Saxon King Athelstan of Wessex was consolidating his kingdom by conquering the Celts. He visited Buryana's shrine on his way to the Scilly Isles, thirty miles to the southwest, and vowed that if he captured the Scillies, he would build a new church in her honour. King Athelstan's expedition was successful, and the stone arches of his magnificent church can still be seen in the north wall of the chancel.

At this time he may have commissioned the fine Celtic cross in St Buryan churchyard. Above a panel of decorated knotwork, Christ reigns from the cross, a triumphant warrior, clothed and booted, with arms outstretched to save. The sculptor carved two similar crosses, one at nearby Sancreed, two miles north of St Buryan, and another now at Lanherne, near St Mawgan-in-Pydar, five miles northeast of Newquay; on these he inscribed his name, Runhol.

In a field a mile northwest of St Buryan, in the hamlet of Alsia, is Buryana's holy well; it provided the village with drinking water, and was also a healing well. Mothers came from far and near with weak and rickety children, to bathe them in the well: rickets is a bone disease found in malnourished children. A nineteenth-century miller's daughter from Alsia recalled that village women fought with the pilgrims to prevent them dipping their babies into the well and contaminating the water.[10]

The area contains a large number of prehistoric ritual and burial monuments, including the Merry Maidens, whose stones form a perfect circle; until the nineteenth century there was a second stone circle nearby. Two medieval crosses stand close by, at the roadside; one is still honoured by the offering of a turnip. Buryana's feast day is 1 May, that of the Celtic goddess of fertility, whom she perhaps came to represent. Another holy well commemorates Buryana at Veryan (another spelling of her name), near Truro, thirty miles northeast.

Three miles southeast of Land's End is the hamlet of St Levan, overlooking a sheltered cove. The sixth-century hermit remembered here was Selevan, who may have been the father of the Cornish missionary, Cybi, whose travels were described in chapter 5. A Selevan is also honoured in southern Brittany. The name 'Selevan' means 'Solomon' in Cornish and Welsh; its modern Irish equivalent is Sullivan. Solomon was a popular name at this time: Celtic Christians were fond of choosing names of biblical characters such as Samson and Daniel, King David and his cantor, Asaph. Selevan's Cornish church is set in a hollow beside a round, fissured rock which was a pre-Christian holy place. Remains of three Celtic crosses stand in the churchyard, one 2.5 metres high. There were originally six of these narrow, elegant crosses, three at each church door.

Across the road, a short track leads down to Porthgwarra Cove. Beside the track is Selevan's holy well and baptistery, which is constructed on a platform above the well. It was built of huge granite slabs. The tiny room measures only 1.5 metres square; its massive walls stand to a height of 1.5 metres. Its roof survived until the eighteenth century. The spring water was good for curing toothache and eye diseases – wells were often believed to cure eye ailments because a well was considered to be an eye on the face of mother earth. When pilgrims had washed in Selevan's well, they slept overnight on the stone floor of his baptistery, in order to be healed. Lower down the track leading to the cove is the hermit's two-roomed chapel and cell, also edged with granite boulders. It was built on an east–west axis; excavation carried out in 1931 uncovered its roughly flagged granite floor.

We know even less about Madron, who gave his name to a hamlet on the moorland, a mile northwest of Penzance. Even today, Maddern is a common surname in the village. Along a signposted track lies Madron's holy well, a small rectangular basin at ground level, overhung by ancient blackthorn bushes: these were considered to be holy trees in Celtic times. Tied to their branches are perhaps a hundred clouties, or pieces of cloth. This custom, still practised across Europe, Asia, Africa and South America, is a way of praying for healing or giving thanks for a cure. The water flows into Madron's baptistery, fifty metres away. The present chapel, with its granite altar slab and seats round its walls, was built in the twelfth century; the earlier baptismal basin is against a corner of the west wall.

After the Reformation, pilgrims continued to visit the chapel and well. In 1641, Joseph Hall, Bishop of Exeter, examined the cure of a cripple who could only crawl for sixteen years, and was 'suddenly so restored to his limbs that I saw him able to walk'. An observer, Francis Coventry, added that the cripple was twenty-eight years old. He spent the night sleeping in front of the altar in the ruined chapel, and washed in the stream flowing down from the well. It took three such visits to cure him, and the cure was complete, for he later enlisted in the Royalist army and was killed at Lyme Regis in Dorset in 1644.[11] Madron well provides water for the village, and in 1750 its water was channelled down the long hill to form the first water supply for Penzance.

Although it is only a village today, Madron was the mother church of Penzance. An inscribed stone of fine whiteish granite in the church provides a glimpse of the early community who worshipped here. Originally a pre-Christian standing stone, it was re-used in the sixth or seventh century to mark a Christian burial. Its inscription suggests that a warrior or nobleman's widow commissioned it for her late husband, who was named 'Fair Slayer'. Above the inscription, the stonemason carved a simple trefoil cross.[12]

 One of Cornwall's chief medieval shrines was that of Piran at Perranporth, seven miles northwest of Truro. Piran was the patron saint of Cornish tin-miners, who flocked to his oratory by the sea. We know almost nothing of his life, but he may have come from Ireland. He had a medieval chapel in Cardiff, and has a number of dedications in Brittany, so Piran was perhaps one of the many missionaries who travelled back and forth between Cornwall and Brittany. Piran's monastery is now buried beneath the sand dunes at Perranporth on the north Cornish coast. The outline of the churchyard probably delineates the boundary wall of his monastery, which was called Lanpiran. A fine Celtic cross still marks the site.

Piran's chapel was excavated several times, and finally reburied in 1981. Now safely cocooned, its walls are of unhewn, uncemented stones, leaning inwards to minimize roof stress. The chapel's east wall perhaps dates from Piran's time; the remainder is early Norman. Before the dunes encroached, Piran's church stood at the head of a small valley. Converts were baptized in a spring which rose beside the chapel and flowed down to the sea. In the ninth century, sand engulfed the buildings, but the Penwortha stream prevented the sand from encroaching further. The monks built a new monastery and a second church on the landward side of the stream.

In the eleventh or twelfth century, a north door was constructed in Piran's first church, to ease the flow of pilgrims, so that they could pass through the chapel to venerate Piran's relics, and leave by the door on the opposite side. A thirteenth-century document describes a reliquary containing Piran's skull, which was placed in a niche above the altar, and a shrine containing his body, which rested on the chancel floor. Piran's small copper bell and his pectoral cross carved out of bone were also preserved, together with his pastoral staff, which was decorated with gold, silver and precious stones. These disappeared in the seventeenth century. At the same time, mining caused the Penwortha stream to go underground, and the monks' second church was gradually engulfed in sand; it survives as a ruin.

In 1325, a monk of St Albans Abbey named John of Tynmouth wrote in his *Life of Piran* that his shrine 'rests in Cornwall above the Severn Sea, fifteen miles from Padstow and twenty-five miles from Mousehole'. A saint's *Life* also served as a guide book; Tynmouth's description of the shrine's location instructed Irish travellers to make for Padstow harbour on the north Cornish coast, and told Breton pilgrims to sail to Mousehole in Paul parish. Piran has a number of dedications in north Cornwall (Perranzabuloe, meaning 'Piran in the sand dunes', Peranchurch, Peranwell), and still more on the south coast facing Brittany (Perranarworthal, Perranwell, Perranuthnoe). He died towards the end of the fifth century.

Celtic travellers generally chose either an outer or an inner sea route from Ireland to Europe. Some sailed directly to western Cornwall, while others crossed to south Wales and landed in eastern Cornwall.[13] The shortest journey to Brittany was from western Cornwall, where the influence of the Breton Church was most strongly felt. In contrast, eastern Cornwall was more deeply affected by the monks of south Wales. We will now travel east of Perranporth and Falmouth, to meet the Cornish missionaries who worked 'above the Severn Sea'.

Chapter eleven

Samson, Petroc
and Eastern Cornwall

IN CELTIC TIMES, eastern Cornwall had a different flavour from the far west. A few Breton missionaries worked in eastern Cornwall, but this region was largely evangelized by Welsh monks. The great monasteries of south Wales were situated close to the coast on the opposite side of the 'Severn Sea', from where it was a short, safe sea journey to Cornwall. Some outstanding individuals set out from the Welsh monasteries across the Severn estuary, chief among them being Samson (*c.* 490–*c.* 565), about whom we know a considerable amount, because we possess a long and interesting *Life of Samson* written by a Breton monk, perhaps as early as the seventh century.

Samson was born in southwest Wales, and came from a wealthy family. His father was from Dyfed and his mother from Gwent. The biographer establishes Samson's credentials as a follower of Christ by recounting that his mother, Anna, was thought to be barren, like Elizabeth in St Luke's gospel.[1] In a dream, Anna is told: 'blessed is your womb, and more blessed is the fruit of your womb', using the gospel words addressed by Elizabeth to Mary, her cousin.[2] When Samson grew up, adds his pious biographer, he healed the sick, cast out devils and raised a dead boy to life, as Jesus did.

The author tells us that Samson was taken as a youth to Illtud's monastery at Llanilltud Fawr in Glamorgan, where Dubricius ordained him as a deacon; Samson's work in Wales was outlined in chapter 4. The biographer betrays his Celtic roots by describing Illtud in druid terminology as 'a most learned magician, who had second sight'. Later, when Samson was ordained as a bishop, fire came from his mouth and nostrils. He captured and killed a huge snake in a cave, and tamed a witch who wielded a 'bloody trident'. These touches would assure the reader that Samson was indeed a true Celtic hero.[3]

Other elements in Samson's *Life* are more prosaic. After becoming a priest, he went to the recently founded community on Ynys Pyr (Caldey Island), off the Pembroke coast, where in time he succeeded Pyr as abbot. He visited Ireland, and spent time in a monastery at Howth, a promontory east of Dublin. Here he acquired a light cart or chariot in which to travel. He put the cart on a boat and returned to the monastery of Llanilltud Fawr in south Wales, where he was invited to become abbot, and was made a bishop in about 521. With his father, Amon, and two companions, he withdrew to a quieter place: they found 'quite a pleasant little fort' near the Welsh bank of the River Severn, where they lived a monastic life together.[4]

Samson then decided to travel as a missionary, so the group sailed to Cornwall, 'with a favourable wind behind them'. The ship would have been large: it contained a crew, tackle and provisions, with Samson and his father, Amon, a cousin and other relatives, together with their personal servants, since Samson's *Life* emphasizes the noble status of his family. The ship also carried Samson's dismantled cart, his books and liturgical vessels, and all the belongings of a group of people intending to emigrate.[5] They landed at Padstow, ten miles northwest of Bodmin, at the mouth of the River Camel, where there used to be a chapel dedicated to Samson.

They continued up the Camel estuary, until they were within two miles of the monastery of Docco. This was situated in the village of St Kew, which was originally named Landocco ('church of Docco'). It is the earliest recorded Cornish monastery. It was probably a daughter house of Llandough in south Glamorgan, which is also named after Docco. A number of crosses surrounding St Kew's church indicate its importance in Celtic times. The author of Samson's *Life* says he was greeted humbly and hospitably by Juvanius, a spokesman for the community.

Juvanius gently explained to Samson that the monks had lapsed from their original ideals, and would prefer not to be judged by so holy a bishop. Samson and his group did not, therefore, visit them. In Samson's day, the monks of Landocco were evidently well educated. They were familiar with both Irish and Latin cultural traditions, as we know from the bilingual gravestone in the church, inscribed in Latin and Irish ogham. This granite stone, roughly shaped like a pillow, was designed to lie at the head of a grave. It is dedicated to a man with the Latin name of Justus. We do not know the exact location of the monastery: it could have been on the site of the present church. St Kew holy well, in the grounds of the former vicarage, was perhaps within the monastic enclosure.

Samson and his party then set off southwards across the Cornish peninsula, using the traditional route from Padstow to Fowey. He sent away the ship that had transported both his companions and his light travelling cart (or *currus* in Latin). Samson acquired a couple of horses to pull the cart, and arranged for a larger wagon (or *plaustrum*) to transport his vessels for worship and his books. As they journeyed southwards they saw a group of pagan people performing a ritual around a statue. A large standing stone stood above them, at the top of a hill. Samson asked what they were doing, and their chieftain explained that they were celebrating the mysteries of their ancestors.

At this point, a boy galloped by, perhaps in a horse race, which could have been a feature of the assembly, and fell from his mount. He lay there unconscious, but after two hours of prayer, Samson cured the lad. He carved a cross with an iron tool on the standing stone, and the chieftain commanded his people to come forward and affirm their baptism. This implies that they had been recently, or nominally, converted to Christianity. The healed boy promised to become one of Samson's followers.[6]

The group of native people accompanied Samson's band southwards for two days, until they reached Golant, where they asked Samson to rid a cave of a fierce serpent. He did so, and the cured youth ran to the chieftain and his war-band to tell them the good news. As a result, the people invited Samson to become their bishop since, apparently, there was as yet no Christian leader in the area. Samson declined, but took over the serpent's cave as a hermitage, and accepted the offer of land on which to build a monastery. Today, local people point out the cave in the west bank of the River Fowey, near Golant village. It is half a mile from the church, which is situated high above the river. Samson's holy well is in a roofed well-house beside the medieval church porch.

The name Golant may derive from the Celtic words meaning 'festival valley' (*gol nant*). Perhaps there used to be a festival here to celebrate Samson ridding the valley of its monster. The monastery that he founded is more likely to have been at Fowey, with its large natural harbour, two miles south of Golant. Fowey's earlier name was Langorthou, which may mean 'enclosure of the war-band', after the group whose chieftain gave the property to Samson. The medieval church at Fowey is a hundred metres from the sheltered beach, and the land slopes towards it, forming a natural slipway. Samson left his father, Amon, in charge of the community. A later abbot appears to have been Berwin, one of Brychan's sons.[7]

A church to the east of Bodmin Moor, in the hamlet of South Hill, two miles northwest of Callington is also named after Samson. A fifth-century grave-marker in the churchyard is inscribed '(the stone of) Cumregnus, the son of Maucus'; it perhaps commemorates one of Samson's converts. The pillar is carved with a *chi-rho* symbol of Christ and decorated with a knotwork panel. There used to be a well nearby dedicated to Samson. South Hill was the mother church of Callington.[8] Beyond Cornwall, one of the Scilly Isles, forty miles southwest of Penzance, also takes its name from Samson.

After leaving Amon in charge of the community at Fowey, Samson embarked with the rest of his followers for Brittany, where he founded Dol on the north coast, and several other monasteries. He was a born leader, and took an active part in Breton politics. He successfully championed one Breton count against another, mobilizing his followers in Guernsey and Jersey. Samson made several journeys to Paris; on one of these, a wheel fell off his much-travelled chariot. He met the Frankish king, Childebert (511–558), and signed the decrees of Church Councils

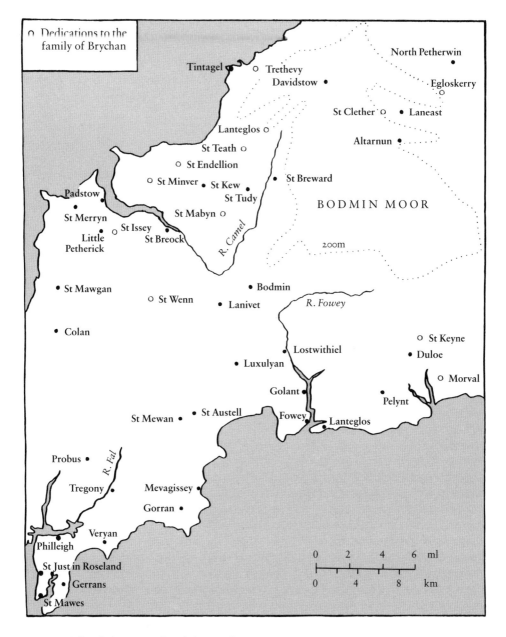

Map 13. *Celtic dedications of mid-Cornwall.*
Celtic missionaries settled mainly above rivers, avoiding the high ground of Bodmin
Moor. Their shortest route from Wales to Brittany followed the valleys of the River
Camel and the River Fowey.

held in Paris in 553 and 557 as 'Samson peccator episcopus' ('sinful Bishop Samson'), using a conventional humble title. He has widespread dedications in eastern Brittany, and others in Normandy associated with his journeys to the Frankish court in Paris.

On his death, Samson's Irish cousin, Magloire, succeeded him as abbot of Dol. Magloire, too, had been educated by Illtud in south Wales, and had accompanied Samson to Brittany. After three years, Magloire retired from Dol and took sixty-two monks to the island of Sark, six miles east of Guernsey, where he settled his new community. Samson's pastoral staff was later acquired by Athelstan, King of Wessex from 924 to 939, for his monastery at Milton Abbas in Dorset.

A close relative of Samson was Mewan. He was born in southeast Wales, like many of the early missionaries, and was brought up in one of Samson's monasteries. When Samson migrated to Cornwall, Mewan is said to have accompanied him, together with a fellow-student named Austell. In Cornwall, the settlements that bear their names are only a mile apart; St Mewan is now almost swallowed up by the larger town of St Austell. Both were within easy reach of Samson's monastery at Fowey (see map 13). Mewan's *Life* relates: 'The two servants of God, St Samson and St Mewan, with their monks, safely cross the seas.... Crowds of men and women flock to hear them preach, among them Privatus, whose sick wife and daughter are healed by the prayers of the holy men.'

Mewan and Austell sailed with Samson to Brittany. On one occasion, Samson sent Mewan, who was still a deacon, on an embassy to a king in southeast Brittany. The journey took Mewan through the forests of central Brittany, where the local chieftain received him kindly and offered him land on which Mewan established the two communities of Gäel and St Meén. The two foundations are four miles apart, and twenty-six miles west of Rennes. Mewan's relative and close friend, the king of Dumnonia in north Brittany, retired to the monastery at Gäel. Mewan was revered in Normandy and throughout Brittany. He is said to have died in old age, followed a week later by Austell. They were buried side by side in the monastery of St Meén.

Another missionary associated with Samson was Breward, whose Celtic name, Branwalader, means 'Raven lord'. He perhaps came from southeast Wales, and is honoured at St Briavels, a church visible for miles around, set on a crest high above the deep Wye Valley. The present church is Norman; Breward's holy well emerges from the hillside below, and was visited for fertility and healing. Breward is said to have accompanied Samson to Cornwall, where another hilltop settlement on the west side of Bodmin Moor, four miles south of Camelford, is named St Breward. An unusual tenth-century wheel cross, decorated with trefoil shapes carved out between each arm, stands in the lower churchyard. Breward is one of a number of Celtic monks who are commemorated around Barnstaple Bay in north Devon, where he is honoured at Braunton, while Branscombe on the south Devon coast, four miles east of Sidmouth, is also named after Breward.

In Brittany, Breladre commemorates Breward, and he may have worked with Samson in the Channel Islands, where he is remembered at St Brelade in the southwest corner of Jersey, overlooking the sea. The tiny Fishermen's Chapel that stands beside the later church is the site of Breward's oratory. This was already a holy place: excavation revealed Neolithic flints and megaliths beneath the site. One of the giant stones had been re-used to form the threshold of Breward's wooden chapel, perhaps to indicate the superior power of the new religion.

The present chapel is decorated with medieval wall-paintings, in which gospel characters wear clothes in the latest fashion of the day. Close by, a stepped 'sanctuary path', one of several in Jersey, leads steeply down to the beach. Until the Reformation, criminals who had taken sanctuary in the church were allowed safe passage down the path to a waiting boat, before banishment from the island.

Three miles southwest of St Breward in north Cornwall lies the settlement of St Tudy. He lived in the fourth century, but we do not know where he was born. Tudy's church contains a Celtic carved stone head, set on the inside wall opposite the porch, and a hogback tombstone 2.5 metres long, constructed in granite for a local seventh-century chieftain. In Brittany, Tudy is associated with two monks whom we met in southwest Cornwall, Corentin and Mawes (see chapter 10). According to his biographer, Tudy was one of three monks proposed as first bishop of Cornouaille, a diocese in western Brittany, but the final vote went to Corentin. His principal monastery was on Ile Tudy in the mouth of the River Odet in western Brittany, ten miles south of Quimper, and churches scattered throughout Brittany are named after him.

The cult of Brioc is linked with that of Tudy both in Brittany and in north Cornwall, where the village of St Breock, just outside Wadebridge, is six miles southwest of the settlement of St Tudy (see map 13). Brioc's church is beside a stream in the small, deep valley of Nansent (Cornish for 'holy valley'). Brioc may have come from Ceredigion in mid-Wales since the church of Llandyfriog in the valley of the River Teifi is named after him. Brioc is remembered in Brittany at Saint-Brieuc on the north coast, where his holy well is found in a shrine built against the cathedral's outer wall. Tudy has two foundations on the nearby coast. Brioc became the patron saint of purse-makers because of his reputation for generosity.

Brioc was one of a number of missionaries with dedications in the Teifi valley of west Wales, whose names are also found in adjacent settlements in mid-Cornwall. In addition, a cluster of churches on the north Somerset coast are also named after these monks, and they have further dedications in north Brittany. Petroc is the most well known of these men, but the surviving sources of his *Life* are late and unreliable. He was a Welsh prince who studied in Ireland and sailed to Cornwall in the early sixth century with his companions.

Petroc landed near Padstow ('Petrocstow') on the River Camel, where he settled with his followers. His *Life* describes his food: 'bread and water, with porridge on Sundays'. His monks worked in the neighbouring countryside, and later the monastery came to own much of the surrounding area. Petroc also had a cell at Little Petherick ('Petroc's little homestead') two miles south of Padstow, beside a tidal creek which flows into the River Camel. There is a well there, and Petroc's *Life* describes him building a mill nearby. It also tells how, true to his austere Irish training, Petroc spent time in the creek, up to his neck in the water, chanting the psalms.

With three companions, Petroc travelled eleven miles southeast to Bodmin, where a hermit named Guron lived in the green, sheltered valley, beside a fast-flowing spring. Guron's well stands beside Bodmin church in a sixteenth-century well-house; below the well, a great volume of water flows through pipes into a trough beside the main road. Petroc's *Life* relates that Guron set out a table with white bread for his four guests. He then left them his dwelling and moved to Gorran, six miles south of St Austell, near the south Cornish coast. Petroc ended his days as a hermit on Bodmin Moor.

The abbot's body was brought back to Padstow, but when the monastery was burnt by the Danes in 981, his monks moved inland to Bodmin for safety, taking with them Petroc's relics, his staff and his handbell. His reliquary can be seen in Bodmin church: it was constructed by Arab craftsmen in Sicily in the twelfth century, and is made of ivory plates bound with brass and decorated with medallions. In the ninth or tenth century, the monks of Padstow annotated a copy of the gospels from Brittany: this is the only surviving manuscript from a Cornish monastery. On its spare leaves and in its margins the monks recorded the liberation of slaves; most of the slaves were Cornish, while most of their owners were Saxon. The Padstow community brought the book to Bodmin when they fled the Viking raids.[9] The monastery at Bodmin flourished during the Saxon period; its monks spread throughout the southwest, where a large number of churches commemorate Petroc. Others are named after him in Wales and Brittany.

Another monk who is remembered in the Teifi estuary on the Welsh coast is Cubert, or Gwbert in Welsh. Three miles northwest of Cardigan, at the river's mouth, the coastal settlement of Gwbert is named after him. A cave on the shore named 'church cave' in Welsh may indicate where Cubert landed. Another church in the parish honours Petroc. On the opposite bank of the River Teifi was a chapel dedicated to Carantoc. Followers of these three monks took their cults southward across the 'Severn Sea'. In north Somerset, the neighbouring churches of Timberscombe and Carhampton are dedicated to Petroc and Carantoc, while on the north Cornish coast, Cubert and Carantoc gave their names to the adjacent parishes of Cubert and Crantock, south of Newquay and the Gannell estuary.[10]

We know little about Cubert or Carantoc. Cubert has two remarkable wells in Holywell Bay, three miles southwest of Newquay. One is in a cave, visible for only an hour at low tide. It is a freshwater pool filled by water dripping from the cave roof, halfway up a series of natural steps in the cave wall, formed by pink and white calcareous deposits. Formerly, the sea level in the bay must have been lower, since pilgrims used to flock to the well in search of healing. Cubert is honoured with another holy well in a ruined chapel in the sand dunes, half a mile away.[11] Higher up, and two miles inland, the parish church of Cubert looks out over the Atlantic Ocean. A pillar cross is built into the outer wall of the porch, and a late sixth-century gravestone re-used in the tower is inscribed: '(the grave of) Conetocus, the son of Tegernomalus'. Cubert or his unknown follower may have baptized Conetocus and erected the simple stone cross.

Even less is known about Carantoc. He was a Welsh monk who may have studied in Ireland; he has two dedications in Ceredigion, and a Cornish church and holy well in Crantock, next door to the village of Cubert. Carantoc's well is in the centre of the village; the walls of the well-house are medieval, but its beehive-shaped stone top is a recent addition.[12] One of the ten or so Cornish monasteries founded in the sixth and seventh centuries was established here. Carantoc's cult spread to north Brittany, where he is commemorated at Carantec.

A cluster of churches in the Teifi valley are dedicated to Mawgan. His followers travelled widely in Wales, to judge by the scattering of dedications to him. In north Wales, the mother church of Ruthin, Llanrhudd, commemorates Mawgan. Ten miles south of Ruthin lies Llangollen ('church of Collen'). Followers of Mawgan and Collen travelled to Cornwall and made foundations in the Newquay area. Mawgan gave his name to the beautiful Vale of Mawgan, with its ancient port of Mawgan Porth and its church of St Mawgan-in-Pydar, where there was another Celtic monastery. Mawgan's well is just inside the churchyard gate. Pydar was one of the six 'hundreds' or land divisions of Cornwall: it was an area which could produce a hundred fighting men.

Mawgan's followers travelled southward to Brittany, stopping at St Mawgan-in-Meneage, on the Lizard peninsula, four miles southeast of

Helston. 'Meneage' means 'land of the monks'. Here, they established another community; a stone pillar on the village green is inscribed '(the stone of) Cnegumus, the son of Genaius', and commemorates an early Christian from the settlement. Setting sail from nearby Mawgan Creek, they continued to northeast Brittany, where Mawgan is honoured in the region around St Malo.

Unlike Mawgan, Collen has no dedications in the Teifi valley. He is remembered in mid-Wales: according to his medieval *Life*, Collen delivered the people in the Vale of Llangollen from a fierce giantess, by slaying her. This may be a symbolic description of how the inhabitants were freed from paganism. Collen is later described living as a hermit on Glastonbury Tor in central Somerset.

Other monks whose cult is recorded at Glastonbury include Kea and Fili. In Cornwall, settlements on opposite sides of the Fal estuary are named after them: Old Kea, two miles south of Truro, and Philleigh, two miles southeast of Kea's church. Collen is also remembered in Cornwall at Colan, three miles south of St Mawgan-in-Pydar. Collen's holy well, half a mile away, cured sore eyes; its water was brought to the church for christenings. It is named 'Lady Nance well'; 'nance' means 'valley' in Cornish, so it is dedicated to Our Lady of the Valley.[13] Collen's *Life* describes him retiring to Llangollen, where his tomb was enshrined in a chapel in the churchyard, until the building was destroyed in the eighteenth century. Breton churches are also named after Collen.

 Among the women who are commemorated in Cornwall is Non, the mother of David, whom we met in chapter 4. She came from Pembrokeshire, and is honoured at Altarnun ('Non's altar') on the northeast side of Bodmin Moor. She has a fine church here beside a fast-flowing stream in a valley. Her holy well is in a field above the church, beside a hawthorn tree. The well feeds a bowssening pool (see opposite), which was used to cure madness by a primitive form of shock therapy. Until the eighteenth century, deranged people were tumbled into the pool by a sudden blow in the chest. They were tossed up and down, accompanied by the chanting of prayers, until they were exhausted. The patients were then taken down to the church, where Masses were sung for their recovery.[14]

As we saw in chapter 4, there are nine early dedications to Non's son, David, in Cornwall. One of these is Davidstow, seven miles northwest of Altarnun. This church in the bleak moorland contains some fine thirteenth-century carved bench ends, including a rare portrait of a minstrel blowing the Cornish bagpipes, an instrument that had been played since Celtic times. Beyond the church is David's holy well, now in a modern well-house; its water is so pure that it is used by Davidstow Creamery.

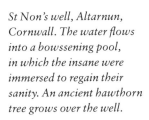

St Non's well, Altarnun, Cornwall. The water flows into a bowssening pool, in which the insane were immersed to regain their sanity. An ancient hawthorn tree grows over the well.

Non is also remembered in southeast Cornwall, at Pelynt, four miles west of Looe. Its name comes from *plou Nent*, which means 'parish of Non'. Her holy well is a mile down the valley in Hobb Park, where a spring emerges from the hillside above the West Looe River. Its well-house is built of flat, unmortared stones; water trickles into a large granite bowl dating from Celtic times, decorated with incised wheel crosses. There used to be a chapel above the well.[15] Non is honoured by a third holy well near St Mawgan-in-Pydar. In Brittany, she is sometimes commemorated as a male companion of David. Non apparently died in western Brittany, and has a fine tomb at Dirinon, ten miles east of Brest.

A final group of Christians who settled in Cornwall brought with them memories of Brychan, a ruler of Brecon in southeast Wales in the fifth century. The origins of this tribal family are discussed in chapter 4, and their dedications across Celtic Britain and Ireland are indicated on map 5. The place-names suggest that while some of the clan returned to Ireland, their original homeland, others travelled southwards, preaching in Devon and Cornwall before continuing to Brittany. They do not appear to have visited western Cornwall, but chose the eastern routes to Europe, working their way across east Cornwall, where a number of adjacent parishes are dedicated to the sons, or more frequently, the daughters of Brychan.[16] Their foundations in mid-Cornwall are each indicated on map 13 by a circle.

A twelfth-century manuscript relates that Brychan's eldest son, Nectan, sailed across the Severn Sea with a number of relatives and followers, landing in Devon near Hartland Point, fourteen miles west of Bideford. Here, Nectan became a hermit in the forest, where his friends visited him once a year. A number of churches around Hartland Point are dedicated to Nectan, and two holy wells at nearby Stoke and Welcombe.

At Trethevy in Cornwall, a mile northeast of Tintagel, is Nectan's Kieve: 'kieve' is Cornish for 'bowl', and describes a rock basin at the foot of a waterfall, from which the River Trevillitt bubbles through a wooded glen before reaching the sea. The glen was known in ancient times: two circular mazes perhaps dating from 2000 BC are carved into the rock face at the seaward end of the glen. Nectan is said to have lived as a hermit at the head of the waterfall, where there are the foundations of a medieval chapel. He may have taken over the properties of an Irish water god named Nechtán, whose well was the source of all knowledge; its flooding waters became the River Boyne.[17]

In Trethevy, Nechtán's well is at the seaward end of the glen, beside the Roman road through north Cornwall. Nearby is a third-century milestone which was perhaps set up when the road was completed. Nectan's *Life* describes him being killed by cattle-rustlers and buried at Hartland Point, where his church at Stoke contained his shrine and his pastoral staff, richly decorated with gold, silver and jewels. A couple of towns in Brittany are named after him.

Nectan's sister, Juliet, is commemorated with a chapel at Tintagel, two miles southwest of Nectan's Kieve. The rocky headland of Tintagel was a royal stronghold in the early sixth century. Its name probably means 'narrow necked fortress': it is almost an island. It is likely that Celtic chieftains moved frequently, for their entourage required more food than any district could supply for long. Tintagel may therefore have been occupied for only a few months each year.[18] However, its chieftains lived in style, and more imported Mediterranean pottery has been found here than at any other sixth-century British or Irish site: pieces of huge oil jars from Tunisia, smaller handled jars from Byzantium and fine red dishes from Carthage. In 1998, fragments of a sixth-century Spanish glass flagon were also found. Some of the red dishes at Tintagel are stamped with a cross, and were probably intended for use in worship.

Overlooking the site, with a magnificent view along the coast in both directions, is Juliet's ruined chapel with its twelfth-century granite altar, and her twin holy wells. From about 600 to 1200, while the fort was abandoned, Juliet's chapel remained in use. She is also commemorated at nearby St Juliot and Lanteglos. Tintagel's parish church, on the mainland opposite, stands within one of Cornwall's earliest cemeteries; it was probably the royal burial-ground for the chieftains who lived in the fort.

A member of Brychan's family called Clether, nicknamed 'the Aged', is commemorated at the village of St Clether on the north side of Bodmin Moor in the valley of the River Inny, eight miles west of Launceston. Here, a spring rises between outcrops of rock. A stream flows down from the spring into Clether's chapel, past the altar. The Normans built a church in his honour higher up the valley, and repaired the well and chapel; for christenings they continued to walk half a mile through the bracken and gorse to Clether's holy well. In the fifteenth century, a granite altar was constructed from three massive slabs. The chapel floor was lowered, so the water would flow out of the chapel into a small covered pool adjoining the chapel's outer wall. Above the pool a shelf was built with a small wooden door, so that the offerings of grateful pilgrims could be retrieved by a priest inside the chapel.

Wenna, one of Brychan's daughters, has a church named after her at St Wenn in mid-Cornwall, six miles west of Bodmin, and another near the southeast coast at Morval, above the West Looe River. She may have been the mother of Cybi, who spent much of his life as a missionary in Wales; his life is described in chapter 5. Wenna's church at Morval is two miles southeast of Cybi's, which stands close to the ancient stone circle at Duloe. Wenna is also commemorated in Brittany, while Rouen in Normandy and St Ouen in Jersey may be named after her.

Three miles northwest of Morval is St Keyne, dedicated to another of Brychan's daughters. After a life of travelling, preaching and building churches, she is described as retiring to Cornwall and settling at St Keyne. Her holy well lies down a steep, leafy lane. There used to be ancient trees beside it: an oak, an elm, an ash and a willow.[19] Keyne is also honoured at the neighbouring church of St Martin's by Looe, which was the mother church of East Looe. She may also be commemorated at Kenwyn, the mother church of Truro.

Other daughters of Brychan gave their names to the villages of St Endellion and St Teath, near the north Cornish coast. Two more of Brychan's daughters were said to be Keria, after whom Egloskerry, four miles west of Launceston, is named, and Adwen, commemorated at Advent. Another was Mabyn, honoured at St Mabyn, four miles north of Bodmin. Minver was described as a daughter of Brynach, Brychan's chaplain and son-in-law. Her hut, chapel and holy well could be seen at St Minver, three miles northeast of Padstow, until the sixteenth century.

Unlike other Celtic kingdoms, Cornwall suffered little from Viking raids: only a few communities such as Padstow were so severely threatened that their monks moved inland for safety. The Saxons gradually pushed the Celts westward through Somerset and Devon, at first to the River Tone, where they captured the Celtic fort at Taunton and so cut off the Celts of the southwest from their northern fellow-Britons. In 935, King Athelstan, grandson of King Alfred the Great, pushed the Celts further west into Cornwall, beyond the River Tamar.

In Northumbria, in the following year, King Athelstan fought and won a fierce battle against combined British forces from Strathclyde, Cumbria, Wales, Cornwall and the Isle of Man. However, Cornish chieftains continued to rule on behalf of their Saxon overlords. Ten years earlier, King Athelstan had set up a Cornish diocese on the Saxon model, based at St Germans, on the west bank of the River Tamar. The Celtic name of this settlement has been lost, but the first bishop of its new cathedral had a Breton name, Conan, so King Athelstan probably confirmed in office the existing Celtic abbot, although he was now answerable to the archbishop of Canterbury.

The Cornish Church continued to evolve in relative peace. Throughout medieval times, Cornwall was a much-travelled route for pilgrims crossing to and from Ireland and mainland Europe. By now, shrines like that of St James of Compostella in northwest Spain were a strong attraction. The ancient road between Padstow at the mouth of the River Camel and Fowey at the mouth of the Fowey River became known as the 'Saints' Way'; the route was twenty-seven miles overland. Halfway lies the settlement of Lanivet, a Celtic church whose founder is unknown. A sixth-century pillar-stone and twelve ancient crosses in the parish indicate the settlement's importance. Medieval pilgrims rested at Lanivet on their way to the great shrines of France and Spain. Others joined them from further east, following the valley of the River Camel as it leaves Bodmin Moor (see map 13). Where the Camel flows through the valley below St Breward, pilgrims paused beside a well dedicated to St James of Compostella; there was a chapel of St James close by.

A number of medieval Cornish miracle plays survive, and Cornish continued to be used in worship. In 1549, Parliament passed an Act of Uniformity, requiring all religious services to be conducted in English. The Cornish leaders replied with spirit: 'We, the Cornish men, whereof certain of us understand no English, utterly refuse this new English (Service)'. In 1600, a Cornish student priest at Valladolid seminary named Richard Pentrey preached in Cornish before the King and Queen of Spain.[20] Only in the last few hundred years has the Cornish language and culture diminished in strength, through pressure from outside forces.

Chapter twelve
The Isle of Man
by Roderick Geddes

FAR FROM BEING an isolated island in the middle of the Irish Sea, Mann was at the centre of sea routes between what are now Scotland, Wales and Ireland. Successive peoples utilized Mann as they moved between the countries that bounded the Irish Sea. During the period when the Celtic Churches were flourishing, Mann formed an important link between the Brittonic territories of Gododdin (the Celtic name for the district around Stirling, beside the Firth of Forth), Strathclyde (or southwestern Scotland) and the fledgling northern Welsh kingdoms.

Although it was not on the most direct route between the British kingdoms, the Isle of Man provided safe harbours and fresh water. The sea journey via Mann was relatively fast; it avoided overland travel through southern Strathclyde and what is now Lancashire and western Cheshire. This land route was made difficult because of the east–west flowing rivers, with their wide, marshy estuaries, the numerous bogs and lakes, and the dense forests, which proved to be barriers for travellers well into the late medieval period.[1] This led to the development of Mann as a strategic link in the western defences of the late Roman and Romano-British regional rulers who were based at Carlisle.

The period when the Celtic saints worked in Mann is notable for its variety. Settlers came from many regions, and each group influenced the development of Christianity on the island. No remotely contemporary native Manx records have survived, but it is fortunate that the Isle of Man regularly appeared in the written and oral records of its neighbours, particularly in Irish annals and in early sources from what is now southern Scotland, preserved in Wales. From their annals, chronicles and folklore it is possible to begin to reconstruct the history of the early Church in Mann.

One of the earliest descriptions of a Christian mission to the Isle of Man is recorded in the *Life of St Ninian* written in 1165, seven hundred years after Ninian's death, by Ailred, Abbot of Rievaulx.[2] Ailred writes that shortly after founding the monastery of Candida Casa at Whithorn in Galloway, Ninian came into conflict with Tudwal, who is described as 'King of Manu'. It has been suggested that 'Manu' could refer to Manau Gododdin, the Brittonic territory beside the Firth of Forth, but there is a stronger argument for the Isle of Man because of references to Tudwal, and more particularly to his descendants, in Welsh sources.[3]

155

It would appear that Tudwal, 'cruel as he was ungodly'[4], was opposed by Ninian himself or by the leader of Ninian's mission on Mann, because of his oppressive rule. There is also a suggestion that conflict may have arisen because the mission was attracting foreigners, 'flocks from many nations'[5], to Mann, and this was disturbing Tudwal. According to Welsh sources, Tudwal was the great-grandson of Magnus Maximus, the general who, after being declared Emperor of Rome by the British-based legions in the late fourth century, reorganized the defensive capabilities of all Roman-held British territories. As part of that policy, the defences around the Solway Firth had been strengthened, with Carlisle re-fortified and developed as a military and later an ecclesiastical centre. Client states with British sub-kings, or *reguli*, were developed in the area, as in the rest of Roman Britain, and Tudwal's position may indicate a continuation of this policy.

Since the role of the sub-kings was to maintain central rule in the face of incursions from unfriendly neighbouring peoples, Tudwal may have seen the influx of people attracted by Ninian's mission as a threat not only to Mann, but to the stability of the whole region. For whatever reason, Tudwal decided to expel the clergy associated with Ninian from the Isle of Man and from all the other territories where they worked. However, upon their expulsion the crops failed and Tudwal was suddenly afflicted with blindness. Ailred's *Life* states that Tudwal commanded a servant to 'fail not to visit the lord bishop, and see him about my obligation for my sin'. Ninian returned, and upon Tudwal's repentance his blindness was lifted and the land again prospered.

Hidden within this story is the possibility of an intriguing historical event. The 'blindness' experienced by Tudwal could have been his adherence to the Pelagian heresy, which had taken a strong hold in Britain at the time. Pelagius taught that people could reach heaven by their own choices, without help from God. Such emphasis on individual responsibility was attractive both theologically and politically to the emerging British kingdoms, with their new sense of national identity.

At this time, Carlisle was a bastion of the orthodox Catholic Church, and there was a strong link between the bishopric of Carlisle and that of Whithorn, where Ninian had established Candida Casa. Ninian's mission to the Isle of Man was possibly intended to combat the native British Pelagian heresy with a native British, but orthodox Catholic, presence. Tudwal's 'cure' may have been his return to the Catholic faith; Christianity on the Isle of Man would have been further consolidated by Ninian's return.

What is certain is that the mission of Ninian on the Isle of Man had a lasting effect. Contemporary records and later church dedications point to the fact that here was a defining influence on the Manx Church. Although the island was under Norse rule from the ninth to the thirteenth centuries, Ninian's influence can still be detected in late medieval times. It is attested by papal records from the late fifteenth century which note that the vicarage of Trinity church at Ramsey in Lezayre was the gift of Ninian's monastery at Whithorn. This suggests the direct involvement of Whithorn in the Manx Church, in the north of the island at the very least, for over a thousand years.

The role of Patrick (*c.* 390–*c.* 461) in the Isle of Man is both pivotal and a matter of extreme conjecture. Many traditions and church dedications are ascribed to him or his disciples, and the later Church of the Norse period used these to validate its pedigree on the island, but none of the references linking Patrick with the Isle of Man can be verified by any contemporary source.

Local tradition states that there was a landing by Patrick, or a shipwreck, on the Isle of Man. This is generally believed to have been on what is now St Patrick's Isle at Peel on the west coast. Other traditions suggest that he landed at 'St Patrick's Isle, Jurby', and as the earliest reference points to the landing being on a promontory, this seems more likely.[6] However, as the former is not mentioned in any sources before the eleventh century and the latter before the tenth, neither can be accepted as historical fact. Since the Church of the Norse period and that of later times used the names of Patrick and other saints to authenticate the pedigree of their site, it is unlikely that Patrick ever visited the island.

There is no doubt, however, that Patrick was working in the area around the western Irish Sea from about 441, when the *Annals* of both Ulster and Innisfallen record: 'Bishop Patrick was approved in the Catholic faith'.[7] This is a significant statement in view of Patrick's subsequent missionary work.

Records from Rome state that Patrick was received by Pope Leo the Great in 442. It is known that Pope Leo was concerned about the continuation of the Pelagian heresy in Britain, and the way it was infiltrating the British Church. No previous missionaries had been able to eradicate it totally. It has been suggested that Patrick was summoned to Rome because Pope Leo wanted to make sure of Patrick's adherence to the Catholic faith[8]; this was possibly the 'approval' mentioned in the Irish annals. Although Patrick had been a bishop since 432 presumably this did not guarantee his orthodoxy, given the prevalence of the Pelagian heresy in Britain at the time.

Patrick appears to have worked as a missionary within, particularly, the field of influence of Ulster. Given this, a visit to the Isle of Man is not beyond the bounds of possibility, for in the volatile political situation at the time, Ulster was attempting to gain control of the regions bordering the northern Irish Sea and, with them, the Isle of Man. However, this would mean that any landing by Patrick on Mann could have been only very brief, late in 442, on his way back from Rome, and unfortunately this cannot be verified. However, there are traces of later missions to the island which are associated indirectly with Patrick, and from these traces we can glimpse the political and ecclesiastical organization of the Isle of Man in the so-called Dark Ages.

St Maughold is referred to in Muirchú's *Life of St Patrick*, written around 690. Maughold appears as 'Macuil moccu Greccae', a local ruler in Ulster in St Patrick's time. He was nicknamed Cyclops because of his legendary cruelty and ungodly behaviour, though perhaps the name derived from the monstrous one-eyed Formorians of Irish legend rather than from a classical source. The Formorians were said to be the pre-Celtic inhabitants of Ireland, an evil people who attacked the Celtic newcomers. It is a fascinating possibility that Maughold may have belonged to this ancient race.

Macuil's character is described as everything that Patrick's was not. When 'he saw St Patrick, radiant with the bright light of faith, and resplendent with some wondrous diadem of heavenly glory, walking on his leisurely way with unshakeable confidence in his doctrine'[9], Macuil decided to kill him, as he had killed travellers often before. However, he also wished to test Patrick, to see if he really was a man of God.

Macuil ordered his followers to place a blanket over one of their party and then called on Patrick and his disciples to 'chant some ... religious spells over him, in the hope that he might be healed'.[10] Patrick expressed no surprise that the man had been taken ill, and when Macuil's followers pulled back the blanket, they found that the man was dead. Patrick was then recognized to be a true man of God and Macuil regretted testing him in that way. He also confessed that he had intended to kill Patrick, and threw himself on his mercy.

Patrick told Macuil that he could not judge him, but that his life was in God's hands: 'As for you, go away unarmed to the sea and cross quickly from this land of Ireland, taking nothing ... with you except some poor little garment to cover your body ... and with the mark of sin on your head'.[11] Macuil was also told to shackle his legs together, throw the key away and set off to sea in a skin boat without any oars. Patrick continued: 'Whatever land divine providence may bring you to, dwell in it and carry out God's commandments there.' The repentant Macuil asked Patrick what would become of the dead man, whereupon 'Patrick ... raised him in that hour, and he came back to life and health'.[12]

Macuil obeyed Patrick's instructions and was carried across the sea to Evonia, Muirchú's name for the Isle of Man. On approaching the shore, shackled and drifting in his skin boat, he was sighted by 'two most admirable men of radiant faith and doctrine, who were the first to teach the word of God and baptism in Evonia, and the islanders were converted to the Catholic faith by their teaching; their names are

Conindri and Rumili'.[13] Macuil remained on the Isle of Man, under the instruction and authority of the two holy men, elsewhere recorded as being named Cynon and Rhun, until he eventually succeeded them as 'bishop and prelate of Ardd Humnann'. The title 'Ardd Humnann' is believed to refer to the upland region of Mann, literally, 'the Hills of Mann'.

Irish annals and Welsh chronicles hint that this story describes a historical event. There is a reference in the *Book of Drogheda* to a local ruler named Indrasaig Mac Cahuil, who granted a considerable amount of land and property to the Church; it was later acquired by the Irish bishopric of Down. Could this be the Macuil of Muirchú's story, who gave his property to the Church before he left Ireland?

On his arrival in Mann, Macuil would have come under the influence of the Brittonic Church based at Whithorn, which was orthodox in its tradition, like that of Patrick. The names of the two bishops in the story, who can be found in Welsh records, would support this. Conindri, or Cynon, was a son of the British prince Brychan (whom we have already met in chapter 4); Brychan was perhaps a sub-king, or *regulus*, like Tudwal. Cynon's mother was an Albanach (or Pictish) woman. Cynon was therefore one of the 'men of the north', the British of Strathclyde, Rheged and Manau Gododdin. Rhun, named in the Macuil tale as Rumili, was formerly a bishop in western Manau Gododdin. So the story suggests that on the Isle of Man there were British missionaries who came not only from Whithorn, but also from the Stirling district, and that of Carlisle and Strathclyde. These northern British Christians had not succumbed to the Pelagian heresy.

Under the influence of the Brittonic Church, which was wholly orthodox, Macuil was converted to the true faith. The repeated mention of the doctrine of both Patrick and the two bishops suggests that this was an ecclesiastical dispute, rather than the conversion of a pagan tyrant. The missions of both Patrick and Ninian could have been concerned with the Pelagian heresy. This may be the reason for Macuil's nickname, Cyclops. He is described as belonging to the one-eyed Formorian race who lived beyond or beneath the sea. There may be a link here with Pelagianism, for the name Pelagius also means 'Seaman'; in modern Welsh the name is 'Morgan'. Perhaps Macuil, or St Maughold as he is referred to on the Isle of Man, was formerly a Pelagian, but was eventually commissioned by the bishop of Carlisle to undertake a mission in the Isle of Man similar to that of Ninian and his followers, and indeed to that of Patrick in Ireland. Maughold's subsequent work in Mann appears to support this.

In his sixty years as bishop in Mann, Maughold organized the Church on the island, and brought it under a central authority.[14] He is said to have ensured that the island was divided into small, equal-sized areas, with a church in each. This led to the Norse system of 'one keeill (or chapel) to each treen (or family's land)'. Through this revolutionary concept, Maughold ensured that every part of the island received the Christian faith. To make sure that his sound teaching was continued, tradition states that Maughold founded a monastery at the place which now bears his name, on the northeast coast of the island. However, the earliest remains of its buildings date from considerably later, around 600.

When we examine the account of Macuil's conversion more closely, the story shifts away from Patrick towards the later Brittonic Church in Mann. Archaeological evidence from the keeill at Knock-y-Dooney on the north coast, facing Galloway, provides evidence of the Brittonic Church in Mann at least a century after Patrick.[15] Why, then, would Muirchú ascribe to Patrick the work of a Brittonic mission? Macuil may have come from Ulster, but the story shows how he was taught the true faith not by Patrick, but by Christian bishops from north Britain.

Muirchú may have had an agenda other than merely telling Patrick's story. At the time when he was writing his *Life of St Patrick*, Armagh was attempting to widen and consolidate its sphere of ecclesiastical influence; to ascribe the conversion of Mann to an Ulsterman who was under the authority of Patrick would further that cause. Are we also seeing confirmation from another source that Ninian's mission to Mann and its continuation by monks from Whithorn was still attracting 'flocks from many nations' to the island?

As we have seen, it is unlikely that Patrick came from Ireland to the Isle of Man. It is also evident that British clergy worked on the island for several centuries. Bearing these facts in mind, we can now examine the Irish missions traditionally associated with St Patrick. One of these is the mission of St Germanus, who is said to have built a cathedral on St Patrick's Isle at Peel. The parish of German was also named after him.

According to a tradition recorded in the *Chronicles of Mann and the Isles*, which were compiled between the twelfth and fourteenth centuries at Rushen Abbey on the island, Germanus was one of Patrick's disciples.[16] He was created a bishop by Patrick, who sent him to the Isle of Man, where he established his seat on St Patrick's Isle. From there he began to convert the local population.

Later writings have suggested that Germanus (which was also the name of a bishop of Auxerre contemporaneous with Patrick) was actually Secundinus, Bishop of Tara at that time, since many of the attributes and stories of the Manx Germanus were also credited to Secundinus. However, since there is no mention of Germanus before the *Chronicles of Mann and the Isles*, there is another possibility: the name Germanus may have been wrongly ascribed to a historical figure who does appear in the Manx Church.

The most likely figure would seem to be St Coemanus, who is mentioned as being the son of a British prince named Brecan (whom we have met earlier as Brychan), and whose mother was from the Cruithnean, or Pictish, people of Ulster.[17] It is possible that the name of Coemanus was later Latinized as 'Germanus', or indeed that he was confused with Germanus of Auxerre. However, if the story of Coemanus is to be believed, and it appears in some Irish sources, we have here a Patrician mission to the Isle of Man, led by Coemanus, a half-British and half-Pictish bishop, who established his seat on St Patrick's Isle and converted the population to the Christian faith.

It is impossible not to recognize the similarities between this story and that of Maughold. The person referred to as Coemanus appears to be the bishop Conindri (or Cynon) whose father was the British prince Brychan and whose mother was an Albanach, or Pict. Again, we see how the work of the Brittonic Church was ascribed to a follower of Patrick from Ulster, possibly to validate claims to Mann by the Church of Ulster.

The history of Mann at this time reflects the same struggle for supremacy. By the late sixth century, the island had become a battle-ground of opposing forces. The Brittonic line of Tudwal still held sway, but it was harassed by foreigners, in particular by Ulster, which was attempting to gain control of the strategic crossroads that Mann represented, and so command the narrow routes across the northern Irish Sea.

In 577, the *Book of Lecan* records that Baetan Mac Cairell, King of Ulster, attacked Mann: 'And Mann was cleared ... of foreigners, so that dominion over it belonged to the Ulstermen from that time forward'.[18] The *Annals of Ulster* confirm the date and describe 'The first expedition of the Uliad (or Ulstermen) to Mann'.[19] The implication of these records is that a major expedition was mounted from Ulster, rather than sporadic raiding. For a time, Baetan Mac Cairell ejected the Brittonic ruling party, and captured the Isle of Man for Ulster. His expedition was apparently a complete success, since they returned home to Ulster the following year. Baetan must have been satisfied that Mann was now firmly within Ulster's sphere of influence.

Baetan may have sought to control Mann in order to protect his interests. At that time a struggle was taking place between the kingdoms of what is now north Wales and that of Strathclyde; Ulster was linked by agreements to both. A close relative of Rhydderch Hael, King of Strathclyde, had recently been killed. It is possible that the kings of Ulster and Strathclyde considered that the ruling family of Mann, which was linked with that of north Wales, was too dangerous a threat to be allowed to remain in power. Although the area was stabilized for a time by the expedition from Ulster, this was not to last long. Within a few years Baetan had died, and the stability that Ulster had looked for in the Irish Sea was shattered by a new force, perhaps the most lasting influence of all upon the Church in the whole of northern Europe.

In 583 a momentous event occurred that is described in almost every contemporary Irish annal and Welsh chronicle; it is even mentioned later in Bede's *Ecclesiastical History of the English Nation* (731). As recorded in the *Annals of Ulster*, this was 'The Battle of Mann, won by Áedán'. Áedán Mac Gabhrainn, King of the Scots in Dalriada, brought his considerable fleet into the Irish Sea and expelled the Ulstermen, their close relatives, from the Isle of Man.

Dalriada had begun as a colony of Ulster; it was situated on the west coast of the Pictish kingdom of Alba, in what is now Argyll. Columba came from Ireland to Dalriada at the invitation of his relative, King Áedán, and became one of the king's chief advisers. When King Áedán captured Mann, the island came under the influence of the Columban Church. Columba was a consummate statesman who worked hard to strengthen the position of Dalriada. His foundation on Iona was to take the lead in a reforming missionary movement that would evangelize most of northern Europe within the next century and a half.

Columba's aim was to tie Church and state irrevocably together, initially in Dalriada, but eventually wherever Dalriadic influence spread. A great source of conflict was Ireland, particularly Ulster, which still claimed authority over its former colony. At the Assembly of Druimm-Cete held in 575, attended by King Áedán and Columba, as we saw in chapter 8, ties were loosened between the high king of Ulster and the king of Dalriada. This gave the Dalriadic fleet independence from Ulster's control, unless the high king requested it. Here there was a careful choice of language in the use of the word 'requested' rather than 'ordered'.

There is no doubt that King Áedán's attack on Mann was part of his policy of achieving independence for Dalriada, and that Columba, his political adviser, was a prime mover in this, although it is never claimed that Columba visited the island. By taking control of Mann, Áedán had secured the southern sea routes, in the same way that an expedition to the Orkneys in 580 had secured his northern borders. More than that, the power of Ulster was broken for the present.

Columba's political skills were considerable, as we have seen. His intention was to expand the influence of his foundation on Iona until it covered the 'Isles of the Sea', which naturally included Mann. This he did within a few short years. The immediate effect of this policy on the Isle of Man was that it no longer feared aggression from its neighbours, and in a comparatively short time the ruling Brittonic dynasty was again in control of the island's affairs. Some Welsh sources suggest that this dynastic line was never actually broken until the Gall-Gael, or Norse-Irish, kingdom was established in Mann over two centuries later. The term *Gall* means 'foreign', and describes the Norsemen who eventually integrated with the Irish Gaels, or Scots. The Gall-Gaels were to create a new and distinctive Manx culture.

In this relatively peaceful period before the arrival of the Norsemen, the Christian Church on Mann was able to consolidate. It was now increasingly linked to the state, in accordance with the policy of Columba and his successors. The construction of buildings at the monastery of Maughold, dating from the seventh century, show that it was developing as an important centre of Christianity on the Isle of Man.

Within fifty years of the establishment of the Columban Church on the Isle of Man, the situation had changed considerably across the whole of the northern British Isles, as former political rivals made peace with one another. Columba and Kentigern (or Mungo) of Glasgow had forged a personal link with each other which had brought Dalriada and Strathclyde together both politically by treaty and ecclesiastically through their commitment to a common mission. They also drew in, by association, Ulster, Mann, the British territory of Rheged around Carlisle, and north Wales.

In the first half of the seventh century, Northumbria assumed a position of political leadership. In 635 St Aidan was invited by King Oswald of Northumbria to come from Iona and establish a Columban monastery on Lindisfarne. This indirectly led to the increasing influence of the Columban Church on Mann. The decorative crosses at Maughold and other sites on the island became increasing Anglian in style. Comparisons with crosses in the north of England suggest that this influence had once more come through Carlisle. Rheged, the kingdom around Carlisle, had now become part of Anglian Northumbria through the marriage of Oswy, King of Northumbria, to Rieinmelth, daughter and heiress of the ruler of Rheged.

There was a flowering of Christianity in Britain in the seventh and eighth centuries, due to the influence of Christian Northumbria and to a new stability resulting from the strengthening of the territories of northern Britain. This had been brought about largely through the policy and influence of the Columban Church. On the Isle of Man, the impact of Columba is seen at many keeill sites. In the parish of Andreas in the north of the island, a bilingual ogham and Latin inscription on a gravestone at Knock-y-Dooney shows a Brittonic influence very similar to that found in south Wales and Cornwall, yet within a mile of this site, another which is virtually contemporaneous has a Columban dedication.[20] British and Columban monks evidently lived as close neighbours on Mann.

It is significant that there are no keeills named after anyone who lived later than Adomnán, Columba's biographer, who died in 704, almost a century before the period of Norse control over the Irish Sea. It was Adomnán and his successors who reformed the Columban Church and brought it into line with that of Rome. It is difficult to know which keeills were founded by British missionaries and which were established by

Columban monks. It may be possible to trace Columban influence by examining the dedications of the Manx keeills. Those attributed to the Norse period may in fact be dedicated to the founder of an earlier Columban keeill on the site, while the later, increasingly Irish, dedications to missionaries such as Conchan, Patrick and German have possibly supplanted dedications to earlier British monks. In the same way, later Irish chroniclers attempted to rewrite the history of the early British missions, as we have already seen.

At the close of the eighth century, the Church on the Isle of Man was firmly under the influence of the Church of Ulster, and Irish clerics had begun to rewrite the history of the British Church on Mann. In the Norse period there was a new shift towards the Western Isles, as Christian settlers from the Hebrides brought new religious and cultural styles to Mann. However, these Christians, too, were influenced by Iona and the orthodox Roman Church which Iona had now come to represent.

Chapter thirteen

Aidan, Cuthbert and Northumbria

AT THE SAME TIME as the Celtic Churches were flourishing, Northumbria was ruled by the Angles. These pagan Germanic tribes came from Denmark and began raiding Britain's east coast in Roman times. In 547 their chieftain, Ida, fought his way north to become the first king of Northumbria. He seized the fortress of Bamburgh, on a rocky outcrop beside the shore, fifteen miles southeast of Berwick-upon-Tweed, and made it his capital. For the next fifty years, the Angles consolidated their position.

Meanwhile, Pope Gregory the Great sent Augustine from Rome to convert the pagan Anglo-Saxons. He arrived in Kent in 597, the year of Columba's death. Augustine was given a church in Canterbury dedicated to Martin of Tours, and spent some years preaching in Kent. He summoned the Celtic bishops to a meeting, possibly at Aust in Gloucestershire, on the English bank of the River Severn, opposite Chepstow. He urged the bishops to consider union with Rome, and to join him in preaching to the Anglo-Saxons. The Celtic bishops replied that they could not abandon their customs without the consent of their people, and so a second meeting was arranged.

This was attended by seven leading Celtic bishops from England and Wales. Augustine would not rise to greet his brother bishops as equals; instead he remained seated and addressed them as subjects. He accused them of celebrating Easter at the wrong time, of administering baptism incorrectly and of failing in their duty to convert the Anglo-Saxons. The Celtic bishops resented Augustine's haughty manner, and were in any case struggling against Anglo-Saxon domination. There was no agreement between them, and Augustine died a few months later, in 604.

Thirteen years later, Princess Ethelburga of Kent travelled to Northumbria to marry the pagan King Edwin, who had recently deposed his brother. The Christian princess was accompanied by her chaplain, Paulinus, whom the pope appointed Bishop of York. Edwin was converted, with all his followers, but within two years he was slain by the pagan King Penda of Mercia and a British king, Cadwallon. Northumbria returned to paganism and Paulinus fled south, taking Ethelburga and her children back to Kent for safety. Paulinus became Bishop of Rochester, where he died.

Meanwhile, Edwin's two nephews had fled to Iona, where they were educated by the monks. The two young men returned to Northumbria

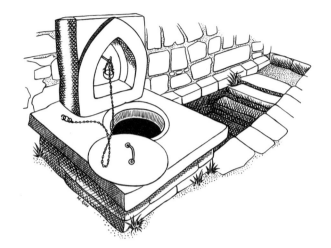

*Kirkoswald well, Cumbria.
King Oswald and St Aidan
traditionally converted the
villagers here, after finding them
worshipping the spirit of the
well. The church is built over
the spring.*

after Edwin's death, seventeen years later. One was killed, but the other, Oswald (604–642), became king at the age of thirty, after defeating Cadwallon. They fought at Heavenfield beside Hadrian's Wall, near Hexham. Oswald set up a wooden cross and assembled his army round it to pray for victory. Although heavily outnumbered, he won the battle, secured his northern border, and set up his royal residence at Bamburgh. He married the daughter of the king of Wessex, and other Anglo-Saxon kings acknowledged him as overlord.

Oswald sent for a bishop from Iona to convert his people: the first abortive mission was led by a monk named Colmán, who returned to Iona, dismissive of Northumbria's 'obstinate, barbarous people'. He was soon replaced by the kindly monk, Aidan, a man of considerable experience, who had been an Irish bishop before he joined the community at Iona. Aidan arrived in Northumbria with twelve companions in 635 and formed a monastic community on an island named Lindisfarne, which is joined to the mainland by a causeway at low tide. Oswald's fort at Bamburgh was just visible from the monastery. Bede recounts that Aidan accepted money and gifts from English lords so that he could buy slaves whom he could educate and train as priests. Aidan established monasteries led by Irish monks at Tynemouth and Barrow, and at Lastingham, six miles northwest of Pickering.

Aidan could not speak English at first, so King Oswald accompanied him on his travels, acting as his translator. They journeyed great distances together throughout Northumbria, preaching the gospel. Across the Pennines, eighty miles southwest of Bamburgh, both men are commemorated in the village of Kirkoswald, six miles north of Penrith. Here, Aidan and Oswald are said to have found the people worshipping the spirit of a spring which flowed out from the hillside. Oswald and Aidan introduced the people to Christianity, and built a church over the spring. Its water flows under the nave and emerges outside the west wall of the church, where it can be drunk from a well (see opposite). There are foundations of Saxon pillars in the chancel, and outside the church, a Saxon ribbed gravestone leans against the wall to the left of the porch. Because the church is built into the hillside, its belfry was placed higher up the hill, so that its bells could be heard.

Oswald was a just and compassionate king. One Easter, Aidan was at Bamburgh, about to bless the royal feast, when Oswald took up a large silver dish of food and had it taken to the poor at the gates, where he gave away both the food and the silver platter. Oswald's reign lasted only eight years: he was killed in 642, fighting King Penda of Mercia. The battle took place at Maserfield, probably near Oswestry on the Welsh border. The town is named after 'Oswald's tree', from a legend that Penda had him hung from a tree before having him dismembered. An ancient well in Oswestry is dedicated to Oswald. In the 1530s John Leland wrote of it: 'there is a chapel of timber over it, and the fountain [is] enclosed with a stone wall'. The chapel no longer remains.

Oswald was soon revered as a royal soldier-saint. Sixty-two English churches are dedicated to him, with others in Europe, particularly in Germany. Oswald's church at Winwick, three miles north of Warrington, is close to another site where the king was claimed to have died. On the arms of a tenth-century wheel cross in Winwick church, Oswald is depicted, suspended head downwards on a pole, being dismembered by Penda's soldiers. On the other arm of the cross, a priest with a bucket fetches holy water from Oswald's well, nearby.

The well can be found in Hermitage Green, a hamlet 1½ miles to the north of Winwick: it is in a field across the road from Monk House. The hamlet is named after the hermit monks who tended the well. Oswestry has a stronger claim to be the site of Oswald's death, but Winwick Quay was the lowest crossing point of the River Mersey, and lay on the old western route to south Britain. Oswald and his army would therefore have travelled through Winwick on their way to fight King Penda, and the army would have returned this way, bearing Oswald's body home to Bamburgh for burial.

After King Oswald's early death, his successor Oswin continued to encourage Aidan's missionary work. King Oswin gave Aidan a horse from the royal stables, but Aidan gave it away to a needy person, since he preferred to travel on foot, like the poor. Among Aidan's friends and followers were a number of women, including Oswald's half-sister, Ebbe (d. 683), who became a nun at the double monastery of Coldingham, nine miles northwest of Berwick-upon-Tweed. It overlooked the sea at St Abb's Head, which is named after Princess Ebbe. The site of the monastery can be found two miles northeast of the village.

Ebbe became abbess of Coldingham, but in her old age, the community of high-born women grew lax. Bede tells us that Adomnán, Abbot of Iona, visited the nuns and reproved them for spending their time weaving fine clothes, making friends with strange men, feasting, drinking and gossiping, instead of praying and studying. A few years after Ebbe's death, the monastery burnt down. Her niece, Etheldreda, founded a community at Ely in East Anglia.

Another of Aidan's friends was Hilda (614–680), who was related to the royal families of Northumbria and East Anglia. When she was thirteen, Hilda was baptized by Paulinus; at the age of thirty-three she decided to join a community in Gaul, but Aidan asked her to remain in Northumbria, where she became abbess of a double monastery at Hartlepool on the coast, seventy-five miles south of Lindisfarne. Hilda later became abbess of Whitby on the cliffs above a harbour settlement, twenty miles south of Hartlepool, where she remained until her death at the age of sixty-six.

At Whitby Hilda created a double monastery which became a centre of learning and the arts. She encouraged Caedmon, an Anglo-Saxon cowherd and lay brother, to write songs and stories to illustrate the scriptures. He composed a *Hymn of Creation*, and is considered to be the first English religious poet. Hilda trained at least five bishops, and hosted the Synod of Whitby in 664, at which she supported the Irish party in the debate over the date of Easter, but accepted the council's decision in favour of Rome.

Little remains of Aidan's monastery on Lindisfarne, since a large twelfth-century abbey was built over it. The name is Celtic and means 'the land by the Lindis', a small stream, now called the Low, which is visible only at low tide. Until recently, residents and visitors had to walk across the sand to Lindisfarne, like their Celtic predecessors, passing the curlew, redshank and other wading birds that comb the shallow waters for food. Aidan's monastery probably consisted of small, simple huts housing one or two monks, perhaps a master and a novice. They would be grouped irregularly round the church. This area was perhaps divided off from the guest house and the other more public buildings. The whole complex would have been enclosed by a bank and ditch. Aidan's successor, Bishop Finán, built a church in the Irish style, of hewn oak covered with reed thatch.[1]

As in other Celtic monasteries, there were outlying hermitages. Four hundred metres southwest of Lindisfarne, St Cuthbert's Isle contains the remains of a seventh-century cell and a later medieval chapel. At low tide, it can be reached on foot from Lindisfarne. Seven miles southeast, Aidan and his successors found a more isolated retreat on the island of Inner Farne. Lindisfarne's monks evangelized much of northeast

Britain; they travelled northwards into Scotland and south into Mercia, East Anglia and Wessex. Monastic craftsmen and artists developed new styles of sculpture and illumination, which they took with them on their missionary journeys.

A vellum factory has been excavated on Lindisfarne, a mile away from the priory; it contained two workshops, a slaughterhouse and the bones of scores of calves. Most of the animals were less than a year old when they were killed; a third of them were only one or two weeks old. The monks produced over a hundred books here; the site was used during the last few years before the Viking raid of 793.

The most beautiful manuscript to have survived is the Lindisfarne Gospel Book, which was written about fifty years after Aidan's death, in memory of St Cuthbert. It would have taken a monk two years to illustrate this book, 258 pages long, using the skins of at least 130 calves. We know the monk's name, because a tenth-century priest named Aldred annotated the final page. He tells us that Eadfrith, Bishop of Lindisfarne, wrote it (probably in the couple of years before his consecration), and that Bishop Ethelwald covered it. He adds that a hermit named Billfrith forged the gold, gilt silver and jewelled ornaments which adorned its cover; this was later lost, probably at the time of the Reformation.[2]

Eadfrith's designs show great beauty, subtlety and sophistication. His curvilinear patterns resemble those found on Celtic metal bowls. He wrote the text in dark brown ink, with pens cut from goose quills or reeds; both were readily available. Eadfrith used a large range of colours; some of the pigments were easily prepared, but others had to be imported. The blue that he used was obtained from lapis lazuli which came from the foothills of the Himalayas, brought to Europe by traders. Aldred added an Anglo-Saxon translation between the lines of Jerome's Latin Vulgate text. Although he probably copied from an earlier source, Aldred's translation is the first surviving example of the gospels in English.[3]

It appears that Aidan did not spend a great deal of time with his community, since we hear of him travelling on lengthy preaching tours, and celebrating Easter not with his monks but with the royal household at Bamburgh. Aidan used to spend the forty days of Lent in solitude on the island of Inner Farne. Bede tells us that Aidan was on Farne when King Penda of Mercia besieged Bamburgh and tried to burn down the royal palace. Aidan saw the flames from a distance, and prayed until the wind changed direction and the castle was saved.[4]

Aidan had established a church in Bamburgh, not far from the palace. Towards the end of King Oswin's reign, Aidan fell ill at Bamburgh, and a shelter was made for him at the west end of the church. The sick man rested here, supported by a wooden beam, which is still preserved in the church. The present building was constructed in the twelfth century by

Augustinian canons. Aidan died here in 651, and his body was taken back to Lindisfarne for burial. After spending only sixteen years in Northumbria, Aidan had established a Christian culture throughout northeast Britain.

The second bishop of Lindisfarne was Finán, an Irish monk who had accompanied Aidan from Iona. During his ten years as bishop, Finán began to send missionaries to other English kingdoms. He converted King Penda's son, Peada, who ruled the Middle Angles; they occupied the area between Bedford and the River Trent. Peada succeeded his father as King of Mercia, and asked Bishop Finán to send him monk bishops for both kingdoms. Two of these were Cedd and Chad, brothers from an Anglian family who had taken their four sons to Lindisfarne to be educated. The four youths had become monks under Aidan, who sent them to Ireland for further experience. While at Lindisfarne, the young men had travelled to Scotland on preaching tours: in chapter 9, we met Cedd and Chad working in Glen Lyon, in the Scottish Highlands.

In 653 Cedd began to preach the gospel in Mercia, and then moved to Essex, where the king of the East Saxons had recently become a Christian. Cedd founded monasteries at Tilbury in the Thames estuary and at Bradwell-on-Sea, on the north shore of the River Blackwater, ten miles south of Colchester. On his visits home to Northumbria, Cedd acted as translator at the Synod of Whitby, and established a monastery at Lastingham in Yorkshire, eighteen miles west of Scarborough. In 664 Cedd was in Lastingham when the community was struck by the plague, which had spread northward from Kent and Essex. One of his own brothers died, and Cedd also caught the disease. Before his death, he sent for his brother, Chad, to replace him as abbot. Chad buried thirty of the monks, including his two brothers.[5] Two holy wells at Lastingham honour Chad and Cedd.

The king of Northumbria then appointed Chad as bishop of York, but he was ousted in 669 by Wilfred, who was supported by Rome. Chad returned to his community at Lastingham, but soon the king of Mercia asked for a bishop, and the new archbishop of Canterbury appointed Chad. There had already been four Celtic bishops working in Mercia, but they were not territorial, and had no authority over a specific area. When the last died, Chad became the first bishop to be responsible for the Church throughout Mercia. This was a vast territory, stretching from Wales to the east coast, and from the River Humber in the north to the Thames. Chad began travelling on foot through his sparsely populated diocese, as his master, Aidan, would have done. When the archbishop of Canterbury gave him a horse, Chad refused to mount it until the archbishop forcibly placed him in the saddle.[6]

Chad made his headquarters at Lichfield, on an ancient holy site. An immense stone buried beneath the high altar of the medieval cathedral appears to be the altar stone of a temple dating from 1000 BC. There was a church here before Chad's time, and he built a monastery nearby. Bede tells us that here Chad 'used to retire with seven or eight monks, in order to pray or study, when he was not busy working or preaching'.[7] The group of monks helped Chad in his work, and after his death one of them succeeded him as bishop. Near the house was a pool, where Chad baptized converts. The cathedral has a fine 'close', or group of church buildings with a surrounding wall. The term comes from the Celtic word *clas*, which means a monastic enclosure.

After only three years as bishop of Lichfield, Chad died when the plague struck again in 672. Thirty years later, the cathedral was built over his tomb. The small timber church probably extended from the present screen to the high altar, and contained Chad's house-shaped shrine, which had a gabled roof, and apertures through which pilgrims could collect dust from the tomb, and take it home to cure sick people and animals. The church was a popular place of pilgrimage, and was rebuilt several times. Visitors arriving in the town were ferried across the Minster Pool to view the shrine.

After Chad's death, Lindisfarne continued to provide missionaries for Mercia. A group of monks from Lindisfarne formed a community at Peterborough; this group, in turn, sent monks to a number of places including Bermondsey in east London, Woking in Surrey, Bredon in Worcestershire and Brixworth, six miles north of Northampton. The imposing early Saxon church at Brixworth has survived almost intact; the large monastic church is built on the plan of a Roman basilica and uses recycled Roman tiles.

In 638 the Angles of Northumbria advanced into Scotland; they captured Edinburgh, then Galloway in the southwest and Fife to the northeast. The Angles kept this territory for almost fifty years, until the Picts defeated them. During this time, Aidan sent monks from Lindisfarne to Old Melrose, situated at a bend of the River Tweed, in the Scottish Borders. Its name means 'bare promontory' (*Máil ros*). Aidan appointed one of his Anglo-Saxon converts, Eata, as its first abbot. The ruins of the twelfth-century Cistercian abbey of Melrose lie 2½ miles west of the earlier monastery.

Aidan sent another group of monks to Jedburgh, twelve miles southeast of Melrose; the abbey crowns a hill above the fast-flowing Jed Water. A group of monastic sculptors worked here from the eighth to the tenth centuries. Some of their carvings survive, including five free-standing crosses and the end panel of a magnificent house-shaped stone shrine: the panel depicts a tree of life, with birds and animals contained in swirling vine tendrils. The shrine probably contained the bones of Boisil (d. *c.* 661), an Irish monk who became the second abbot of Melrose.

Boisil's reputation for holiness and learning attracted a youth named Cuthbert to Old Melrose in 651. As a boy, he had been fostered in a nearby Christian household; at the age of eighteen, while working as a shepherd, Cuthbert decided to enter the community. When Boisil went on preaching tours through the surrounding countryside, the young monk accompanied him. Cuthbert also went on longer missions from Melrose: he sailed to the kingdom of Fife on the Scottish east coast, and also travelled further north to work among the Picts near Loch Tay. His cave retreat at Weem in Glen Lyon was described in chapter 9.

In about 659, Boisil became abbot of Melrose, when Eata was sent 120 miles south to found a new monastery at Ripon in north Yorkshire. Cuthbert, now aged twenty-five, accompanied Abbot Eata and became guestmaster of the small community. They stayed here only two years, however, before being ousted by Wilfred, an ambitious monk who had trained at Lindisfarne and later studied in Rome. Wilfred enjoyed royal favour, and the king appointed him to be abbot instead of Eata. Wilfred introduced the Benedictine rule, and built a new stone church with a fine crypt, which survived the Viking raids. The underground chapel was perhaps designed to store the relics of saints that Wilfred had brought back from Rome, planning to install them in the new churches which he hoped to build.

Since Eata, Cuthbert and the Celtic group could no longer live freely at Ripon, they returned north to Melrose. Three years later, the community was struck by the plague, and the elderly Boisil became ill. Cuthbert was also infected, but survived, and for a week he read St John's Gospel to the dying man. Bede describes Cuthbert asking the old monk what he would like to have read to him. Boisil replied: 'The Gospel of John; I have a copy consisting of seven quarto sheets. With God's help, we can read one each day, and meditate on it as best we can'.[8]

 On the death of Finán, Colmán (d. 676) had become the third abbot bishop of Lindisfarne. Like his two predecessors, he was an Irish monk from Iona. In Colmán's time, Wilfred's pro-Roman faction lobbied at the royal court until the king ordered that a council be convened to decide whether Northumbria should follow Celtic or Roman traditions. The synod was held at Whitby in 664, and the main debate took place between Colmán and Wilfred. The king favoured the Irish position, but felt compelled by Wilfred's arguments, and the debate was concluded. Colmán resigned as abbot of Lindisfarne and returned to Iona, taking with him most of the Celtic monks and thirty Anglo-Saxons. From Iona they continued to Ireland, and made a new settlement on the island of Inishbofin off the Galway coast.

In 664, Eata of Melrose replaced Colmán as abbot of Lindisfarne; he brought Cuthbert with him as prior. He chose Cuthbert as an assistant since he was an experienced monk with good sense and discretion, who would help him to manage a community that was now divided by the conflict between the Celtic and Roman Churches. After the Synod of Whitby, Cuthbert adopted Roman customs; he gradually and patiently won over the remaining dissident monks to his point of view. From Lindisfarne, Cuthbert travelled eighteen miles north to the double monastery of Coldingham, where his abbess, Princess Ebbe, had problems with the luxurious lifestyle of her nuns, as we have seen, and with the tension between Celtic and Roman practice. He used the tiny island adjoining Lindisfarne, now known as St Cuthbert's Isle, as a solitary retreat.

After ten years as prior of Lindisfarne, Cuthbert became a hermit on Inner Farne. He built a circular hut of earth and stone, with a small opening in the roof to allow daylight to enter. He constructed a small, rectangular oratory and a guest house; a medieval chapel was later built on the site. There were no trees on the island; Cuthbert carved out a well from the rock, and sowed seed in the shallow soil. Wheat failed to germinate, but he succeeded in growing barley for bread. Cuthbert remained in touch with Church affairs, and was frequently visited for his wise advice. He remained on Inner Farne for ten years, until a delegation of monks and bishops begged him to return. Now aged fifty, he became Bishop of Lindisfarne, and once more began to preach and teach.

Cuthbert had only two more years to live, but during that time he travelled throughout the diocese. Several times he followed Hadrian's Wall westward to visit Carlisle. Six miles west of Newcastle upon Tyne, Cuthbert is said to have preached at Heddon-on-the-Wall. Halfway along the Wall, at Housesteads, an overhanging rock to the west of the Roman fort is named Cuddy's Crag after Cuthbert. He was responsible for the church in Carlisle, where there was a double monastery whose abbess was a sister of the Anglian Queen Iurminburg.

One of Cuthbert's friends named Herbert lived as a hermit in Cumbria on an island in Derwentwater. Herbert used to travel to Lindisfarne each year to visit Cuthbert. Their final meeting was in Carlisle; both were to die the following year. There are remains of a circular stone building on St Herbert's Island, which may have been his hut. Friar's Crag, a mile south of Keswick, marks the spot where pilgrims set out to visit Herbert in his island hermitage, with its beautiful view of lake and mountains.

In 687 Cuthbert returned to Inner Farne to die. Monks from Lindisfarne visited him regularly, but in the last week of his life, violent storms prevented them from reaching Cuthbert for five days. Bede tells us that a group of monks, including Cuthbert's attendant, Herefrith, finally managed to land, and found their master weak and sick. He had been sitting in the guest house for a week, unable to move. Bede relates that he heard what happened from an old monk who was one of the party, whom Herefrith had told: 'I warmed some water and washed his feet, which had an ulcer ... that needed attention. I also warmed some wine which I had brought, and begged him to taste it, for I could see from his face that he was exhausted by pain and hunger. When I had finished serving him, he sat quietly on the couch, and I sat beside him.'[9]

The monks carried Cuthbert to his hut, and later to the chapel, where he died peacefully among his friends. His body was brought back to Lindisfarne for burial. Eleven years later in 698, the monks dug up Cuthbert's remains in order to enshrine them. The brothers had prepared an oak chest decorated with carvings of Christ surrounded by the four evangelists, the Virgin and child, and angels. Meanwhile, the Lindisfarne Gospels had been illuminated in Cuthbert's honour. His body was found to be undecayed; it was placed in the oak casket, together with his belongings, including the gold cross that he wore, decorated with red garnets. The casket was laid in the sanctuary of the church, and pilgrims flocked to the shrine.

Ninety years later, Vikings began to raid the coast. In 793, Lindisfarne was sacked by Norwegian marauders. At the time of the raid, the Northumbrian scholar, Alcuin, was working in France as a teacher, at the invitation of the Emperor Charlemagne. He wrote five letters to England about the raid. In one addressed to the king of Northumbria he exclaimed: 'No one ever thought that such an attack could be made from the sea. But now St Cuthbert's church is splashed with priests' blood and robbed of all its ornaments. It is the holiest place in Britain, but these pagans have made it their hunting ground.' The advanced technology of the Viking ships made the attack possible. It was followed by a succession of raids on other monasteries: on Wearmouth and Jarrow, where Bede had lived, in 794, on Iona in 795, and then by other attacks in Ireland and France.[10]

The monks soon returned to Lindisfarne, but grew increasingly uneasy as other monasteries were destroyed. Hilda's community at Whitby was thoroughly sacked in about 800, and Iona was raided again in 802 and 806. In 875 the monks of Lindisfarne decided to leave their island home, taking their treasures with them, including the oak casket containing Cuthbert's body, and the Lindisfarne Gospels. For seven years they journeyed through Northumbria, in search of a safer place. They reached Workington on the west coast of Cumbria and tried to embark for Ireland, but a storm swept one of their manuscripts overboard and they abandoned the attempt. They travelled into southwest Scotland, where Kirkudbright in Galloway is named after Cuthbert.

Scattered across Northumbria are churches where the monks rested with Cuthbert's body. They spent some years at Chester-le-Street, five miles north of Durham, where Aldred the priest inserted his Anglo-

Saxon translation between the Latin lines of the Lindisfarne Gospels, and added the final paragraph telling us who created and decorated the manuscript. At this time, King Athelstan of Wessex, the grandson of Alfred the Great, gave the monks forty-five kilograms of silver, two gospel books and a *Life of Cuthbert*, in honour of their saint. In 883 the monks took Cuthbert's body to Ripon, where it rested for a hundred years, until the monks fled again before marauding Danes, who eventually destroyed Wilfred's church and wiped out the monastery where Cuthbert and Eata had lived.

In 995 the monks finally chose a new location for their monastery at Durham, on a rocky hill surrounded on three sides by the River Wear. Here, they built a stone church over Cuthbert's tomb. A hundred years later, work began on the magnificent cathedral that stands on the site today, with its giant Norman pillars and its beautifully proportioned façade. Substantial parts of Cuthbert's oak coffin can be seen, together with his jewelled cross, some vestments and his portable altar. The survival of so many belongings of an early saint is extraordinary.

The Viking raids on monastic settlements brought confusion to the Celtic Churches and caused the dispersal of many communities. The marauders were not anti-Christian, but were attracted by the riches they found in monasteries, which were poorly defended, unlike chieftains' forts. Monks who were not murdered were captured and sold as slaves. The Vikings were not the first Germanic raiders to threaten the Celts. In a series of migrations in the fifth century, Angles from Schleswig-Holstein, Jutes from Jutland and Saxons from Lower Saxony in northwest Germany had overrun Britain. The Vikings of Norway and Denmark were their kinsmen. But by the eighth century, the new wave of raiders had developed long, flexible and lightweight boats that could handle rough seas, yet travel up rivers in water only a metre deep. They could penetrate far inland, and had no need for harbours, since they could run their ships onto a beach without damage.

The word 'Viking' probably comes from the Old Norse word *vík* meaning a bay or creek: Vikings were associated with the sea. Much of the Scandinavian coast consists of mountains bordering deep fjords; overcrowding and shortage of land impelled the Norsemen to seek new territory. Raids were seen as feats of heroic valour, and were regulated by Viking law: it was forbidden to attack traders or farmers, women or a man who was already engaged in a fight. Norse raiders were not invincible; they were often defeated, but they generally returned to attack another year.

Scandinavians spoke a single language, but the Vikings were never one nation: their loyalty was to their clan. From coalitions of clans, the three kingdoms of Norway, Sweden and Denmark were gradually formed. By

800, Norwegians began to colonize the Isles of Orkney and Shetland, while Danes began to settle in eastern England from 850. During the next three hundred years, Norsemen terrorized France, Italy and Germany, Byzantium and the Arab Empire. The raiders were normally farmers or fulltime soldiers. By 860, the Vikings had permanent bases abroad; they could now stay away from Scandinavia for years at a time.

As they began to settle in Britain and intermarry, these dynamic people brought new gifts of poetry and artistry, with new forms of administration and justice. They developed great market towns, for they were experienced merchants. We do not know when they became Christian: the three earliest churches in Scandinavia are found in trading centres, and may have been established by foreigners. Viking merchants were happy to submit to baptism when that was a condition of being allowed to trade with Christians. *Egil's Saga*, written in Iceland in the thirteenth century, describes the custom among soldiers and merchants of accepting provisional baptism so that they could live alongside both pagans and Christians, yet follow whichever faith was more agreeable to them.[11]

In 865, Danish warriors landed in East Anglia, acquired horses and became a mounted, mobile army. Two years later they captured York, from where they controlled Northumbria. It is thought that Lindisfarne was attacked not by Danes, however, but by Norwegians based in Orkney. It is not known when they conquered the Isles of Orkney and Shetland, or whether this was a peaceful process. A Pictish hoard was found buried in the eighth-century church on St Ninian's Isle, the mother church of Shetland. The silver treasures may have been brought to the church by a wealthy Pict, to protect them during a Norse raid. Since he did not return to collect his wealth, perhaps he was murdered. The Picts may have been wiped out or enslaved by the Vikings: the place-names of Orkney and Shetland are all Norse, which suggests that Pictish culture was swamped or obliterated.[12]

The twelfth-century *Saga of the Men of Orkney* describes how Svein Asleifarson, a wealthy Orkney farmer on the island of Gairsay, spent each winter at home, where he entertained eighty men at his own expense in his great drinking hall. In the spring he supervised the sowing of his crops, then went off plundering in the Hebrides and in Ireland, on what he called his 'Spring trip'. He would sail home in late summer to supervise the harvest, and then set off raiding on his 'Autumn trip'. He returned again for a winter of feasting.[13] This was a pattern followed by ancient warrior peoples: campaigns alternated with the vital tasks of sowing and harvesting.

Throughout the eighth century, Norwegians based in Orkney and the Hebrides plundered Irish monasteries. Their first recorded raid took place in 795, but, to put this in perspective, Irish annals record the burning of at least thirty monasteries before this date by rival Irish tribes. In 807 the monks of Cork and Clonfert fought against each other so viciously that many of them were slain. By this time, the Vikings were becoming Christian. A small Irish casket shrine containing relics wrapped in a silk cloth was found in Denmark; it is now in the National Museum, Copenhagen. An inscription on the shrine, carved in Norse runes, reads 'Ranvaig owns this casket'; it was perhaps a gift from an Irish monastery to a Danish church.[14]

Norsemen fortified sea bases that grew into Ireland's first towns; they established Dublin in 841. In the following century, a Danish king of Dublin named Anlaf retired to Iona as a monk, while only six years later, in 986, a Viking group raided Iona and killed its abbot. Eleven years later still, King Magnus Barelegs of Norway visited Iona to pay homage at the shrine of Columba: Viking groups did not all embrace Christianity at the same time.

Irish monastic craftsmen were influenced by Scandinavian art. Fine examples of this are the twelfth-century crozier of the abbots of Clonmacnoise, with its trailing tendrils and interlace designs, and the processional cross of Cong in County Mayo, with its biting, ribbon-like animals.

Bishop from a Viking chess set found on Lewis in the Hebrides (Royal Museum of Scotland, Edinburgh).

At the southern tip of the Outer Hebrides, the island of Barra, five miles wide, was a haven for Viking pirates, who launched raids in several directions, using Barra as a base. They also settled here: three place-names end in a Norse suffix meaning a shieling, or summer pastoral settlement. The Norwegians may have lived alongside Celtic Christians: the island's name, Barra, is another form of St Finbar's name, while an islet to the south is named Pabbay, meaning 'hermit's isle' in Norse. Viking sagas describe Norsemen who drove out Barra's Celtic rulers in the mid-ninth century, in order to use the island as a base for plunder, while keeping contact with their relatives in Norway and Iceland.[15]

Pagan graves of both men and women indicate that the Norwegians brought their wives, but within a hundred years they had accepted Christianity. A grave-slab was discovered at Finbar's church with an ornamented Celtic cross on one side and an inscription in Norse runes on the other which reads: 'This cross was raised for Thorgerth, daughter of Steinr'. This suggests that the cemetery remained a Christian burial-ground during the Viking period.[16] At the opposite end of the Hebrides, a Norse chess set was discovered on the Isle of Lewis. Its wide-eyed Viking bishop raises his right hand in blessing, while with his left he firmly holds his pastoral staff (see previous page).

Manx crosses tell a similar story of integration. An elegant, tapering wheel-headed cross at Old Kirk Braddan in the southeast of the island, dating from the late tenth or early eleventh century, commemorates Fiac, who has an Irish name, although his father, Thorlief, and his uncle, Hafr, have Norse names. Presumably, Fiac's mother was Irish. At Kirk Michael on the northwest coast, there is a wheel-headed cross-slab, decorated on each side with interlaced patterns. A long inscription carved in Old Norse runes tells us that it was commissioned by a Celt for his father, who bore a Norse name: 'Melbrigdi, son of Athakan the smith, erected this cross for his soul, (saved from) sin'.

The inscription continues, 'but Gaut made it, and all in Man'. This refers to a Viking immigrant named Gaut, who founded a school of sculpture on the island. Gaut signed himself on another grave-slab as 'Gaut, son of Bjorn, from Kuli', so he probably came from the Isle of Coll in the Hebrides, where Columba's monks once grew grain to feed the community on Iona. Gaut's simple, attractive style is evident on other crosses around the island.[17]

It is probable that Gaut learnt his trade as a sculptor in the northwest of England, which was colonized by Norsemen from Ireland and the Scottish islands in the early tenth century; the decoration on Anglo-Scandinavian crosses in Northumbria has much in common with those on the Isle of Man. Northumbria was a region where Celtic faith and culture fused with that of both ruling Angles and Viking invaders. An outstanding example of such integration is the Ruthwell cross, which was perhaps set up on the sea shore in the early eighth century as a boundary-marker between the Anglians of Northumbria to the east and the Britons of Galloway and Strathclyde to the west.

The cross now stands in Ruthwell church, ten miles southeast of Dumfries. The carvings on the tall cross, five metres high, express the rich faith of its unknown sculptor. Beneath a figure of Christ in glory appears an ancient Celtic theme: St Anthony and Paul the Hermit, breaking bread in the desert. The loaf they share symbolizes the breaking of bread at meals and in worship which lies at the heart of monastic life. Along the side-panels of the cross, birds and beasts play among vine tendrils, resembling those on the shrine of Boisil, Cuthbert's teacher, at Jedburgh Abbey.

The central figure on the cross is Christ portrayed as a triumphant warrior, with a moustache in Germanic style, not a beard. He wears a cloak and sash, and clasps his hands, at peace. Inscribed both in Latin and in Anglo-Saxon runes is a poem, *The Dream of the Rood*. Its theme is one dear to warrior peoples, Celts, Saxons and Vikings alike: Christ, the young hero, fights a great battle, wounded and bloodstained, yet victorious. The story is told by the rood, or tree of the cross:

> 'I raised a great king,
> liege-lord of heaven....
> I dared not bow down.
>
> Men reviled us both.
> I was all moist with blood
> which poured from his side....
>
> I saw it all,
> overwhelmed with grief,
> wounded with arrow shafts.
>
> They laid him down, limb-weary.
> They stood at the corpse's head:
> they saw the Lord of heaven.'

Women are also carved on the cross: the Angel Gabriel greets Our Lady, and Magdalen tenderly washes the feet of her Lord. There is space for all in the tribe whose chief is the liege-lord of heaven.

Chapter fourteen

Celtic Saints: Passionate Wanderers

WHAT WAS IT LIKE to live as a holy man or woman in the early British Church? What energized the Celtic missionaries? Few early texts survive to tell us how these people understood their calling or perceived their life unfolding. Irish monks often described their life as a *peregrinatio pro Christi*, or exile for Christ. The early monks of the Near East journeyed into the desert in order to meet God in solitude; Irish monks sailed across oceans in search of similar empty places where they could encounter God in stillness. Often they set out with no geographical destination in mind, letting the winds and currents guide them.

Many such men and women lived and died quietly, their actions unrecorded. For others, life unfolded differently: they began to preach their faith to the non-Christians among whom they lived. Their followers commemorated them in place-names, and inscriptions on tombstones record the names of men and women whom they baptized. As they journeyed among pagan peoples, some became missionaries; they travelled widely, sharing the beliefs they held dear. Patrick was such a man: a fifth-century bishop on the edge of the crumbling Roman Empire, who crossed the sea to bring Christianity to an alien people.

Patrick's autobiographical *Confession* is one of the few documents that tell us how an early British Christian perceived himself. Looking back in old age, Patrick saw his journey through life as a response to an inner calling. It had been an unexpected call, which he first heard as a teenager in Ireland: 'I was taken as a captive to Ireland, like so many thousands of others.... At that time I was ignorant of the true God ... but he made me aware of my unbelief.'[1] Patrick felt his life take on a new direction: 'I was like a stone lying deep in the mud, until the Mighty One came and, in pity, lifted me up. He truly raised me aloft and set me on the top of the rampart.'[2]

In chapter 2 we looked at Patrick's description of how he learnt to find God through long hours of prayer in the woods and mountains, in summer and winter. This is one of the few accounts of a Celtic holy man preparing himself for his life's work. Through his deepening relationship with God, Patrick gradually became equipped for his future task. He reflected on this process: 'I felt within myself a formidable strength coming from God.... Through his response to me, a poor, ignorant pupil, I was often forewarned about many things. So where did I get this wisdom? It was not in me before, since I did not care about God.'[3]

From this point onwards, Patrick described his work as a collaboration between God and himself. One way in which he heard God's voice was through paying attention to his dreams: 'One night I had a dream in which I heard a voice saying to me ... "Soon you will return to your own country." Not long afterwards, I heard an answer to the dream, which said, "See! Your ship is prepared!". But the ship was far off, perhaps two hundred miles away, in a place where I had never been before, where I knew nobody. Shortly after that, I ran away from the man to whom I had been bound for six years. At last, I arrived at the ship. I had travelled in the power of God, who guided my steps towards what was good.'[4]

Among the various ways that Patrick learnt to listen to God, he continued to discern his call through interpreting his dreams: 'A few years later, I was back with my parents in Britain.... It was there that I dreamt of a man who seemed to come from Ireland. His name was Victoricius, and he was carrying more letters than I could count. He gave one of them to me, and I read aloud where it began, "The voice of the Irish". As I read the opening, I thought I could hear the voices of people living beside the forest of Foclut, near the Western Sea. They all seemed to be shouting: "Holy lad, please come back again and walk among us". I was pierced to the heart, and could read no further. Then I awoke.'[5]

Patrick followed the dream and returned to Ireland. As his life unfolded, he came to see himself as a messenger of God, entrusted with the task of establishing Christian communities in the foreign land where he now lived: 'We should fish well and carefully.... It is truly our task to cast our nets and catch a multitude, a vast crowd, for God, so that everywhere there might be priests who can baptize and preach to a people in want and in need.... This is what the Lord urges and teaches in the gospel, where he says: "Go now, teach all nations".'[6]

Patrick's view of the world was stable and certain. He knew the scriptures intimately, and had deeply absorbed them. His *Confession* is a tissue of biblical quotations, and he saw himself as a Christian following in the steps of Jesus, carrying out his instructions in considerable detail. Patrick also had a panoramic world-view: he took literally the command of Jesus to 'go and baptize all peoples, even to the ends of the earth'. By sailing to Ireland, at the western edge of the Roman world, Patrick believed that he was helping to complete the task that Jesus gave his followers.

The first Christians expected that the world would come to an end when they had taken the gospel to the ends of the earth. Patrick felt he was playing a part in this great venture: 'Look! We bear witness to the fact that the gospel has been preached to the farthest limits where people live.... I came to the remotest places where no one else had ever gone, in order to baptize people, ordain priests, and strengthen their faith.'[7] He was handing on something precious: 'It is right to preach boldly everywhere, in God's name, so that even after my death I may leave something of value to the many thousands, my brothers and sisters, sons and daughters, whom I have baptized in the Lord.'[8]

This task was also an honour: 'God has given me a great gift that through me many people might be born in God and later brought to fullness of life. Through me, clergy were ordained for them everywhere, to care for this people who have only recently come to belief.' He was proud of the fact that, like the apostles in the early Church, he preached without being a financial burden to anyone: 'When I baptized all those thousands, did I hope to receive a halfpenny from any of them? Just tell me, and I will repay it! Or when the Lord ordained priests everywhere through my feeble efforts, and I freely gave them my services, did I ask them for so much as the price of a pair of shoes?'[9]

In the *Confession* there are a few examples of Patrick's attempts to convert pagans. When he took a ship from Ireland, he remained with the captain and crew: 'We reached land three days later, and for four weeks we made our way through a barren landscape. Their food ran out and they were starving. Then the captain said to me: "Now, Christian, explain to us why we are in this mess. You say that your God is great and powerful, so why can't you pray for us?" ... So I boldly said to them: "Turn in trust with your whole heart to the Lord my God, to whom nothing is impossible, and today he will send you food." With God's help, that is what happened. A herd of pigs appeared on the road, just in front of us.'[10]

He encountered opposition to his work, and felt the hostility of his fellow-bishops particularly keenly: 'I was attacked by some of my superiors, who opposed me in my burdensome office of bishop. They confronted me with my failings. I was truly struck down and falling, and felt I might never recover, but the Lord kindly spared me, a stranger in a foreign land.' Others tried to dissuade Patrick from his task: 'There were many who criticised my mission. They kept talking behind my back, saying to each other, "Why does this man put himself in such danger among these enemies who do not know God?"'[11]

Patrick could tolerate opposition because he felt lovingly supported by God, often in quite practical ways: 'As we travelled, the Lord looked after us with food and dry shelter each day, until after a fortnight we reached a place where people lived.' God's support enabled Patrick to endure dangers of every kind: 'Each day I expect to be killed or waylaid, or taken back into slavery or assaulted in some other way.... But I have flung myself into the hands of the all-powerful God, who rules everywhere.'[12]

Patrick retained a serene confidence because he set his work against a broader horizon. His life and death were part of a larger canvas; his only task was to follow his calling to the end: 'I pray that God will give me perseverance, and allow me to prove a faithful witness, until the point when I pass from this life ., On that day, we shall all arise in the brightness of the sun, that is, in the glory of Christ Jesus, our redeemer.'[13]

Patrick's stable view of the world was probably shared by many holy men and women of the early British Church. It was a Christian vision of life which had not changed greatly during the preceding centuries. As the Celtic missionaries saw it, they were helping to weave a tapestry whose parameters were eternal, and this gave them a sense of freedom and safety. They were content to journey with and for God, since the tapestry was in place, and they were weaving it according to God's design.

These men and women felt at home on planet earth; although they might have no fixed geographical destination, their wandering was focused, even ordered. Their love for God energized them and gave meaning to their journeying. They were engaged in a passionate relationship with the creator of their universe, and this gave an eternal dimension to their adventures. They wandered lovingly, confident that they were not alone. Their understanding of the world and their place within it was inevitably limited, but the devotion and learning of these passionate wanderers inspired the whole of medieval Europe. They have given us, too, a unique and lasting legacy.

Gazetteer

Listed below are sites on mainland Britain that are described in the text and may be difficult to find.

ENGLAND

Altarnun Cornwall *St Non's well and bowssening pool*	With the churchyard wall on your left, walk along the road leading northeast, up the hill. Enter the second field on your right, by way of a track. The bowssening pool and hawthorn tree beside St Non's well are now visible on the right, across the corner of the field.
Brampton Cumbria *St Martin's church*	Take A6071 northwest, out of the town centre. At the brow of the hill, pass the college on your left, then turn left along a signed road to the cemetery. After half a mile, you pass the modern cemetery on your left; continue to the end of the road. Collect the chapel key from the farm to your right, and enter the churchyard to your left.
Brougham Ninekirks Cumbria *St Ninian's church*	Take A66 east past Penrith. After almost four miles, a signed footpath leads left across fields for a mile, following the winding River Eamont. The church is then visible in a hollow.
Castle Sowerby Cumbria *St Kentigern's church and well*	There is no village here, only a country house. Leave the M6 at junction 5 and take B5305, signed Sebergham. Halfway there, turn left for Lamonby. Castle Sowerby is then signed. The well is in the churchyard wall, beside the road.
Colan Cornwall *Lady Nance well*	Take A392 from St Columb Road towards Quintrell Downs. In the hamlet of Mountjoy, turn right down a rutted track. After half a mile, you reach a group of cottages. The well is under the trees, beside a stream to the right of the track.

Davidstow Cornwall *St David's well*	Davidstow church is beside A395. Walk east along the road, downhill past the church. Before reaching the church hall, turn left along a signed track, over a stile. The well is now visible in the field ahead of you.
Holywell Bay Cornwall *St Cubert's two wells*	To visit the well on the beach, ascertain low tide. The well is visible only for an hour, and is almost half an hour's walk from the road. Drive through Cubert to Holywell Bay. At the end of the road, take the track across the dunes to the beach. Walk to your right, round the bay. The well is in the third cave, up a flight of natural steps, against the left wall of the cave. To visit the well in the dunes, park where the road ends. Take the track and turn right through the dunes, roughly following the stream. Keep to its left bank. Enter the golf course, but at once bear right, downhill. Pick up the track through a copse beside the stream. The well chapel is on the left, before a flight of steps that leads up to the golf course again.
Madron Cornwall *St Madron's well and baptistery*	Madron is northwest of Penzance on B3312. Drive through the village and turn right after half a mile. The well is ten minutes' walk along a signed track to the right. Continue to the baptistery.
Nectan's Kieve Cornwall *Nectan's cell, waterfall and well*	Take B3263 north from Tintagel through Bossiney to Trethevy. When the road descends to the valley, park and walk inland along the glen, or else continue along the road as it ascends, and park in a lay-by to your left, beside a telephone kiosk. Walk up the lane opposite you, to the left of the pub. The well is on the left, opposite St Piran's chapel on the right, which is worth a visit. Turn right just before St Piran's chapel, and the road leads to the glen. Follow the path left along the river. After twenty minutes' walk, climb up to the

site of Nectan's cell, beside a tea garden. You can continue down to the waterfall.

Oswestry
Shropshire
St Oswald's well

Travelling south on the main road through the town, pass the church on your right. Turn right at the crossroads, which have traffic lights. Turn right into Oswald Place, and continue past a school (right) and tennis courts (left). The well is close to the road in a small park on the left.

Pelynt
Cornwall
St Non's well

From Pelynt, take either minor road east down a steep hill to Watergate. Turn left onto the road for Duloe. Before crossing the bridge over the West Looe River, bear left up a steep road signed 'Hobb Park'. At the top of the hill, park at the cattle grid. The well is signed in the first field on the right. Go through the gate and turn left. After three minutes' walk, you can see the well below the hedge, in a fenced enclosure.

Perranporth
Cornwall
St Piran's church and cross

Take B3285 from Goonhavern in the direction of Perranporth. The 'lost church' is signed right, at a sharp bend in the road. Turn right here, and park in a lay-by opposite the first road to the right. Take the footpath left across Penhale Sands, then bear right, following some of the many white marker-posts. After fifteen minutes, look for a tall Celtic cross on a rise ahead of you, or ask a fellow-walker. The ruined church is visible in the sand beyond the cross.

St Breward
Cornwall
St James' well

In St Breward, ask for the road to Combe. It leads downhill, westwards, towards the River Camel. Before reaching the river, fork right where the aviary is signed. Seventy metres before a house on the left named Chapel Barn, turn right up a signed footpath. After five minutes' walk, the well will be on your right.

St Buryan Cornwall *St Buryana's well*	Take B3283 southwest out of St Buryan, going towards Land's End. Turn right for the hamlet of Alsia. In Alsia, ask for the well, and look for five large stone steps leading up through a hedge on your left. The well is in the second field ahead of you, in a bank to the right of the stream.
St Clether Cornwall *St Clether's chapel and well*	From Launceston, take A395, signed Camelford. After seven miles turn left along the narrow road signed to St Clether church. After a mile, park at the church. Walk through the churchyard, left of the church. Go through the kissing gate, and keep to the path through the field for half a mile, following the white markers. The chapel and well are now ahead of you.
St Kew Cornwall *St Kew's monastery and well*	The church is on the site of the monastery. With the church and telephone kiosk to your right, walk along the main road out of the village for five minutes, following the high wall of the former vicarage. Turn right; the well is just inside the front gate of the vicarage, to the left.
St Levan Cornwall *St Selevan's baptistery, well and cell*	Take B3283 from St Buryan towards Land's End. A mile after Treen, turn left, signed Porthcurno. Continue past Porthcurno to St Levan, where the road ends. Take the footpath opposite the churchyard, leading down to Porthgwarra Cove. Walk for ten minutes, bearing left at the fork. You will see the baptistery and well ahead of you. Continue down the rough track. As it bends left, St Selevan's cell is on the left, before the footbridge over the stream.
Winwick Lancashire *St Oswald's well*	Approach Winwick from M6, junction 22, or M62, junction 9. Drive through the village, with the church on your left, on a high green. Continue 1½ miles to Hermitage Green. Pass The Hermit pub on your right. After a bend in the road, as it rises up a hill, the well is in the field to your

left, but before visiting the well, continue driving to the crest of the hill, and ask permission at the farmhouse on your left. You can park here. When you enter the field, walk right, along the hedge, for three minutes. The well is in a fenced enclosure to your left.

Woolston
Shropshire
St Winifred's well

Take A5 southwards past Oswestry. At the roundabout, continue on A483. Take the second left, through Ball, to Woolston. The hamlet is not named as you enter it; turn left into it at the T-junction. Park, and as the road bends right, walk left down a lane signed 'access to houses only'. At the end of the lane, a gate on the right gives access to a footpath leading to the courthouse. The well is behind the house.

SCOTLAND

Broughton
Scottish Borders
St Llôlan's cell

Broughton is on A701 between Biggar and Peebles. Travelling north on A701, enter Broughton. Pass B7016 on your left. Stop at the village store on your left, and ask for the key to St Llôlan's chapel in the cemetery. Continue to the next exit left. As you turn into it, you will see the old church and cemetery up a lane, through a gate, on the right. The cell is actually Llôlan's tiny church, with a modern turfed roof.

Callander
Stirling
St Kessóg's Mound

Enter Callander from the south, on A81. Cross the River Teith. Just over the bridge, a cemetery behind a wall on the left is all that remains of Kessóg's church. Turn left, then left again, into the large car park. Kessóg's Mound is now between you and the cemetery, surrounded by grass, with the river to your right.

Drumelzier
Scottish Borders
Merlin's altarstone

From Peebles, take A72 west. Turn left on B712 through Stobo, where Kentigern's church is up a lane to the right, and worth a visit. Continue on A72. Just before crossing the River Tweed, turn right into a minor road which leads to Broughton. The first farm on your left is Altarstone Farm. The square boulder is in the hedge to the right of the road, opposite the farm entrance.

Dunadd
Argyll
Dunadd fort

Travel north on A816 from Lochgilphead. After four miles, turn left along a signed track, and park at the base of the fort.

Ellary
Argyll
St Columba's cave

This is at the head of Loch Caolisport in Knapdale. It can be reached on foot from Kilmory, but not by car. Instead, drive south on A83 from Lochgilphead. Turn right on B8024. After five miles, turn right through Achahoish, and after three miles, St Columba's cave is signed along a short track to the right.

Hoddam
Dumfries and Galloway
St Kentigern's church

In Gretna Green, take A75 west, past Annan. Turn right on B723. Park near the bridge over the River Annan, at the entrance to Hoddam Castle. Cross the bridge on foot, and follow a footpath to the right along the river bank for five minutes. The cemetery of Kentigern's church is ahead of you, with the foundations of a chapel.

Kinkardine
Fife
St Llôlan's church

Cross Kinkardine Bridge into Fife. Turn left through the town and ask for the Church of Scotland cemetery, which is off to the right, on a rise overlooking the rest of the town. The cemetery is on the right side of the road, and surrounds St Llôlan's church.

Rosneath
West Dunbartonshire
St Modan's church and cross

From Helensburgh, take A814 north. At the head of Gare Loch, turn left on B833 to Rosneath. The Church of Scotland is on the main road through Rosneath, in a large open churchyard on the right. Drive behind it, to the ruins of the medieval church. The Celtic cross is in the modern church, which is open on Sunday mornings.

Tyndrum Stirling *St Fillan's priory and pool*	Take A82 west from Crianlarich. Turn right up a signed track to Kirkton Farm, over a slender bridge. Park facing the ancient cemetery, which is on a mound. The ruined priory is beneath trees to the left. Return to A82 and continue westwards. Stop where the road crosses the River Dochart, beside a track on the right which leads to Auchtertyre Farm. Do not drive up the track. Instead, with the track to your left, walk from A82 towards the river. The pool is a shallow stretch of water near the opposite bank.
Whithorn Dumfries and Galloway *St Ninian's cave*	Take A747 west from Whithorn. Follow signs to St Ninian's cave, Physgill. Park where the road ends. Follow the path to the right through Physgill Glen for half a mile. Turn right at the beach. The cave is ahead of you.

WALES

Aberaeron Ceredigion *St David's monastery of Henfynyw*	Aberaeron is twelve miles south of Aberystwyth on A487. Continue south from Aberaeron on A487, up a hill. Before you reach a signed road to Henfynyw on the left, and a roundabout, pull into a lay-by on the right, in front of a cemetery. The chapel in the cemetery is on the site of David's monastery.
Berriew Powys *Maen Beuno* ('Beuno's Stone')	Berriew is five miles southwest of Welshpool. Take A483 south from Welshpool. Turn right to Berriew. There are ancient yew trees in the churchyard. Walk along the road to the River Rhiw, where Beuno was said to have been frightened by a Saxon warrior on the opposite bank. To find Beuno's Stone, drive back along the road, with the Red Lion pub to your right, as if for Newtown. At the A483 junction, continue into Dyffryn Lane (unsigned), past a few houses and a lay-by. Beuno's Stone is on the right, beside the hedge.

Clorach
Anglesey
Wells of Saints Seiriol and Cybi

Clorach is near Llanerchymedd, ten miles east of Holyhead. With the church on your right, take B5111 out of the town. Fork left along the Maenaddwyn road before you reach the brow of the hill. Pass Clorach Farm on the left, and continue to where the road crosses a small stream. Listen for the sound of water. Seiriol's well is just visible to the right of the road, flowing through a square stone pool, under the hedge. Cybi's well, to the left of the road, was destroyed when the bridge was built.

Dyserth
Denbighshire
St Cwyfan's church, waterfall and well

Dyserth is four miles southeast of Rhyl. Travelling from Rhyl on B5119, the church and waterfall are on your left. To find the well, which is now dry, drive back along the road, with the church on your right. Turn right at the main road. The well is soon visible in a square, stone well-house, beside the road on the right.

Foel
Powys
St Tydecho's church

Foel is fifteen miles west of Welshpool, on A458. Drive through the village on A458. After the last houses, look up the hillside on your right. You can spot the church ahead of you. Turn right along the first lane, then fork left. The track ascends steeply to the church. It is possible to turn at the top.

Llanbadrig
Anglesey
St Patrick's church

Llanbadrig is fifteen miles northeast of Holyhead, on the north coast of Anglesey. Take A5025 east from Cemais. At Neuadd, take the track left down to the cliffs. You soon reach Llanbadrig. The church is open from May to September, 10am to 12 noon and 2pm to 4pm.

Llandderfel
Gwynedd
St Derfel's church

Llandderfel is five miles east of Bala. The church is on a rise, near the end of the village. The key can be obtained from the former vicarage, now a nursing home, up the road, across from the church.

Llanfyllin
Powys
St Mullins' church
(Myllin in Welsh) and
well

Llanfyllin is eight miles northwest of Welshpool. Entering Llanfyllin from the west on A490, the church is to the left of the main street. Soon there is a sign to turn right for the well. Turn up this street, and right again at the top. Continue up the hill, park, and walk another hundred metres on foot. As the track bends left, the well is on the right, beneath a great sycamore tree.

Llangwyfan
Anglesey
St Cwyfan's church and
island

In Aberffraw, take A4080 heading northwest for Holyhead. After a mile, turn left along a rough road into a motorbike racing area. Pass its entrance kiosk, where you can check directions. Continue along the road, and fork right. Park where the road ends. St Cwyfan's islet is ahead of you.

Llangybi
Ceredigion
St Cybi's well

Llangybi is on A485, four miles northeast of Lampeter. Drive southwest past the church on A485 for a quarter of a mile, until you reach a Nonconformist chapel on your left. The well is signed across the main road on your right, under a hedge.

Llanidan
Anglesey
St Nidan's church

Visits are possible only on weekdays. Llanidan is on a private estate near the Anglesey shore, three miles southwest of Llanfair P.G., on A4080. One and a half miles after the exit right for Llanddaniel Fab, turn left at the first crossroads, which has a lodge on the corner, into a long drive. Park at the end. Ring the bell at the locked gate; the groundsman will appear with a key.

Llanstinan
Pembrokeshire
St Justinian's church

Llanstinan is two miles southeast of Fishguard, off A40. Watch for a sign on the left, beside a disused quarry. Park in the lay-by, then walk for ten minutes along the signed footpath, through the Cleddau valley. Turn left through a farmyard. The church is on low ground in front of you.

Pennant Melangell
Powys
St Melangell's church

Pennant Melangell is fifteen miles south-east of Bala. Take B4391 to Llangynog. You pass Llangynog church on your right. Just past the churchyard, turn sharp right, and drive two miles along a single track road up to the head of the valley, where the road ends at Pennant Melangell. The church is open daily.

Pistyll
Gwynedd
St Beuno's church

Pistyll is in the Lleyn peninsula, five miles northwest of Pwllheli. Drive northeast from Nefyn through the hamlet of Pistyll. At the end of the village, turn sharp left down a steep, signed track. Park beside the churchyard. If you approach it from the opposite direction, it is easy to miss the sign for the church.

St David's
Pembrokeshire
St Non's well and chapel

Drive through St David's. The road to the well and chapel is clearly signed. Continue for a mile, following the signs. Park, then walk downhill. The well is on the left, and the ruined chapel is ahead of you; a few prehistoric standing stones encircle the field.

Notes

Chapter one: The Origins of Celtic Christianity

1. E. G. Bowen, *Saints, Seaways and Settlements in the Celtic Lands* (Cardiff), 1969, p. 180
2. W. J. Watson, *The History of the Celtic Place-names of Scotland* (Edinburgh), 1993, pp. 274, 278
3. O. Davies, *Celtic Christianity in Early Medieval Wales: the Origins of the Welsh Spiritual Tradition* (Cardiff), 1996, p. 143
4. A. M. Allchin, *Pennant Melangell* (Oswestry), 1994, pp. 44–46
5. S. Toulson, *Celtic Journeys in Scotland and the North of England* (London), 1995, p. 4
6. B. Colgrave and R. A. Mynors (eds), *Bede's Ecclesiastical History of the English People*, (Oxford), 1969, Bk 1, ch. 7
7. 1 Corinthians. 11:18–22
8. K. Cameron 'Eccles in English Place-names', in M. W. Barley and R. P. Hanson (eds), *Christianity in Britain, 300–700*, Papers presented to the Conference on Christianity in Roman and Sub-Roman Britain, held at the University of Nottingham, 17–20 April 1967 (Leicester), 1968, pp. 87–91
9. M. Fulford, *Calleva Atrebatum: a Guide to the Roman Town at Silchester* (Gloucester), 1997, p. 23
10. P. Wilkinson, 'Church found in ruins of fort at Hadrian's Wall', in *The Times*, 25 July 1998
11. C. Thomas, *Christianity in Roman Britain to AD 500* (London), 1981, pp. 221–23
12. R. Goodburn, *The Roman Villa, Chedworth* (London), 1994, p. 24
13. J. Toynbee, 'Pagan Motifs and Practices in Christian Art and Ritual', in Barley and Hanson (eds), *op. cit.*, pp. 180–86

14. D. Neal, *Lullingstone Roman Villa* (London), 1991, pp. 8, 23
15. D. Keys, 'Archaeologists unearth Capital's first Cathedral', in *The Independent*, 3 April 1995
16. C. Guest, *The Mabinogion* (New York), 1997, p. 56
17. E. G. Bowen, *The Settlements of the Celtic Saints in Wales* (Cardiff), 1954, pp. 21–23
18. Sulpicius Severus: *The Life of Martin of Tours*, in J. P. Migne (ed.), *Patrologia Latina*, vol. 20, columns 159–222 (Paris), 1844ff.

Chapter two: Patrick and the Early Irish Church

1. C. Thomas, *And Shall These Mute Stones Speak?* (Cardiff), 1994, p. 28
2. *Ibid.*, pp. 28–30
3. *Ibid.*, pp. 33–34
4. Rufinus: 'Historium Monachorum in Aegypto', Latin version in J. P. Migne (ed.), *Patrologia Latina*, vol. 21, columns 387–462 (Paris), 1844ff.
5. B. Ward, *The Lives of the Desert Fathers* (London), 1981, p. 10
6. Bowen, *op. cit.*, 1969, pp. 130–31
7. C. Thomas, 'Cellular Meanings, Monastic Beginnings', in *Emania*, 13, 1995, pp. 51–57
8. Watson, *op. cit.*, p. 187
9. S. Lincoln, *Declan of Ardmore* (Cork), 1995, pp. 2–9
10. *Ibid.*, pp. 33–41
11. *Ibid.*, p. 32
12. A. Chetan and D. Brueton, *The Sacred Yew* (London), 1994, pp. 53–57
13. M. Low, *Celtic Christianity and Nature* (Dundonald, Northern Ireland), 1996, pp. 82–100
14. Patrick: *Confession*, 16, based on D. R. Howlett, *The Book of Letters of St Patrick the Bishop* (Dublin), 1994; J. Skinner, *The Confession of St Patrick*

and *Letter to Coroticus* (New York),
1998; T. O'Loughlin, *St Patrick: the Man and his Works* (London), 1999
15. Patrick: *Confession*, 23
16. Patrick: *Confession*, 10
17. Patrick: *Confession*, 28
18. Bowen, *op. cit.*, 1969, pp. 126–27
19. Exodus 2:1–4
20. M. C. Millard, 'The Channel Coracle', in *The Coracle Society*, vol. 2, May 1991
21. Julius Caesar, 'The Civil War', Bk. 1, in J. M. Carter (ed., trans.), *The Civil War, Books I and II, Julius Caesar* (Warminster), 1991
22. D. Gent, 'Did Caesar see Coracles?', in *The Coracle Society*, vol. 3, February 1992
23. P. Badge, 'The Boyne Curragh', in *The Coracle Society*, vol. 4, June 1993
24. P. Faulkner, in *The Coracle Society*, autumn 1997
25. T. Severin, *The Brendan Voyage* (New York), 1978
26. G. Jenkins, 'The Coracle Man', in *The Coracle Society*, vol. 1, 1990

Chapter three: Irish Nuns, Monks and Missionaries

1. M. Low, 'Canaire of Inis Cathaig', in G. Márkus (ed.), *The Radical Tradition* (London), 1992, p. 27
2. Low, *op. cit.*, 1996, p. 158
3. C. Manning, *Early Irish Monasteries* (Dublin), 1995, pp. 16, 29
4. D. P. Mould, *Ireland of the Saints* (London), 1953, pp. 63–64
5. Watson, *op. cit.*, p. 275
6. Manning, *op. cit.*, p. 44
7. P. Harbison, *Ancient Irish Monuments* (Dublin), 1997, p. 34
8. Severin, *op. cit.*, pp. 14–15
9. M. Bragg, *Credo* (London), 1996, pp. 85–87, reproduced by kind permission of the author
10. Mould, *op. cit.*, p. 96
11. Based on K. Jackson (trans.), *A Celtic Miscellany* (London), 1971; Low, 1996, *op. cit.*
12. G. Moorhouse, *Sun Dancing: a Medieval Vision* (London), 1997

13. D. Farmer, *The Oxford Dictionary of Saints* (Oxford), 1984, pp. 255–56
14. Based on Jackson, *op. cit.*; R. Van der Weyer, *Celtic Fire: an Anthology of Celtic Christian Literature* (London), 1990; Low, 1996, *op. cit.*
15. Based on Jackson, *op. cit.*; Low, 1996, *op. cit.*

Chapter four: David and South Wales

1. Davies, *op. cit.*, pp. 7–8
2. Bowen, *op. cit.*, 1954, pp. 16–19
3. Thomas, *op. cit.*, 1994, pp. 27, 41
4. Bowen, *op. cit.*, 1954, pp. 19–23
5. M. Redknap, *The Christian Celts* (Cardiff), 1991, p. 36
6. Davies, *op. cit.*, pp. 10, 26–27
7. Thomas, *op. cit.*, 1994, pp. 144–45
8. Thomas, *op. cit.*, 1994, pp. 145–50
9. Thomas, *op. cit.*, 1994, pp. 150–51
10. Bowen, 1954, *op. cit.*, p. 27
11. E. Campbell, 'New Finds of Post-Roman Imported Pottery and Glass from South Wales', in *Archaeologica Cambrensis*, vol. 138, 1989–1990, pp. 59–63
12. F. Jones, *The Holy Wells of Wales* (Cardiff), 1992, p. 43
13. M. Forrest Brewster, 'Gildas the Wise: St Kilda and Dumbarton's Neglected Saint', in *St Kilda Mail*, vol. 20, 1996
14. M. Costen, *The Origins of Somerset* (Manchester), 1992, pp. 70, 74
15. *Tenby Observer*, 23 September 1988
16. E. G. Bowen, *The St David of History. Dewi Sant: Our Founder Saint*. Address given to the Friends of St David's Cathedral (Aberystwyth), 1982, pp. 11–13, 20–23
17. *Ibid.*, pp. 7–15, 32
18. *Ibid.*, pp. 14, 18
19. *Ibid.*, pp. 9–10
20. Davies, *op. cit.*, p. 23
21. Jones, *op. cit.*, p. 41
22. van der Weyer, *op. cit.*, pp. 70–72
23. Davies, *op. cit.*, pp. 45–48
24. Redknap, *op. cit.*, p. 77
25. P. Berresford Ellis, *Celtic Inheritance* (London), 1992, pp. 56–59

Chapter five: Celtic North Wales

1. Bowen, *op. cit.*, 1969, p. 203
2. L. Macinnes, *Anglesey: A Guide to Ancient and Historic Sites on the Isle of Anglesey* (Cardiff), 1994, pp. 20–24
3. Jones, *op. cit.*, pp. 142–43
4. *Ibid.*, pp. 15, 159
5. *Ibid.*, pp. 74, 151
6. Bowen, *op. cit.*, 1954, pp. 92–94
7. Bowen, *op. cit.*, 1969, p. 201
8. C. Kightly, *Mwynhewch Sir Ddinbych Ganoloesol* (Denbigh), 1998, p. 18
9. N. Pennick, *The Celtic Saints* (London), 1997, p. 51
10. Jones, *op. cit.*, p. 178
11. D. Senogles, *A History of Part of the Parish of Llandysilio* (Anglesey), 1991, p. 2
12. Based on Pennick, *op. cit.*, and others
13. Jones, *op. cit.*, pp. 81, 198
14. Kightly, *op. cit.*, p. 14
15. Kightly, *op. cit.*, p. 15

Chapter six: Beuno and Winifred

1. Matthew 25:36
2. Davies, *op. cit.*, pp. 17–19, 143
3. S. Baring-Gould, *Lives of the Saints* (London), 1898, vol. 13, pp. 70–72
4. Jones, *op. cit.*, p. 70
5. C. David, *St Winefride's Well: a History and Guide* (Kildare), 1993, p. 20
6. Chetan and Brueton, *op. cit.*, pp. 55, 153
7. J. and C. Bord, *Sacred Waters: Holy Wells and Water Lore in Britain and Ireland* (London), 1986, pp. 74–75, 171
8. C. Thomas, *Celtic Britain* (London), 1986, p. 114

Chapter seven: Ninian, Kentigern and Strathclyde

1. C. Thomas, 'The Evidence from North Britain', in Barley and Hanson (eds), *op. cit.*, pp. 111–16
2. P. Hill, *Whithorn and St Ninian; the Excavation of a Monastic Town, 1984–91* (Stroud), 1998
3. Toulson, *op. cit.*, p. 11
4. Watson, *op. cit.*, pp. 159–60
5. Watson, *op. cit.*, p. 296
6. I. Macdonald, *St Ninian (The Life of St Ninian by Aelred of Rievaulx)* (Edinburgh), 1993a, p. 51
7. Cumberland and Westmoreland Antiquarian Society, 'St Martin's Church, Brampton', in *Transactions of the Cumberland and Westmoreland Antiquarian Society*, vol. 82, 1982
8. I. Macdonald, *St Mungo (The Life of Saint Mungo by Jocelyn of Furness)* (Edinburgh), 1993b, p. 29
9. *Ibid.*, pp. 29–30
10. J. Marsden, *The Illustrated Columcille* (London), 1991, pp. 52, 68
11. J. Randall and C. Seymour, *Stobo Kirk* (Selkirk), 1997, pp. 8–9
12. *Prophecy concerning Artbranan*, in Marsden, *op. cit.*, p. 78
13. Toulson, *op. cit.*, pp. 6, 59
14. Bowen, *op. cit.*, 1969, p. 25
15. *Prophecy on the Arrival of St Cainnech*, in Marsden, *op. cit.*, p. 61

Chapter eight: Columba and Argyll

1. Marsden, *op. cit.*, pp. 28–29
2. *Ibid.*, pp. 28–29, 145
3. *Ibid.*, pp. 34–35
4. J. Dunbar and I. Fisher, *Iona: a Guide to the Monuments* (Edinburgh), 1995, p. 30
5. Watson, *op. cit.*, p. 89
6. Marsden, *op. cit.*, pp. 35–38
7. Watson, *op. cit.*, p. 289

Chapter nine: The Pictish Church

1. Watson, *op. cit.*, p. 61
2. *Ibid.*, pp. 62–63
3. Thomas, *op. cit.*, 1994, pp. 161–71
4. *Ibid.*, pp. 161–71
5. *Ibid.*, p. 104
6. Toulson, *op. cit.*, p. 137
7. Watson, *op. cit.*, p. 233
8. A. Ritchie, *Meigle Museum: Pictish Carved Stones* (Edinburgh), 1997, p. 6
9. *Ibid.*, p. 16
10. *Ibid.*, p. 16
11. Watson, *op. cit.*, pp. 310–12
12. N. Atkinson, *Aberlemno to Glamis* (Balgavies, Angus), 1997, pp. 4–5
13. Colgrave and Mynors (eds), *op. cit.*, Bk 5, ch. 21
14. Atkinson, *op. cit.*, pp. 8–9

15. Colgrave and Mynors (eds), *op. cit.*, Bk 5, ch. 21
16. Marsden, *op. cit.*, pp. 93–94
17. R. Fawcett, *St Andrews Cathedral* (Edinburgh), 1993, p. 4
18. *Ibid.*, pp. 4–5
19. *Ibid.*, p. 6
20. Davies, *op. cit.*, p. 47
21. Colgrave and Mynors (eds), *op. cit.*, Bk 5, ch. 25
22. Marsden, *op. cit.*, p. 13
23. Marsden, *op. cit.*, pp. 14–15
24. Colgrave and Mynors (eds), *op. cit.*, Bk 5, ch. 25
25. Chetan and Brueton, *op. cit.*, pp. 47–49
26. *Miracle of Broichan, the Druid*, in Marsden, *op. cit.*, p. 125
27. Pennick, *op. cit.*, p. 119

Chapter ten: The Southwest: Somerset and Cornwall

1. P. Leach, *Shepton Mallet: Romano Britons and Early Christians in Somerset* (Birmingham), 1991, pp. 9, 24
2. *Ibid.*, p. 24
3. Costen, *op. cit.*, p. 47
4. *Ibid.*, p. 75
5. *Ibid.*, p. 77
6. Thomas, *op. cit.*, 1986, pp. 61–63
7. N. Johnson and P. Rose, *Cornwall's Archaeological Heritage* (Truro), 1993, pp. 11–12
8. Thomas, *op. cit.*, 1994, p. 316
9. *Ibid.*, pp. 197–200
10. M. and L. Quiller-Couch, *Ancient and Holy Wells of Cornwall* (London), 1894, pp. 4–5
11. *Ibid.*, pp. 126–27
12. Thomas, 1994, *op. cit.*, p. 291
13. Bowen, *op. cit.*, 1969, p. 109

Chapter eleven: Samson, Petroc and Eastern Cornwall

1. Luke 1:7
2. Luke 1:42
3. Davies, *op. cit.*, p. 43
4. Thomas, *op. cit.*, 1994, p. 227
5. *Ibid.*, p. 233
6. *Ibid.*, pp. 229–30
7. *Ibid.*, pp. 231–32

8. J. Meyrick, *A Pilgrim's Guide to the Holy Wells of Cornwall* (Falmouth), 1982, p. 133
9. J. Chapman, *St Petroc* (Bodmin), 1995, p. 4
10. Bowen, *op. cit.*, 1954, pp. 89–91
11. Meyrick, *op. cit.*, p. 36
12. *Ibid.*, p. 112
13. *Ibid.*, p. 34
14. Quiller-Couch, *op. cit.*, pp. 171–74
15. *Ibid.*, pp. 175–78
16. Bowen, *op. cit.*, 1969, p. 182
17. A. Cotterell, *Celtic Mythology* (London), 1997, pp. 47, 68
18. Thomas, *op. cit.*, 1994, p. 214
19. Quiller-Couch, *op. cit.*, pp. 107–112
20. Berresford Ellis, *op. cit.*, p. 68

Chapter twelve: The Isle of Man

1. D. Moore (ed.), *The Irish Sea Province in Archaeology and History* (Cardiff), 1970
2. J. Mac Queen, *St Nynia* (Edinburgh), 1961
3. D. Brooke, *Wild Men and Holy Places* (Edinburgh), 1994
4. Ailred of Rievaulx, 'Life of St Ninian', in MacQueen (ed.), *op. cit.*
5. *Ibid.*
6. L. Bieler (ed.), *Four Latin Lives of St Patrick* (Dublin), 1971
7. S. Mac Airt and G. Mac Niocall (eds), *Annals of Ulster Part 1* (Dublin), 1983
8. W. S. Dempsey, *The Story of the Catholic Church in the Isle of Man* (Bradley Hall Press), 1958
9. P. M. C. Kermode, *Manx Crosses* (Belgavies, Angus), 1907, reprinted 1994
10. *Ibid.*
11. *Ibid.*
12. *Ibid.*
13. *Ibid.*
14. Dempsey, *op. cit.*
15. P. M. C. Kermode (ed.), *The Manx Archaeological Survey* vols 1–5, and vol. 6 (Douglas, Isle of Man), 1909–18, reprinted 1968
16. G. Broderick (trans.), *Chronicles of the Kings of Man and the Isles* (Douglas, Isle of Man), 1979
17. Dempsey, *op. cit.*

18. Kermode, *op. cit.*, 1968
19. Mac Airt and Mac Niocall, *op. cit.*
20. Kermode, *op. cit.*, 1968

Chapter thirteen: Aidan, Cuthbert and Northumbria

1. E. Cambridge, *Lindisfarne Priory and Holy Island* (London), 1995, p. 8
2. J. Backhouse, *The Lindisfarne Gospels* (Oxford), 1991, pp. 7–17
3. *Ibid.*, pp. 17–32
4. Colgrave and Mynors (eds), *op. cit.*, Bk 3, ch. 26
5. J. Austerberry, *Chad, Bishop and Saint* (Derby), 1984, p. 5
6. *Ibid.*, pp. 7–8
7. Colgrave and Mynors (eds), *op. cit.*, Bk 4, ch. 3
8. Bede: *The Life and Miracles of St Cuthbert*, ch. 8, in Colgrave and Mynors (eds), *op. cit.*
9. Bede: *The Life and Miracles of St Cuthbert*, ch. 37, in Colgrave and Mynors (eds), *op. cit.*
10. M. Magnusson, *Vikings!* (London), 1980, pp. 31–34
11. *Ibid.*, p. 71
12. *Ibid.*, pp. 252–53
13. A. Ritchie and D. Breeze, *Invaders of Scotland* (Edinburgh), 1991, pp. 37–38

14. Magnusson, *op. cit.*, pp. 157–58
15. A. Macquarrie, *Cille Barra* (Droitwich), 1989, pp. 10–11
16. *Ibid.*, p. 12
17. A. M. Cubbon, *The Art of the Manx Crosses* (Douglas, Isle of Man), 1977, pp. 19–20, 28

Chapter fourteen: Celtic Saints: Passionate Wanderers

1. Patrick: *Confession*, 12, based on D. R. Howlett, *The Book of Letters of St Patrick the Bishop* (Dublin), 1994; J. Skinner, *The Confession of St Patrick and Letter to Coroticus* (New York), 1998; T. O'Loughlin, *St Patrick: the Man and his Works* (London), 1999
2. *Ibid.*, 12
3. *Ibid.*, 30, 36, 37
4. *Ibid.*, 17
5. *Ibid.*, 23
6. *Ibid.*, 40
7. *Ibid.*, 34, 51
8. *Ibid.*, 14
9. *Ibid.*, 38, 50
10. *Ibid.*, 19
11. *Ibid.*, 26, 46
12. *Ibid.*, 22, 55
13. *Ibid.*, 58, 59

Bibliography

Allchin, A. M., *Pennant Melangell* (Oswestry), 1994

Atkinson, N., *Aberlemno to Glamis* (Balgavies), 1997

Austerberry, J., *Chad, Bishop and Saint* (Derby), 1984

Backhouse, J., *The Lindisfarne Gospels* (Oxford), 1991

Badge, P., 'The Boyne Curragh', in *The Coracle Society*, vol. 4, June 1993

Baring-Gould, S., *Lives of the Saints* (London), 1898

Berresford Ellis, P., *Celtic Inheritance* (London), 1992

Bieler, L. (ed.), *Four Latin Lives of St Patrick* (Dublin), 1971

Bord, J. and C., *Sacred Waters: Holy Wells and Water Lore in Britain and Ireland* (London), 1986

Bowen, E. G., *The Settlements of the Celtic Saints in Wales* (Cardiff), 1954

——, *Saints, Seaways and Settlements in the Celtic Lands* (Cardiff), 1969

——, *Britain and the Western Seaways* (London), 1972

——, *The St David of History. Dewi Sant: Our Founder Saint*, Address given to the Friends of St David's Cathedral (Aberystwyth), 1982

Bragg, M., *Credo* (London), 1996

Broderick, G. (trans.), *Chronicles of the Kings of Man and the Isles* (Douglas), 1979

Brooke, D., *Wild Men and Holy Places* (Edinburgh), 1994

Cambridge, E., *Lindisfarne Priory and Holy Island* (London), 1995

Cameron, K., 'Eccles in English Place-names', in Barley, M. W., and Hanson, R. P. (eds), *Christianity in Britain, 300–700*, Papers presented to the Conference on Christianity in Roman and Sub-Roman Britain, held at the University of Nottingham, 17–20 April 1967 (Leicester), 1968

Campbell, E., 'New Finds of Post-Roman Imported Pottery and Glass from South Wales', in *Archaeologica Cambrensis*, vol. 138, 1989–1990

Chapman, J., *St Petroc* (Bodmin), 1995

Charles-Edwards, T., *St Winefride and her Well: the Historical Background* (Holywell), n.d.

Chetan, A., and Brueton, D., *The Sacred Yew* (London), 1994

Colgrave, B., and Mynors, R. A. (eds), *Bede's Ecclesiastical History of the English People* (Oxford), 1969

Costen, M., *The Origins of Somerset* (Manchester), 1992

Cotterell, A., *Celtic Mythology* (London), 1997

Cubbon, A. M., *The Art of the Manx Crosses* (Douglas), 1977

Cumberland and Westmoreland Antiquarian Society, 'St Martin's Church, Brampton', in *Transactions of the Cumberland and Westmoreland Antiquarian Society*, vol. 82, 1982

Cunliffe, B., *The Celtic World* (London), 1992

David, C., *St Winefride's Well: a History and Guide* (Kildare), 1993

Davies, O., *Celtic Christianity in Early Medieval Wales: the Origins of the Welsh Spiritual Tradition* (Cardiff), 1996

Dempsey, W. S., *The Story of the Catholic Church in the Isle of Man* (Bradley), 1958

Doble, G. (Attwater, D., ed.), *The Saints of Cornwall*, 5 vols (Truro), 1960–1970

Dunbar, J., and Fisher, I., *Iona: a Guide to the Monuments* (Edinburgh), 1995

Farmer, D., *The Oxford Dictionary of Saints* (Oxford), 1984

Faulkner, P., article in *The Coracle Society*, autumn 1997

Fawcett, R., *St Andrews Cathedral* (Edinburgh), 1993

Forrest Brewster, M., 'Gildas the Wise: St Kilda and Dumbarton's Neglected Saint', in *St Kilda Mail*, vol. 20, 1996

Fulford, M., *Calleva Atrebatum: a Guide to the Roman Town at Silchester* (Gloucester), 1997

Gent, D., 'Did Caesar See Coracles?', in *The Coracle Society*, vol. 3, February 1992

Goodburn, R., *The Roman Villa, Chedworth* (London), 1994

Gould, B., and Fisher, J. (Bryce, D., ed.), *Lives of the British Saints*, Wales, 1990

Gregory, D., *Country Churchyards in Wales* (Llanwrst), 1991

Guest, C., *The Mabinogion* (New York), 1997

Harbison, P., *Ancient Irish Monuments* (Dublin), 1997

Hill, P., *Whithorn and St Ninian; the Excavation of a Monastic Town, 1984–91* (Stroud), 1998

Howlett, D. R., *The Book of Letters of St Patrick the Bishop* (Dublin), 1994

Jackson, K. (trans.), *A Celtic Miscellany* (London), 1971

Jenkins, G., 'The Coracle Man', in *The Coracle Society*, vol. 1, 1990

Johnson, N., and Rose, P., *Cornwall's Archaeological Heritage* (Truro), 1993

Jones, F., *The Holy Wells of Wales* (Cardiff), 1992

Kermode, P. M. C., *Manx Crosses* (Balgavies), 1907, reprinted 1994

——, *The Manx Archaeological Survey*, vols 1–5, and vol. 6 (Douglas), 1909–18, reprinted 1968

Keys, D., 'Archaeologists Unearth Capital's First Cathedral', in *The Independent*, 3 April 1995

Kightly, C., *Mwynhewch Sir Ddinbych Ganoloesol* (Denbigh), 1998

Lane-Davies, A., *Holy Wells of Cornwall* (Cornwall), 1970

Leach, P., *Shepton Mallet: Romano Britons and Early Christians in Somerset* (Birmingham), 1991

Leask, H., and Wheeler, H., *St Patrick's Rock, Cashel*, 1990

Leggat, P. O. and D. V., *The Healing Wells: Cornish Cults and Customs* (Redruth), 1987

Lincoln, S., *Declan of Ardmore* (Cork), 1995

Low, M., 'Canaire of Inis Cathaig', in G. Márkus (ed.), *The Radical Tradition* (London), 1992

——, *Celtic Christianity and Nature* (Dundonald), 1996

Mac Airt, S., and Mac Niocall, G. (eds), *Annals of Ulster*, Part 1 (Dublin), 1983

Mac Airt, S. (trans.), *Annals of Innisfallen* (Dublin), 1988

Macdonald, I., *Saint Columba* (Selections from the Life of Saint Columba by Adamnan), Edinburgh, 1992

——, *St Mungo (The Life of Saint Mungo by Jocelyn of Furness)* (Edinburgh), 1993

——, *St Ninian (The Life of St Ninian by Aelred of Rievaulx)* (Edinburgh), 1993

Macinnes, L., *Anglesey: A Guide to the Ancient and Historic Sites on the Isle of Anglesey* (Cardiff), 1994

Macquarrie, A., *Cille Barra* (Droitwich), 1989

Mac Queen, J., *St Nynia* (Edinburgh), 1961

Magnusson, M., *Vikings!* (London), 1980

Manning, C., *Early Irish Monasteries* (Dublin), 1995

Marsden, J., *The Illustrated Columcille* (London), 1991

Marshall, D., *History of Bute* (Bute), 1992

Meyrick, J., *A Pilgrim's Guide to the Holy Wells of Cornwall* (Falmouth), 1982

Migne, J. P. (ed.), *Patrologia Latina* (Paris), 1844ff.

Millard, M. C., 'The Channel Coracle', in *The Coracle Society*, vol. 2, May 1991

Moore, D. (ed), *The Irish Sea Province in Archaeology and History* (Cardiff), 1970

Moorhouse, G., *Sun Dancing: a Medieval Vision* (London), 1997

Mould, D. P., *Ireland of the Saints* (London), 1953

Neal, D., *Lullingstone Roman Villa* (London), 1991

O'Loughlin, T., *St Patrick: the Man and his Works* (London), 1999

Orme, N. (ed.), *Nicholas Roscarrock's Lives of the Saints: Cornwall and Devon* (Exeter), 1992

Pennick, N., *The Celtic Saints* (London), 1997

Quiller-Couch, M. and L., *Ancient and Holy Wells of Cornwall* (London), 1894

Quine, D., *St Kilda Revisited* (Frome), 1982

Randall, J., and Seymour, C., *Stobo Kirk* (Selkirk), 1997

Redknap, M., *The Christian Celts* (Cardiff), 1991

Ritchie, A., *Meigle Museum: Pictish Carved Stones* (Edinburgh), 1997

———, and Breeze, D., *Invaders of Scotland* (Edinburgh), 1991

Room, A., *A Dictionary of Irish Place-names* (Belfast), 1994

Salter, M., *The Old Parish Churches of Mid-Wales* (Malvern), 1991

———, *The Old Parish Churches of North Wales* (Malvern), 1993

Senogles, D., *A History of Part of the Parish of Llandysilio* (Llanfair P. G., Anglesey), 1991

Severin, T., *The Brendan Voyage* (New York), 1978

Sharkey, J., *Celtic High Crosses of Wales* (Llanwrst), 1998

Sharp, M., *Holy Places of Celtic Britain* (London), 1997

Smith, D., *Celtic Travellers: Scotland in the Age of the Saints* (Edinburgh), 1997

Thomas, C., 'The Evidence from North Britain', in Barley, M. W., and Hanson, R. P. (eds), *Christianity in Britain, 300–700,* Papers presented to the Conference on Christianity in Roman and Sub-Roman Britain, held at the University of Nottingham, 17–20 April 1967 (Leicester), 1968

———, *Britain and Ireland in Early Christian Times, AD 400–800* (London), 1971

———, *Christianity in Roman Britain to AD 500* (London), 1981

———, *Celtic Britain* (London), 1986

———, *And Shall These Mute Stones Speak?* (Cardiff), 1994

———, 'Cellular Meanings, Monastic Beginnings', in *Emania*, 13, 1995

Toulson, S., *Celtic Journeys in Scotland and the North of England* (London), 1995

———, *The Celtic Year: A Celebration of Celtic Christian Saints, Sites and Festivals* (Dorset), 1996

Toynbee, J., 'Pagan Motifs and Practices in Christian Art and Ritual', in Barley, M. W., and Hanson, R. P. (eds), *Christianity in Britain, 300–700,* Papers presented to the Conference on Christianity in Roman and Sub-Roman Britain, held at the University of Nottingham, 17–20 April 1967 (Leicester), 1968

Van der Weyer, R., *Celtic Fire: an Anthology of Celtic Christian Literature* (London), 1990

Wadell, H., *The Desert Fathers* (New York), 1998

Ward, B., *The Lives of the Desert Fathers* (London), 1981

Watson, W. J., *The History of the Celtic Place-names of Scotland* (Edinburgh), 1993

Wilkinson, P., 'Church found in ruins of fort at Hadrian's Wall', in *The Times*, 25 July 1998

Winterbottom, M. (ed.), *Gildas: The Ruin of Britain and Other Works* (*Arthurian Period Sources* no. 7) (Chichester), 1978

Wooding, J. M., *Communication and Commerce along the Western Sealanes* (Oxford), 1996

Zaczek, I., *The Art of the Celts* (London), 1997

Index